POLITIQUE, DÉMOCRATIE ET CULTURE AUX ÉTATS-UNIS À L'ÈRE DU NUMÉRIQUE

Sous la direction de
Élisabeth Boulot

POLITIQUE, DÉMOCRATIE ET CULTURE AUX ÉTATS-UNIS À L'ÈRE DU NUMÉRIQUE

5-7, rue de l'Ecole-Polytechnique, 75005 Paris

http://www.librairieharmattan.com
diffusion.harmattan@wanadoo.fr
harmattan1@wanadoo.fr

ISBN : 978-2-296-55562-4
EAN : 9782296555624

Préface

Selon la dernière enquête faite par le *Pew Research Center* 79% des Américains, toutes générations confondues, utilisent l'Internet[1]. Certes les 18-33 ans sont les plus nombreux à s'en servir pour aller sur les réseaux sociaux ou lire des blogs, mais ces derniers deviennent de plus en plus prisés par toutes les tranches d'âges comme source d'information et moyen d'expression. L'objectif des auteurs qui ont contribué à cet ouvrage est d'examiner les incidences, au cours de ces quinze dernières années, du passage d'un espace public dominé par les médias de masse à un espace public en réseaux sur la vie politique aux Etats-Unis, sur les valeurs fondatrices de sa démocratie et sur l'émergence d'une nouvelle forme de culture politique.

La place prépondérante prise par ce nouveau média a profondément transformé la production de l'information et la communication entre les citoyens et les hommes politiques. **Aurélie Godet** rappelle que les conservateurs qui jusqu'à la fin des années quatre-vingt-dix mobilisaient leurs partisans, attaquaient leurs adversaires et collectaient des fonds grâce aux *talk shows* diffusés sur les radios locales, furent les premiers à comprendre le rôle crucial que cette nouvelle technologie pouvait jouer afin de mobiliser les citoyens. La décision de Matt Drudge de mettre au grand jour sur la Toile les relations de Bill Clinton avec Monica Lewinsky servit de révélateur. Des sites communautaires furent par la suite créés pour orchestrer une campagne et organiser des manifestations afin d'obtenir la destitution du président. John McCain, candidat malheureux aux primaires en 1999, réalisa bien avant ses rivaux, l'importance que la maîtrise de l'Internet pouvait avoir pour gagner la course à la Maison-Blanche, en particulier pour susciter le soutien financier de ses partisans. Au cours de la campagne présidentielle, en 2002, la blogosphère de droite fut l'un des artisans de la victoire de George W. Bush non seulement pour collecter des fonds et inciter les

[1]Kathryn Zickuhr, « Generation 2010 », Pew Internet and American Life Project, *Pew Research Center*, http://pewinternet.org/Reports/Generations-2010.aspx. Ils sont pour la plus grande majorité d'entre eux connectés grâce aux services proposés par les câblo-opérateurs et se servent de plus en plus de leur téléphone mobile pour suivre l'information en direct.

électeurs à voter pour lui mais aussi pour disséminer sur la Toile des insinuations tendant à accréditer la thèse qu'en Floride le candidat était victime d'une tentative de fraude perpétrée par ses adversaires politiques. Après avoir retracé l'ascension fulgurante des blogs conservateurs et les raisons de leur position dominante jusqu'en 2003, elle étudie les facteurs qui ont causé le déclin de leur influence et pose la question de leur résurgence, depuis 2009, avec l'apparition du mouvement du *Tea party*.

A partir de 2002 les progressistes, indignés par la manière dont la bataille électorale pour la présidence en 2000 avait été tranchée et irrités par la défaite des Démocrates en 2004 due selon eux à l'immobilisme des caciques du parti, ont pris leur revanche. Les *netroots*[2] ayant peu à peu fleuri sur la Toile ont su rallier à leur cause de très nombreux militants et les mobiliser dans le but de faire naître, à l'échelle nationale, un mouvement que Jerome Armstrong et Markos Moulitsas Zùniga ont qualifié de « populiste » et « patriotique »[3] afin que leurs voix soient entendues et que leur soit restitué le pouvoir de décision au sein du Parti démocrate pour créer une nouvelle dynamique et renouer avec la victoire. L'usage très novateur de l'Internet par Howard Dean durant sa campagne pour la présidence en 2004, les conforta dans leur entreprise. Une fois nommé président du Conseil national du parti, celui-ci fit en sorte que le fruit de leurs efforts se traduise dans les urnes dès 2006. En effet pour lui, l'Internet est « l'outil le plus significatif pour encourager la démocratie depuis la presse à imprimer, étant donné que le pouvoir ne repose plus sur un système de message centralisé mais sur des électeurs qui exigent que les hommes politiques les écoutent avant de s'adresser à eux »[4]. Selon les auteurs, cette nouvelle génération de militants n'aurait pas été en mesure de contester les stratégies du parti sans les *netroots* car

---

[2] Ce terme a été créé par le blogueur Jerome Armstrong (*MyDD.com*) pour désigner les blogs progressistes. Aujourd'hui pour s'en démarquer, les conservateurs utilisent le terme *rightroots*.

[3] Jerome Armstrong, Markos Moulitsas Zùniga (*DailyKos.com*), *Crashing the Gate: Netroots, Grassroots, and the Rise of People-Powered Politics*, White River Junction, VT: Chelsea Green, 2006, p. xvii.

[4] Lowell Feld, Nate Wilcox, *Netroots Rising: How a Citizen Army of Bloggers and Online Activists Is Changing American Politics*. Wesport, CT: Praeger, 2008, p. 170, « *The Internet is the most significant tool for building democracy since the invention of the printing press. Power is shifting away from centralized messaging and towards voters who demand that politicians listen to them before speaking to them* ».

ils « n'avaient ni les moyens financiers, ni les contacts, ni le pedigree pour entrer dans le monde fermé de l'appareil du parti. Mais dans l'univers démocratique de l'activisme en ligne [ils] n'avaient pas besoin de cela pour [se] faire entendre »[5]. Sans aucun doute le candidat Obama a su tirer les leçons de ces événements, profiter de la rénovation qui s'opérait dans son parti et choisir une équipe de campagne capable d'utiliser l'Internet. Pour Matthew R. Kerbel, il s'agit d'une « campagne hybride »[6]. **Aurélie Blot** consacre son étude à examiner dans quelle mesure la stratégie d'Obama de miser sur les possibilités offertes par ce nouveau média pour obtenir le soutien des jeunes électeurs a été décisive dans son élection. En effet, 43 millions d'Américains, soit 20% du corps électoral, ont entre 18 et 29 ans et se servent principalement de l'Internet pour suivre l'actualité. Ils consultent les pages *web*, dialoguent sur les réseaux sociaux, visionnent des vidéos sur *YouTube* ou lisent les blogs. Or, les études citées montrent que cette stratégie a fait la différence dès les primaires, permettant au candidat d'amasser un capital de sympathie et de récolter suffisamment de dons pour passer du statut d'*outsider* à celui de présidentiable. Comparant Barack Obama à John Kennedy, dont la victoire est attribuée à son aisance au cours des débats avec son adversaire à la télévision, elle argue qu'il a su apparaître aux yeux des électeurs, grâce à son e-campagne, comme un président capable « d'instaurer le changement » et de mobiliser un électorat particulièrement volatil par sa présence sur tous les sites de réseaux sociaux ; elle souligne, cependant, que l'Internet – média interactif – a été un atout parce qu'il était en adéquation avec le message du candidat : restaurer des liens authentiques avec les électeurs, délivrer une promesse d'espoir pour l'avenir.

---

[5] Jerome Armstrong, Markos Moulitsas Zùniga, *op. cit.*, « *We did not have the money, the connections or the pedigree to break into the insular world of traditional politics. But in the democratic world of online activism, we didn't need those things to be heard* », p. xv.

[6] En effet le candidat s'est entouré à la fois de conseillers chargés d'organiser une campagne traditionnelle mais il s'est aussi assuré qu'à l'échelon local les volontaires avaient les moyens et la liberté de s'organiser et d'agir. Il a su également concilier les exigences d'une campagne télévisuelle formatée et maintenir un contact régulier avec les membres des réseaux sociaux ainsi qu'une présence efficace sur d'autres sites du *Net.* Matthew R. Kerbel, *Netroots. Online Progressives and the Transformation of American Politics*, Boulder, CO: Paradigm Publishers, 2009, chapitre 7.

La question de la relation entre blogueurs et journalistes a été soulevée par de très nombreux auteurs[7]. **Erica Johnson** teste le bien fondé, des affirmations de Tom Rosenstiel et Bill Kovach, dans un rapport publié par le *Pew Research Center*. Pour les auteurs, durant la campagne présidentielle en 2008, « les deux médias – l'ancien et le nouveau – ont été interdépendants et souvent complémentaires (...) rarement en compétition, ils ont été une source d'information mutuelle »[8]. Son étude de cas porte sur trois jours : du 2 au 4 novembre 2008. Elle analyse le point de vue sur les différents candidats exprimé dans un échantillon de dix blogs représentatifs de toutes les tendances sur l'échiquier politique, des plus « libérales » aux plus conservatrices, examine la fréquence des mises à jour en fonction de l'actualité et la qualité des informations postées. Les données collectées sont ensuite comparées à celles fournies par l'analyse de trois quotidiens du nord-est des Etats-Unis, choisis en fonction du nombre de leurs lecteurs. Cette étude, bien que limitée, démontre la pertinence des conclusions de Bill Kovach et Tom Rosenstiel et confirme la principale différence entre blogueurs et journalistes : les premiers revendiquant leur droit à prendre parti, au nom de la liberté d'expression, alors que les seconds s'efforcent de respecter les règles déontologiques de la profession : maintenir une certaine neutralité dans leur présentation des informations et cantonner l'expression d'opinions politiques aux éditoriaux[9].

Les trois contributions suivantes considèrent une question qui fait débat : l'Internet est-il un média qui favorise l'engagement des citoyens, une nouvelle forme de démocratie coopérative et participative ? Présente-t-il, au contraire, des dangers pour une démocratie libérale comme celle qui existe aux Etats-Unis ? **Elisabeth Boulot** s'est penchée sur les enjeux et les défis auxquels sont confrontés les responsables politiques et les juges lorsqu'il s'agit de préserver la liberté d'expression et l'accès à

---

[7] Certains d'entre eux les prénomment des e-journalistes ou des journalistes citoyens, d'autres les considèrent comme des amateurs.

[8] Bill Kovach, Tom Rosenstiel, « Lessons of the Election », *State of the News Media 2009,* Pew Project for Excellence in Journalism, « *(...) the old and the new media were interdependent and often complementary. (...) The two media were hardly in competition. They informed each other* ».

[9] Ceci conduit certains auteurs à considérer les blogueurs comme ayant une part de responsabilité dans l'accroissement de la polarisation de la vie politique aux Etats-Unis, voir dans la bibliographie : Davis 2009, Perlmutter 2008, Sunstein, 2002 et 2007, Thompson 2003, Tunney et Monagan, 2010.

l'information sur la Toile, en dépit des pressions économiques et de la nécessité d'assurer la sécurité nationale. Après avoir exposé les motifs qui ont conduit la Cour suprême en 1997 à affranchir l'Internet – à la différence des autres médias électroniques – de la tutelle de la *Federal Communications Commission*, au nom du premier amendement, elle évalue l'impact de cette décision sur le développement de ce média, puis examine les menaces qui pèsent sur la « neutralité du Net », à la fois à cause des avancées technologiques, des impératifs économiques et de la volonté des Etats de réduire le plus possible le modèle de gouvernance horizontale qui a présidé à sa construction afin d'en faire un espace public proche de celui des médias traditionnels. Le récent e-G8 a montré combien ces questions sont brûlantes et sources de divisions entre les Etats. **Jean-Marie Ruiz** s'est attaché à élucider les causes des réactions particulièrement violentes de la classe politique aux Etats-Unis à l'affaire WikiLeaks, après avoir souligné qu'elles étaient pour le moins surprenantes dans un pays dont la Constitution protège la liberté d'expression, qui a inscrit dans la loi le principe de l'accès des citoyens à l'information[10] et de la part d'une administration qui s'était engagée au respect des ces droits. L'affaire WikiLeaks[11] posant la question des limites de la transparence, prendre en compte la relation ambivalente que la diplomatie américaine a entretenue, au cours de son histoire, avec le secret d'état est l'une des réponses possibles. Or, à l'ère numérique, comme l'illustre le site WikiLeaks, la séparation entre les coulisses et la

[10] *Freedom of Information Act* (1966).

[11] De nombreux rapprochements ont été faits entre cette affaire et celle de la publication « des papiers du Pentagone » en 1971 par le *New York Times* et le *Washington Post*. Il y a cependant des différences importantes entre les deux, certaines sont d'ordre matériel. Les documents dérobés n'étaient pas des données brutes mais des rapports classés secret défense. Ils pouvaient être publiés tels quels, si l'on excepte un certain nombre de précautions d'usage. La quantité de copies était sans commune mesure, étant donné les moyens de l'époque. De plus, la diffusion se limita aux journaux américains, le monde étant encore séparé en deux blocs et la guerre au Vietnam l'une des conséquences de cette division. L'identité de la source ne fut connue que lorsque Mark W. Felt, alors âgé de 91 ans, décida de divulguer cette information en 2005, Bob Woodward et Carl Bernstein ayant toujours refusé de révéler l'identité de celui que l'on surnommait « Gorge Profonde ». Enfin, la Cour suprême des Etats-Unis autorisa, contre l'avis de l'administration Nixon, la publication des documents (*New York Times v. U.S.*, 403 U.S. 713, 1971) défendant vigoureusement le droit de la presse d'informer les citoyens à propos de cette guerre très impopulaire. Daniel Ellsberg fut emprisonné puis libéré.

scène devient floue. Pour comprendre la virulente condamnation des agissements de Julien Assange par plusieurs des membres de l'administration Obama, il convient également de prendre conscience des difficultés d'un président qui a dû se démarquer à la fois de la politique étrangère « néo-impérialiste » de son prédécesseur et d'une administration ayant érigé le secret d'état en principe après les attentats du 11 septembre. Chercher à réconcilier le droit des citoyens à être informés et la sécurité nationale ne va pas sans heurts. **Virginie Picquet** aborde également la question des limites de la transparence mais par un autre biais. Examinant l'impact des *netroots* sur le débat politique aux Etats-Unis, elle met en lumière leurs avantages. Ils ont, entre autres, rendu la parole aux citoyens et suscité leur engagement politique, donné à des candidats considérés comme des *outsiders* la possibilité de gagner une élection et révélé des informations que les médias traditionnels ont tendance à laisser dans l'ombre. En favorisant la prise de parole, les *netroots* facilitent la circulation des informations et ont pour objectif une plus grande « transparence » de la société et par conséquent des décisions prises par les gouvernements. Mais cette intense circulation des informations *entre* les individus s'accompagne d'une mise en commun d'informations *sur* les individus. Certes, elle oblige les hommes politiques à s'expliquer et à rendre compte mais elle rend la frontière entre vie publique et vie privée de plus en plus poreuse ce qui n'est pas sans danger et pose la question de ce qu'il est légitime de mettre sur la Toile[12]. La démocratie s'enrichit-elle de la circulation de l'information en « temps réel » ?

Les deux derniers articles examinent différents imaginaires politiques : dans l'un le relationnel prime et la politique est prise en charge par les individus et les groupes sociaux, le « nous » l'emporte sur le « ils », dans un autre l'internaute construit son propre univers autour de son moi virtuel pour ne plus s'intéresser qu'à ce que Cass R.

[12] La demande de plus de transparence de la part des hommes politiques s'appuie aux Etats-Unis sur la thèse que la libre circulation des idées dans la sphère publique préserve la démocratie ; voici les termes choisis par le juge Louis Brandeis pour défendre dans l'arrêt *Whitney v. California*, ce principe énoncé dans le premier amendement : « *If there be time to expose through discussion the falsehood and fallacies (...) the remedy to be applied is more speech, not enforced silence* » (274 U.S. 357, 377, 1943). L'élargissement de l'espace public induit pas la communication en ligne, a-t-il rendu cette thèse caduque ?

Sunstein[13] appelle le *Daily Me*, c'est-à-dire ses propres contacts : amis sur les réseaux sociaux, forums de discussions, blogs, articles de presse ou programmes télévisés choisis uniquement parce qu'ils correspondent aux idées auxquelles on souscrit. Leur émergence est le fruit de la révolution numérique, ils sont en devenir. L'Internet a décloisonné le débat politique, facilité la création de communautés en ligne transnationales qui se rassemblent dans le monde physique pour agir ; les *netroots* ont fait découvrir aux citoyens les vertus de l'auto-organisation et le partage des cultures. Quelles vont être les incidences de cette expérience de la démocratie à l'échelle planétaire sur les politiques nationales et locales alors que, dans le même temps, chacun s'est créé un moi dans le cyberspace ? **Christian Moraru** argue que le citoyen internaute est conduit à repenser sa relation à son pays et au monde qui l'entoure, mais aussi à « l'autre ». Deux voies s'ouvrent à lui, l'une « égocentrée » : une utilisation individualiste de ces nouvelles technologies au profit de celui qui s'en sert en tant que consommateur ; l'autre implique une nouvelle éthique, une nouvelle « écologie politique et culturelle » : un « être ensemble » qui préserve l'individualité de chacun, instaure une plus grande authenticité dans les relations humaines, privilégie le face-à-face plutôt que l'interface, la délibération, le partage des ressources et des les projets communautaires. L'Internet fait-il vraiment bouger les lignes du pouvoir politique ou est-ce une illusion ? Il est coutumier aujourd'hui d'opposer l'univers participatif du *web* et sa gouvernance horizontale à celui des médias de masse où l'information est sélectionnée, présentée et expliquée par un professionnel à un public passif, selon les règles d'une communication qui s'effectue « du haut vers le bas ». Cependant, comme le démontre Richard Grusin et Jay D. Bolter[14], l'apparition d'un nouveau média induit une transformation des médias existants ; la télévision n'a pas échappé à cette règle, la présentation des informations a été reformatée : elle est maintenant présentée en continu. De plus la segmentation du petit écran, sur le modèle de celui d'un ordinateur,

---

[13] Cass R. Sunstein, *Republic.com 02*, Princeton, NJ: Princeton University Press, 2007. Ces pratiques sont pernicieuses pour la démocratie car elles enferment l'internaute dans un "cocon". En conséquence, il n'est plus exposé à des points de vue différents du sien.

[14] Richard Grusin et Jay D. Bolter, *Remediation. Understanding the New Media*, Cambridge, MA: MIT Press, 2000.

donne une illusion d'ubiquité, même si la spécificité de la télévision reste la présentation des événements « en direct » à un public de masse. **Daniel Burns**, à travers une étude de cas, s'interroge sur la validité d'un modèle de transmission de ce qui prétend être de l'information, comme sur l'opportunité de perpétuer la nostalgie d'une vision impérialiste du monde entretenue par George W. Bush. Il analyse la manière dont Glenn Beck s'est servi de l'affaire des 9 de Tarnac et du tract *L'Insurrection qui vient* pour agiter une fois encore, le spectre du complot et l'existence d'ennemis toujours plus menaçants pour les Américains. L'étude faite par Richard Hofstadter du style paranoïaque en politique aux Etats-Unis[15], et celle d'Emily Apter sur le concept de « *oneworldedness* »[16], servent de fil conducteur pour mettre en lumière les stratégies d'un présentateur omniscient afin de donner à son auditoire une vision du monde qui privilégie les valeurs conservatrices. Sous couvert d'une apparente impartialité et de la noble mission d'expliquer les événements à l'Américain lambda, il n'hésite pas à faire la promotion de ses propres écrits par le biais d'une lecture tronquée du tract et réutilise à l'envi le même schéma pour présenter les révolutions dans les pays arabes et susciter la crainte d'un effet de contagion. Glenn Beck a maintenant disparu des écrans de *Fox News*. Ceci signifie-t-il pourtant que ce type de rapport avec le public n'est plus crédible aujourd'hui, même si la paranoïa peut resurgir à tout moment dans la vie politique américaine comme le montre les réactions à l'affaire WikiLeaks ?

Certaines des contributions rassemblées dans cet ouvrage ont fait l'objet d'une communication lors d'une journée d'étude sur les *netroots*, à l'Université Paris Est Marne-la-Vallée le 17 juin 2010. C'est grâce au soutien de Marie-Françoise Alamichel et de William Dow, à la participation active des étudiants de première année du Master Langues et Civilisations Aires Anglophones, à celle des collègues qui ont pris part à ce projet et aux anglicistes de l'UFR, qu'elle a pu être organisée et donner lieu à de fructueux débats. C'est à eux tous que j'adresse mes chaleureux remerciements.

Elisabeth Boulot

[15] Richard Hofstadter, *The Paranoid Style in American Politics and Other Essays*, 1965; New York: Vintage, 2008.
[16] Emily S. Apter, « On Oneworldedness: Or Paranoia as a World System », *American Literary History*, vol. 18, n° 2, 2006, p. 365-389.

Liste alphabétique des auteurs

Aurélie BLOT (Université Paris Ouest Nanterre La Défense)
Campagne virtuelle et élection réelle, quel rôle a joué l'outil Internet dans l'élection présidentielle de Barack Obama ?

Elisabeth BOULOT (Université Paris Est Marne-la-Vallée)
Protéger la liberté d'expression et l'accès à l'information sur l'Internet. Enjeux et défis.

Daniel BURNS (University of North Carolina Greensboro)
On the U.S. Reception of L'Insurrection qui vient.

Aurélie GODET (Université Michel Montaigne Bordeaux 3)
The "Other Netroots": A Study of Online Conservative Activism from 1998 to 2010.

Erica JOHNSON (Université Paris Est Créteil)
Developing Democratic Debate: A Case Study of American Political Blogs and the Mainstream Print Media in the Run-up to the 2008 Presidential Election.

Christian MORARU (University of North Carolina Greensboro)
Rerouting Politics: Networks, Netroots, and the U.S. Cultural Imaginary.

Virginie PICQUET (Université d'Angers)
L'Impact des netroots sur le débat politique et la démocratie américaine : à la fois positif et pernicieux.

Jean-Marie RUIZ (Université de Savoie)
Le bruit et la fureur : WikiLeaks contre l'administration Obama.

Internet et vie politique aux Etats-Unis

The "Other Netroots": A Study of Online Conservative Activism from 1998 to 2010

Despite all the talk about the blogosphere being *"one community"*[1], a sort of "*giant communal brain*"[2], and about its potential for realizing what Jürgen Habermas called a "*public sphere*,"[3] the Internet political world has been sharply divided along ideological lines since the closing years of the 20th century. There are the progressive netroots on the one hand (clustered around sites like Democratic Underground, DailyKos, Huffington Post, or Tom Paine) and, on the other, the conservative netroots (dominated by sites like FreeRepublic and blogs like Instapundit, Michelle Malkin, Newsbusters or Red State).

As has been noted by numerous scholars, the two universes do not really communicate. 54.6% of conservative traffic and 69% of progressive traffic go to the top 10 blogs representing their respective ideologies. Webmasters tend to filter reader feedback according to the ideological tendency of the website. Political bloggers are much more likely to link to others who share their political predispositions. Cross-overs tend to be labelled as "trolls," that is, provocateurs interested in starting a flame war.

The result appears to be a growing fragmentation and specialization of the Internet political sphere, so that for the most part what we have

---

[1] Markos Moulitsas Zùniga, quoted in Kathy Kiely, "'Freewheeling 'Bloggers' Are Rewriting Rules of Journalism", *USA Today*, December 30, 2003.

[2] Andrew Sullivan, *idem*.

[3] "*By 'public sphere', we mean first of all a domain of our social life in which such a thing as public opinion can be formed. Access to the public sphere is open in principle to all citizens. A portion of the public sphere is constituted in every conversation in which private persons come together to form a public.*" Jürgen Habermas, "The Public Sphere: An Encyclopedia Article", *New German Critique* 3, Autumn 1964, p. 49. Habermas distinguishes between "*mere opinions*" and "public *opinion*": the latter requires "*a public that engages in rational discussion.*"

are separate zones of discourse with no room for centrist thought. Gary Thompson's metaphor of "*bubbles*" isolating writers by ideology[4] or Cass R. Sunstein's concept of conservative and progressive blogs as "*echo chambers*"[5] seem particular relevant here.

The progressive netroots have been described at length since 2004 by people such as Eric Boehlert, Jerome Armstrong, and Matthew R. Kerbel.[6] The literature on online conservative activism, however, remains scarce. This paper will attempt to even the field by summarizing the evolution of the online conservative infrastructure over the past ten years; in so doing, it will provide tentative answers to three sets of questions:

(1) Why do online conservative militants seem to be "losing" since 2004? Could this change in the near future?
(2) What do conservative activists do online? Do they use the Internet differently from liberals or progressives?
(3) How do the conservative "netroots" interact with the conservative "elite"? To what degree can they be said to influence elected officials, right-wing intellectuals, and Republican Party operatives?

1. A short history of the online conservative infrastructure from 1998 to 2008

The era of dominance: 1998-2004

After successfully using talk radio for a decade to speak to their supporters, target opponents and raise money for political campaigns, American conservatives quickly jumped on the Internet train in the 1990s.

---

[4] Gary Thompson, "Weblogs, Warblogs, the Public Sphere, and Bubbles", *Transformations* 7, September 2003.

[5] Cass R. Sunstein, *Republic.com*, Princeton, NJ: Princeton University Press, 2002.

[6] Eric Boehlert, *Bloggers on the Bus: How the Internet Changed Politics and the Press*, New York: Free Press, 2009; Jerome Armstrong and Markos Moulitsas Zúniga, *Crashing the Gate: Netroots, Grassroots, and the Rise of People-Powered Politics*, White River Junction, VT: Chelsea Green, 2006; Matthew R. Kerbel, *Netroots: Online Progressives and the Transformation of American Politics*, Boulder, CO: Paradigm Publishers, 2009.

In January 1998, a young gossip hound named Matt Drudge caught wind of a story that *Newsweek* was considering running, a story about President Bill Clinton's affair with a young White House intern named Monica Lewinsky. When *Newsweek*'s editors decided not to print it, Drudge posted it on his protoblog The Drudge Report, which he had created two years before. Drudge made no pretense of objectivity in telling the story. Yet he forced the mainstream news organizations to follow the stories he pushed. His website, often called "*the granddaddy of all blogs*," quickly stood unrivalled in its effectiveness.

Community news sites like FreeRepublic, NewsMax, and WorldNetDaily also earned their stripes during the impeachment imbroglio by providing an outlet for Republican critiques of the liberal media. A few weeks before President Clinton's impeachment by the House, FreeRepublic sponsored a rally that drew an estimated 5,000 to 6,000 pro-impeachment protestors to the Washington Monument. It later sponsored a dinner honouring the House impeachment managers, which 1,200 people attended.

In 2000, FreeRepublic, NewsMax, and WorldNetDaily.com galvanized the political right in support of George W. Bush. FreeRepublic which at that time had 47,000 registered users and generated 75,000 visitors and 2 million page views a day, sponsored pro-Bush rallies in San Francisco and in Florida. NewsMax raised money for an advertising campaign accusing Democrats of election fraud in Florida. Its fundraising letter accused the media of "*dirty tricks*" and said: "*Our country teeters on the edge of a Constitutional crisis the likes of which we have never witnessed.*"[7]

But it was John McCain who first realized the potential of the Internet in a presidential race, running an experimental set of targeted banner ads during his ill-fated 1999 primary battle against George W. Bush. McCain's campaign was considered the cutting edge of fundraising after raising $3 million in the 10 days following the New Hampshire primary. This event led social media consultant J. D. Lasica to talk of "*the right's dominance over the web*" in 2000.[8]

---

[7] A copy of the letter can be seen at: http://the firing line.com/forums/archive/ index. http://thefiringline.com/forums/archive/index.php/t-48037.html.

[8] "*As for the right's dominance over the web, I happen to think several factors come into play. Chief among them: the demographics of online users still skew conservative (remember that Bush trounced Gore in Youth-e-Vote.net's online poll of young voters*

American conservative dominance on the Internet never ceased to increase between 2001 and 2003. After a company called Pyra Labs, which has since been acquired by Google, developed Blogger.com, software that allowed Internet users to create Web pages without using the complicated computer coding known as HTML, dozens of popular conservative blogs were created, among which:

1. Instapundit, operated by University of Tennessee Law professor Glenn Reynolds.
2. The Daily Dish, created by conservative libertarian journalist Andrew Sullivan.
3. RealClearPolitics, started by Tom Bevan, a former advertising executive, aged 34, with no experience in either politics or journalism.
4. GOPUSA, an Internet publication for conservative Republicans run by Bobby Eberle, a Houston engineer with, again, no previous journalism experience. Eberle scored an interview with President Bush's top political adviser, Karl Rove, in 2002.
5. Little Green Footballs, which defended the war in Iraq and referenced news reports in such a way as to disparage non-Fox News-style presentation.
6. PowerLine, a multiauthor conservative blog that was named *Time Magazine*'s "Blog of the Year" in 2004 (i.e, two years after launch).
7. RedState.com, a conservative community blog intentionally set up to allow any registered user to contribute their original content to the site.

One of the most prominent characteristics of these blogs was that they linked to each other a lot, indeed with greater frequency than leftwing blogs. This linking practice gave them higher rankings in Google search results, which in turn brought more readers to them in a kind of "snowball effect".

---

taken in the days before the election, though among actual voters aged 18-25, Gore beat Bush); the right is far better funded than the left; and the political camp out of power tends to be the hungrier, more active, and more vocal". J. D. Lasica, "Election News from the Wired Right", *Online Journalism Review*, November 11, 2000.

The « Other Netroots »

When the first coherent study of the blogosphere was conducted in July of 2003, it revealed two important trends in the online political landscape: (1) blog traffic was highly concentrated in a small number of top-tier blogs. Blogs 7-100 combined had approximately the same number of page views as the top 6; (2) conservative bloggers vastly outpaced progressives in terms of total traffic. The top-ranked blog Instapundit, had as much traffic as the next 5 sites combined and was 3 times larger than any other blog.[9] Studies suggested that as of 2003, the conservative blogosphere was 2 or 3 times as large as the progressive blogosphere and held a commanding lead in terms of overall traffic.

The Republican Party could not ignore the potential of the conservative grassroots during the 2004 presidential campaign. Indeed, the Bush campaign tried to encourage them by posting a link to "Bloggers for Bush" on its campaign website. Jimmy Orr, the head of the White House's Internet activities, admitted that many in the administration read blogs every day to keep up to date on the issues that were receiving voters' attention.[10] Republican representative Jack Kingston (R-GA) even organized a series of blogging seminars and conference calls that brought together GOP aides on Capitol Hill with popular right-leaning bloggers.[11] Relationships with Republican operatives, however, remained a bit tense throughout. "*To read this stuff is to drink politics from a fire hose. There's so much of it that it's hard to process*," said Terry Holt, spokesman for President Bush's campaign, in 2003.[12]

In the end, the real political successes of the conservative netroots were not so much founded in grassroots organizing or campaign fundraising as in combating liberal media coverage. Conservative blogs created major messaging problems for Democratic Senator Tom Daschle

---

9 Results quoted in Chris Bowers and Matthew Stoller, "Emergence of the Progressive Blogosphere: A New Force in American Politics", New Politics Institute, August 10, 2005, http://newpolitics.net/node/87?full_report=1.

10 Dan Froomkin, "White House Goes to he Blogs", *The Washington Post*, August 17, 2004.

11 Eric Pfeiffer, "GOP Urged to Make Greater Use of Blogs", *The Washington Times*, April 13, 2006.

12 Quoted in Kathy Kiely, "'Freewheeling 'Bloggers' Are Rewriting Rules of Journalism", *USA Today*, December 30, 2003.

in 2003, chummed the Swift Boat Veterans for Truth in 2004 and, of course, led the charge against Dan Rather.

In 2004, Dan Rather, then a senior journalist with CBS, reported on six documents that his network received that they claimed were from the files of President Bush's commanding officer when he served in the National Guard as a young man. The documents seemed to show that Bush was derelict in his duty. Rather reported on the news show that his network had analyzed the documents and found them to be legitimate. Within hours of the report, several right-leaning bloggers began their own check on the authenticity of the documents. They found their own expert who claimed that the documents were forgeries and several blogs such as FreeRepublic, PowerLine, and Little Green Footballs began asking their readers to put pressure on CBS to withdraw their story. Finally blogger Matt Drudge became involved and this triggered the Associated Press to pick up the challenge to Rather's report. In the end CBS withdrew their report, fired the producer of Rather's show and forced Rather to apologize. He ended up retiring in 2005 – a year earlier than expected. Rather had been a long-time nemesis of conservatives who saw him as the supreme embodiment of the liberal bias in the press. His apology and early retirement brought them great satisfaction.

As late as 2004, it therefore appeared to many observers as though there was a slight conservative advantage on the web, at least in the political blogosphere. One of the most heavily-cited article on the blogosphere, Lada Adamic and Natalie Glance's 2005 paper, "The Political Blogosphere and the 2004 Election: Divided They Blog" used hyperlink maps to demonstrate that leftwing and rightwing netroots operated as largely independent neighbourhoods and, noting that conservatives linked to one another with greater frequency, implied that the Right was, if anything, leading in this arena.[13] Robert Ackland conducted a follow-up study with the same dataset and found that conservative bloggers were indeed more "prominent" online, with 9 of the 10 most prominent political bloggers coming from the conservative blogosphere.[14]

---

[13] Lada Adamic and Natalie Glance, "The Political Blogosphere and the 2004 U.S. Election: Divided They Blog", March 4 2005. http://www.blogpulse.com/papers/2005/AdamicGlanceBlogWWW.pdf.

[14] Robert Ackland, "Mapping the U.S. Political Blogosphere: Are Conservative Bloggers More Prominent?", May 7 2005, http://voson.anu.edu.au/papers/polblogs.pdf.

Ironically, the fortunes of the conservative movement online started to change at the very moment when its dominance started to be validated by most media researchers.

The era of decline: 2004-2008

After the 2004 presidential campaign, the progressive netroots made a surprise resurgence. While Instapundit almost doubled the size of its audience between 2003 and 2005, DailyKos, now the second largest political blog in the world behind the Huffington Post, increased its audience nearly 30 times over.[15] As of July 2005, it received more than four times as many monthly visits as Instapundit. While FreeRepublic had long been understood to be the largest political community on the web, Democratic Underground almost entirely closed the traffic difference with its conservative rival in the months following John Kerry's defeat. All in all, the progressive blogosphere grew from less big than the conservative blogosphere to nearly double its size between 2005 and 2008. Its trajectory furthermore indicated a maturation from the ideological polarization of netroots groups such as MoveOn or CodePink to the online ObamaNation that recruited political moderates as well as partisans. Progressives were neither the innovators nor the early adopters of online communication but they became, in innovation theory parlance, "*the early majority*".[16]

Conservatives continually tried to develop parallel organizations to those that had risen to prominence in the American left. But, as Internet scholar Dave Karpf has convincingly shown in his work, most of these attempts were failures, resulting in a gap in online infrastructure between the left and the right.[17] RedState.com, which had legitimately claimed to be "the" conservative community hub since 2004, never emerged as a central hub for conservative bloggers. In 2009, RedState received roughly 50,000 visits per day – ten times less than the most-trafficked conservative site, HotAir.com, and 17 times less than DailyKos. In terms

[15] Chris Bowers and Matthew Stoller, "Emergence of the Progressive Blogosphere: A New Force in American Politics", New Politics Institute, August 10, 2005.

[16] Cf. Everett M. Rogers, *Diffusion of Innovations*, Glencoe, IL: Free Press, 1962.

[17] David Karpf, "Unexpected Transformations: The Internet's Effect on Political Associations in American Politics", Ph.D. dissertation, University of Pennsylvania, June 2009. See especially chapter 7.

of comment activity and hyperlink authority, the site likewise scored unexceptional numbers when compared to other elite political blogs. According to the Blogosphere Authority Index – an aggregate ranking system devised by David Karpf, that tracks the elite progressive and conservative blog networks by taking into account four distinct measures of strength: network centrality, link density, site traffic, and community activity – RedState.com was the 9th most trafficked conservative blog in November 2007 and it fell to 19th place during the 2008 election season.

The only blogs that rose in the rankings between 2004 and 2008 were solo-author affairs that lacked the community blog structure and did not generate political activity. Their audiences acted as readers, not as participants. While the progressive netroots empowered a new set of insurgent leaders within the progressive coalition, the conservative blogosphere remained ruled by long-time media critics (Hugh Hewitt, Brent Bozell) and existing contributors to Fox News (Michelle Malkin). For reasons we will detail later, conservative attempts at developing community blogs did not attract high levels of readership, hyperlinking, or participation.

There were several attempts at launching a "MoveOn for conservatives". Founded in 2003, RightMarch was the first such attempt. Heralded in mass media coverage and promoted by wealthy Republican backers, it promised to be "*the 'Rapid Response Force' against the ongoing liberal onslaught*".[18] It never lived up to conservatives' expectations however, failing to do much of anything with the large e-mail list it claimed to have developed. According to the data collected by *the Center for Responsive Politics*, RightMarch sent $60,750 in the 2004 election cycle, versus MoveOn's $31.8 million. In 2006, RightMarch raised $102,699 while MoveOn brought in $28.1 million. They improved against their standard in 2008, raising $646,089, but this hardly compared to the $38.4 million raised by MoveOn in the cycle.[19]

A promising competitor to RightMarch, TheVanguard.org, was founded in March 2006 by a group of tech-savvy conservative leaders. With a strong base of sophisticated Internet entrepreneurs who had previously started the popular online financial transaction site

[18] See the "About Us" section of its website: http://www.rightmarch.com/about.htm.

[19] RightMarch data available at: http://www.opensecrets.org/pacs/lookup2.php?cycle=2008&strID=C00386482. MoveOn data available at: http://www.opensecrets.org/pacs/lookup2.php?strID=C00341396.

paypal.com, TheVanguard seemed better positioned to keep pace with MoveOn's breakneck pace of technological innovation. Despite heavy promotion from the outset and a collection of conservative activist heavyweights on their board and staff, the organization never fully coalesced. Today, 4 years after launching, the website of the organization in still in Beta version and its blog contains only one post.

Freedom's Watch, meanwhile, was launched by a collection of former Bush administration appointees and staffers with an initial wave of ads that countered MoveOn's controversial "Betray-Us" newspaper ad in the summer of 2007. Aided by a reported budget of $200 million, this group was heralded as, finally, a successful conservative response. That excitement lasted little more than 3 months. The organization was almost solely funded by conservative casino mogul Sheldon Adelson. After Adelson's company, Las Vegas Sands Corp., lost 95% of its stock value in the 2008 market tank, he withdrew his funding and the group announced that it would permanently shut up shop at the end of the year.

During the 2008 presidential election campaign, intense coverage of some stories by the conservative blogosphere (e.g. the scandals over Pastor Jeremiah Wright or Barack Obama's comment that "*bitter*" small-town voters "*cling to guns or religion*") threatened to erase the Democratic ticket's lead in the polls. Record numbers of bloggers attended and covered the political conventions, and an increasing number of bloggers was employed by the presidential campaigns. Within days of her nomination, Sarah Palin – the first woman to be nominated for the vice-presidential office by the Republican Party – became far and away the most searched-for political figure in America, and reigned supreme over the blogosphere as the subject of more posts than Biden, McCain, and Obama. Even Palin herself acknowledged the role Internet users played in breaking and spinning news about her, blaming "*bloggers in their parents' basement*" for "*talking garbage*," sowing controversy, and spurring negative coverage. But the conservative netroots were nonetheless outgunned by the progressive ones, notably in the area of online advertising. The Democrats used a fundraising tool, ActBlue, which let users set their own endorsement list and easily interface with a blog's infrastructure – including an embedded fundraising thermometer that let visitors see how close the site was coming to its goal. This malleable approach to fundraising proved invaluable in lowering the infrastructure costs of smaller web-based activist groups and outstandingly effective.

The same could not be said for ActBlue's right-wing equivalents. Launched in 2006, the RightRoots fundraising site was meant to be a Republican counter to ActBlue. But, crucially, it set out its own list of endorsees, developed by a small circle of prominent conservative bloggers and insiders, and chose not to give users the ability to develop their own lists. Rightroots essentially fell into disuse in the 2008 election cycle, replaced by SlateCard, which suffered from the similar top-down management challenges. SlateCard raised nearly $650,000 for Republican candidates and committees in the 2008 election cycle, setting the combined fundraising totals of the two Republican answers to ActBlue at around $1 million in two cycles. ActBlue, meanwhile, raised over $85 million between 2004 and 2009.

There is one interesting exception to this story of conservative online fundraising failure, however: the Ron Paul primary campaign. Paul, an antiwar populist Republican, harnessed the power of the Internet. More popular online than he was in the polls, he raised a lot of money on the Internet: an astonishing $6.1 million from contributors by 37,000 backers. The "Paulites" are best-known for their single-day "moneybomb" on November 5th, 2007, which raised somewhere between $3.75 and $5 million. They also used meetup-style tools pioneered by the Dean campaign to promote local actions throughout the country and a medium called Vlogging or video blogging to promote his candidacy. Videos of his supporters across the country talking to him were posted on YouTube. Each candidate had a site on YouTube but Ron Paul's got more hits than any other. Positively ridiculed by the elite conservative blogosphere, banished from comment threads wherever they popped up during the 2008 primary season, Ron Paul supporters functioned as an outparty of sorts within the conservative coalition. And while the network of elite conservative consultants, party operatives, and politicians has consistently tried and failed to build web-based participatory communities, the one limited success has come from the vocal minority.

Since 2004, according to a George Washington University study, the Internet Democrats outnumber the more conservative Internet Republicans by almost 2 to 1 among what the study calls "Online

Political Citizens".[20] According to the Blogosphere Authority Index devised by David Karpf, here were the top 20 political blogs in December 2008:

1. DailyKos (liberal)
2. Huffington Post (liberal)
3. Talking Points Memo (liberal)
4. Hot Air (conservative)
5. Atrios (liberal)
6. Crooks and Liars (liberal)
7. Firedoglake (liberal)
8. Michelle Malkin (conservative)
9. Newsbusters (conservative)
10. Think Progress (liberal)
11. Washington Monthly (liberal)
12. Instapundit (conservative)
13. American Thinker (conservative)
14. Ace of Spades HQ (conservative)
15. Little Green Footballs (conservative)
16. American Blog (liberal)
17. Volokh Conspiracy (conservative)
18. Digby (liberal)
19. Feministing (liberal)
20. Jihad Watch (conservative)[21]

Seven of the top 10 political blogs were progressive in nature, indicating a clear advantage to the progressive bloggers. Adamic and Glance's initial findings remain correct with relation to blogrolls. The average conservative blogroll in this study had 129 links, while the average progressive blog had 72. Conservative bloggers were more generous with their links, it seemed, but this generosity was diffuse. Only 7 conservative blogs were listed in over 50% of all included blogrolls, which was surprising given the outstandingly large number of average

[20] "Political Influentials Online in the 2004 Presidential Campaign", Institute for Politics, Democracy and the Internet, Graduate School of Political Management, George Washington University, February 5, 2004, http://www.gwu.edu/~media/pressrelease.cfm?ann_id=10462.

[21] David Karpf, "Blogosphere Authority Index", December 14, 2008, http://www.blogosphereauthorityindex.com/default.asp?archive=bai_Dec142008.mdb.

links. The rich-get-richer pattern did not seem to hold true for the conservative blogosphere any more.

The top sites in the conservative blogosphere acted less as central hubs than did the top sites in the progressive blogosphere. It is likely that this is tied to a disparity between the architecture of the elite blogs. It appears as though "community blogging" architecture was more heartily distributed through the progressive than conservative blogosphere. Dailykos.com included over 1,000 user-generated "diaries" per week, providing far more content for potential hyperlinking. Huffingtonpost.com received submissions from hundreds of well-known authors, including many elite bloggers who also maintained their own personal sites. Two of the top three conservative sites – MichelleMalkin.com and Instapundit.com – employed a simpler "individual blogging" architecture, also called "closed authorship".

After the top 4 progressive sites, however, a convergence between the progressive and conservative authority scores could be observed. The difference between the liberal and conservative blogosphere lied therefore in the hub sites – the elite of the elite. Dailykos.com was roughly 50% larger than the entire conservative blogosphere! There was simply no comparable entity in the conservative political universe.

2. How can the decline of the conservative online infrastructure be explained?

Structural/ideological cause: conservatism is incompatible with the democratic structure of the Internet

Since 2004, while attracting far fewer headlines, the progressive blogosphere has therefore become larger than the conservative blogosphere, to great financial benefit for their favoured political candidates. Two competing explanations for this gap can be laid out: the first being structural and ideological, the second contextual.

The first hypothesis is that conservatism is, at some underlying level, incompatible with the democratic structure of the Internet and that its "top-down" ideology is better adapted to talk radio as a medium. It is true that conservative bloggers do not seem comfortable with community organizing. Some of them do encourage their readers to vote for or contact elected officials, suggesting that they believe they can motivate their readers to become politically active and engaged. Buttressing more traditional campaign activities, they sometimes serve as campaign workers collecting money, disseminating information, organizing events, and even publishing campaign literature. But the core of their activity seems to be informing and acting as media watchdogs.[22] Conservative bloggers like to provide their readers with links to reports and articles found elsewhere. They frequently receive their information from Republican operatives and reiterate talking points that are generated from inside formal conservative institutions. Conservative bloggers also write posts that detect errors, omissions or biases in the media. Most of them see their role as acting as a check of what they perceive as the liberal tendencies of the mainstream media, thus following the model of Matt Drudge of the Drudge Report. In 2007, while only 27 out of the 40 liberal bloggers surveyed by Laura McKenna and Antoinette Pole reported that they engaged in watchdog activities, 57 out of 63 conservative bloggers wrote watchdog posts[23]. Unsurprisingly, the only conservative blog with community features that rose through the rankings between 2004 and 2008 was Newsbusters, which as the blogging feature of the conservative Media Research Center, holds as its central mission "*exposing and combating liberal media bias*".[24] Conservative blogging appears therefore limited to disseminating information and criticizing the traditional media, as opposed to mobilizing for or against electoral or legislative efforts. This has led scholars to conclude that, while left-wing blogs organize themselves around horizontal dialogue, right-wing blogs appear therefore as more hierarchical.[25]

Not unlike conservative bloggers, the people behind Slatecard and Rightroots, RightMarch and the Vanguard are unwilling to abandon a top-down approach to political activism and to welcome a more dynamic, collaborative Web 2.0 "Rightosphere". They have all failed to give their users the sort of participatory toolset offered by their successful progressive counterparts. They refuse the malleability of an

---

[22] Laura McKenna and Antoinette Pole, "What Do Bloggers Do: An Average Day on an Average Political Blog", *Public Opinion*, n° 134, 2008, p. 97-108.

[23] Laura McKenna and Antoinette Pole, "What Do Bloggers Do: An Average Day on an Average Political Blog", p. 105.

[24] See the Newsbusters website, http://newsbusters.org.

[25] Henry Farrell, "Do the Netroots Matter?", *The American Prospect*, August 13, 2009.

ActBlue or the agenda-setting responsiveness of a MoveOn because they are ideologically more attuned to a conservative culture of clearly-defined hierarchical roles. Moreover, being members of offline communities such as churches, they seem to believe that conservatism online should be anchored in an already existing conservative infrastructure. Instead of building independent online communities, forging a new constituency group, a new set of leaders, and a new forest of social relationships like the progressive netroots have done, they tend to "*us[e] their existing offline communities to generate websites that reinforce their politics and their ideology*".[26] The single most important difference between the two netroots is therefore this: while the progressive netroots have introduced new actors into the political scene, the right-wing netroots have facilitated further organization of what was already a fairly coherent political world.

The Republican Party network does not seem to believe in the power of netroots either. It is not the case that Republicans do not "get it" with regards to new media technologies and campaign techniques. Patrick Ruffini, Michael Turk, Jon Henke and other bloggers are Republican strategists held in high regard within the technology consulting community. The crucial difference between these individuals and their Democratic counterparts is their "soft power" within the party network. The Democratic Party quickly absorbed the progressive netroots after 2004 and the "Internet people" within elite Democratic circles are now considered key players. In Republican circles, they are still relegated to the periphery. Former Reagan speechwriter Peggy Noonan made fun of conservative bloggers during the 2008 campaign, after exalting them in the *Wall Street Journal* in 2005. A few days after John McCain's defeat in the 2008 presidential election, a group of long-time, elite Republicans – including Grover Norquist of Americans for Tax Reform and Tony Perkins of the Family Research Council – gathered at the home of Brent Bozell, President of the Media Research Center. Ruffini, Turk, and Henke were not invited, leading them to launch two websites, RebuildtheParty.com and NextGenGOP.com that featured an online petition urging the candidates for RNC Chair to embrace and fund online infrastructure.

---

[26] Chris Bowers and Matthew Stoller, "Emergence of the Progressive Blogosphere: A New Force in American Politics", *op. cit.*

The difficulties with treating the structural hypothesis as a sufficient explanation are threefold, however. Firstly, it does not account for previous eras of grassroots conservatism in U. S. history. After all, both the Goldwater-era conservatives and Ralph Reed's Christian Coalition in the 1990s engaged in grassroots community organizing. Community organizing is not an activity solely appreciated by the left.

The second concern is that if the Internet is a medium naturally adapted to the political left, then a left-wing online advantage should be observed in other countries as well. Data from the United Kingdom suggest otherwise: British online conservatives seem to have developed an online advantage.[27] One may of course argue that British conservatism and American conservatism are very different entities, but this would further undermine the ideologically deterministic thesis. If there are various brands of conservatism, then the Internet is not an inherently "progressive" medium, it is just a medium ill-suited to the Republican Party circa 2004-2009.

The third concern with the thesis is its teleological nature: "Progressives dominate online, therefore the Internet is a progressive medium". Such an argument also maintains that talk radio is inherently a conservative medium, because conservatives dominate the airwaves. A 2007 study by the Pew Internet and American Life Project finds only marginal partisan differences in Internet usage, with 55% of Republicans, 61% of Democrats, and 48% of independents looking online for news about politics, and 49% of Republicans, 50% of Democrats, and 48% of independents using the Internet, email, or text messaging "*to learn about the campaign and engage in the political process*".[28] While we can grant that ideology has some impact on the development of online infrastructure today, evidence from history and from cross-national comparison cautions against making too much of this explanation.

---

[27] David Karpf, "Unexpected Transformations: The Internet's Effect on Political Associations in American Politics", p. 240.

[28] Lee Rainie, Aaron Smith, "The Internet and the 2008 Election", Research Report, Pew Internet and American Life Project, 2008, http://www.pewinternet.org/Reports/2008/The-Internet-and-the-2008-Election.aspx.

Contextual cause: out-of-power parties/candidates/movements tend to favour technological innovation

These very critiques of the structural/ideological thesis point to an alternative argument. At the organizational, candidate, and party network levels, there are several incentives that lead us to expect the party out of power to more aggressively adopt new communication tools and campaign tactics:

(1) For new organizations, storming the castle is a lot more fun. It also proves to be the case that organizing as the opposition to government policymakers is a more successful business model.

(2) For candidates, innovative campaign strategies offer an opportunity to change the rules of the game, a strategy which is more appealing to those dark horse candidates who are expected to have only an outside chance under the existing rules.

(3) Within party networks, new campaign technologies are introduced by a new set of elite actors displacing the previous set of established actors, and that displacement is more likely to happen when a party has been losing elections and is searching for new ideas.

These three perspectives combine to form the "outparty innovation incentives" thesis developed by David Karpf[29]. According to this thesis, the party that is out of power will usually innovate more. If the widely-shared expectation is that you are going to lose, you should try to alter the rules of the game. And since formal campaign law rules are not alterable, that leaves technological and strategic innovations as the best opportunity.

This thesis is strongly supported by the history of presidential campaigns and interest group mobilization:

(1) Previous periods of strong grassroots conservatism, as seen with the Goldwater era and the Christian Coalition, all occurred when the Democratic Party was in power.

---

[29] David Karpf, "Unexpected Transformations: The Internet's Effect on Political Associations in American Politics", p. 242-250.

(2) Membership of the Sierra Club more than doubled after Ronald Reagan assumed the Presidency, since the organization was able to cast Secretary of the Interior James Watt as an identifiable villain attacking environmental protection. Bill Clinton's election led to a membership decrease among various leftwing interest groups, a decrease that stopped when Newt Gingrich was elected Speaker of the House in 1994 and launched his "Contract with America."

(3) In the 2000 primaries, the McCain campaign was viewed as the pioneer in online fundraising. Given the candidate's 2008 admission that he himself never used email or the Internet, one can safely surmise that this was not because of a personal predisposition in favour of new campaign technologies. Rather, George W. Bush was the established forerunner, and the McCain campaign embraced ostentatious innovations in order to change the campaign dynamics.

(4) Between 2003 and 2008, MoveOn only developed a substantial membership base and reputation when it became the central outlet for the anti-Iraq war movement. For several years, the organization was able to unite its membership under the banner of opposing the Bush Administration's most controversial initiative, a strategy that proved a critical element of their fundraising model.

Today, voices on both the left and the right connect the decline of the conservative netroots in the 2004-2008 period with the fact that the Republicans then controlled the Presidency (and, from 2004 to 2006, Congress). According to libertarian blogger Jon Henke, "*A substantial part of the [decline of the right-wing netroots] is attributable to simple cyclical dynamics. While the Right has been in power, defending the status quo, the Left has been storming the castle*".[30] In other words, Henke thinks that, because the Republican Party was in power from 2000 to 2008, the conservative netroots neglected to evolve and remained devoted to their web 1.0 model. Joe Trippi, campaign manager for Howard Dean's 2004 presidential bid, said more or less the same thing in his memoir *The Revolution Will Not Be Televised*:

> *Internet's roots in the open-source Arpanet, its hacker culture, and its decentralized, scattered architecture make it difficult for big, establishment*

[30] Jon Henke, "The Online Right", June 3, 2008. See http://www.thenextright.com/jon-henke/the-online-right#comments.

candidates, companies and media to gain control of it. And the establishment loathes what it can't control. It is difficult for establishment candidates, companies and media to gain control of the Internet because of its decentralized and scattered nature.[31]

Trippi felt that insurgent candidates and companies that challenge that status quo and have a forward-looking vision have an advantage on the Internet as it is a forward-looking medium that embraces change.

If the outparty thesis is to be trusted, it then follows that we ought to see increases in conservative interest group activism, including the birth of new, Internet-mediated conservative organizations, now that the Obama administration has been elected and is attempting to enact its policy agenda.

3. A rebirth of online conservative activism since 2009?

The Tea Party protests and their online counterpart

Recent events provide relatively strong support for this assertion. The conservative group AmericanSolutions.com was launched in August 2008 to support the "Drill Here, Drill Now, Pay Less" oil and gas proposal promoted by Newt Gingrich. The site garnered substantial media exposure and built a sizable email-based member list.

Spring 2009 brought the start of TV host Glenn Beck's side gig as a social organizer through his 9.12 Project. The numbers 9 and 12 referred to a checklist of principles such as "*I believe in God and He is the center of my life*"; "*I work hard for what I have and I will share it with who I want to. Government cannot force me to be charitable*" and values such as honesty, hope and courage, but their greater significance lay in the allusion to September 11. "*The day after America was attacked, we were not obsessed with Red States, Blue States or political parties,*" the project's mission read. "*We want to get everyone thinking like it is September 12, 2001 again. Inclusiveness was the point.*"[32] A website was quickly launched (www.the912-project.com) to promote the group

[31] Joe Trippi, *The Revolution Will Not Be Televised*, New York: HarperCollins, 2004, p. 102.

[32] Cf. "The 9/12 Project – Principles and Values", http://the912-project.com/test/about/the-9-principles-12-values/.

and several local 9-12 groups formed soon after in cities across the United States.

Spring 2009 also saw the birth of the Tea Party movement, a patriotic, anti-tax, mostly Libertarian movement using rhetoric in a way very similar to that of the 1964 Goldwater campaign. The April 15th, 2009 "Tax Day Tea Party" protests included hundreds of thousands of conservative participants in simultaneous protests around the country, organized through a website (www.TaxDayTeaParty.com) and promoted through social community tools like Twitter and Facebook, the political blogosphere and conservative media outlets. "*If there was a central theme to the proceedings, it was probably best expressed in the refrain 'Can you hear us now?,' conveying a long-standing grievance that the political class in Washington was unresponsive to the needs and worries of ordinary Americans*", explained Ben McGrath in a *New Yorker* profile of the movement.[33]

As spring passed into summer, the scores of local Tea Party gatherings turned to hundreds, and then thousands. More than 1,000 Tea Party groups united around a new website, (www.teapartypatriots.com), "*a centralized web destination for decentralized malcontents*".[34] The anti-Obama guerrilla also discovered a new playing field: town hall meetings organized by Democratic officials to promote the president's healthcare reform. FreedomWorks, an organization created in 1984 by former House Republican majority leader Dick Armey, put a "Health Care training kit" at their disposal on its website, suggesting that they ask Obama's representatives specific questions.

On September 8th, 2009, the White House announced the resignation of Anthony Van Jones as "special adviser to the president for green jobs, enterprise and innovation." Van Jones had been the target of numerous conservative bloggers and online activists for his past radical commitments. Glenn Beck, for example, had made Jones a frequent target on his show, reporting his participation during the 1990s in the former Bay Area collective STORM (Standing Together to Organize a Revolutionary Movement), which supported Marxist principles and militant, direct action. The Jones story reached a tipping point on

[33] Ben McGrath, "The Movement. The Rise of Tea Party Activism", *The New Yorker*, February 1, 2010, http://www.newyorker.com/reporting/2010/02/01/100201fa_facts_mcgrath.
[34] *Idem.*

September 3rd when the conservative blog Gateway Pundit reported that Jones had signed a petition in 2004 that called for congressional hearings and other investigations into whether the George W. Bush administration had allowed the September 11 attacks to occur as a pretext for war in the oil-rich Middle East. The following day, Republican Senator Kit Bond called for a hearing to probe Jones' "*fitness*" to serve as a presidential adviser via Twitter. Afraid that his case might endanger Obama's fights for health care and clean energy, Jones responded by handing in his resignation.

On September 9th, 2009, at 9pm, conservative activists organized the largest online Tea Party, using Twitter to send up their 140 character or less rants, slogans and sneers against the Obama administration. For two months conservative Twitter members had been promoting this grassroots effort by posting and reposting a "tweet" that read "*Largest Twitter Tea Party Ever 09-09-09 at 9 pm EST. Please RT http://www.TwitterTeaParty.com*". This simple message with an easily remembered time and date kicked off a weekend's worth of Tea Party events across the county with all eyes in Washington, D.C., for the much-anticipated 9:12 event spoken of by Glenn Beck. Dave Davidson, organizer of the event and founder of TEApublican.com, a free member site where Tea Party Patriots across the country could synergize online, explained, "*By having the Twitter Tea Party just a few days before 9:12 it lays a foundation for Americans to mobilize together and even make last minute plans to attend a local event.*"[35]

When September 12th arrived, everybody was surprised by the apparent strength of the new movement, as measured by the crowds who made the pilgrimage to the Capitol for a Taxpayer March on Washington, swarming the Mall with signs reading "*'1984' Is Not an Instruction Manual*" and "*The Zoo Has an African Lion and the White House Has a Lyin' African!*" Politics is ultimately a numbers game, and the natural excitement surrounding 9.12 drove crowd estimates upward, from an early figure of sixty thousand, reported by ABC News, into the hundreds of thousands and across the million mark, eventually nearing two million – an upper limit of some significance, because 1.8 million

[35] "Today's Twitter Party Will Be Largest Online Tea Party Ever", Free Press Release, September 9, 2009, http://www.free-press-release.com/news-today-s-twitter-tea-party-will-be-largest-online-tea-party-ever-1252486780.html.

was the figure commonly reported in mainstream media outlets as the attendance at President Obama's Inauguration. The fact that the mainstream media generally declined to acknowledge the parallel, regarding the marchers as a loud and motley long tail of disaffection, and not a silent majority, only hardened their resolve. Once again, the event was sponsored by prominent conservative figures like Rick Santelli or Glenn Beck and financed by conservative organizations like FreedomWorks or Americans for Tax Reform, but came to life thanks to online organizing and advertising.

On February 4-6, 2010, the first Tea Party national convention was held in Nashville, attended by 600 people. Prepared by a new online activist group named the Tea Party Nation[36], it received broad media coverage as former GOP Vice-Presidential Candidate, Sarah Palin, was the featured speaker. Finally, the Republican Party seized control of the House of Representatives in the 2010 mid-term election, effectively landing three Tea Party candidates – Rand Paul, Ron Paul's son, Marco Rubio, and Nikki Haley – a seat in Congress or a governorship.

All in all, it seems that these Tea Party protests are on the way to becoming a long-term hub for conservative political organizing, as if communities needed to have a high-profile opponent to organize against. Does the solid online infrastructure on which they are based really signal a revival of conservative online activism?

Weaknesses of the movement

Before a rebirth of conservative online activism can be predicted in the years to come, one should be careful to distinguish between the Tea Party movement and the Republican Party. While the Democratic Party has, to a certain extent,[37] embraced the "progressive netroots" since

[36] See their website: www.teapartynation.com.

[37] Henry Farrell argues that, while the netroots have had a genuine impact in the 2008 election, the president they helped to elect has no use for their style of politics, even as he steals some of their tricks. "*Although Obama's advisers were very interested indeed in learning from the netroots, they had no interest in working with bloggers who might disrupt their control over messaging and money. Instead, they built their own blogging and online fundraising structures from scratch, combining a traditional campaign organization with new network capacities in what Matthew Kerbel describes in his book* Netroots *as a 'hybrid' structure*". Henry Farrell, "Do the Netroots Matter?", *The American Prospect*, August 13, 2009. In other words, Obama has taken the parts of

2004, the Republican Party seems a little bit embarrassed about this new grassroots mobilization. It has tried to court it by sending representatives at Tea Party events. House minority leader Mike Pence thus spoke at the September 12th 2009 demonstration – and using Tea Party symbols – the former Republican National Committee chairman, Michael Steele, used teacups as props during a speech in December 2009. It has even tried to co-opt it by creating rival organizations like the Tea Party Nation or the Tea Party Express – a road show funded by a political action committee called "Our Country Deserves Better" – and federating local branches through GOP-friendly organizations like FreedomWorks, Americans for Tax Reform, the Club for Growth, Campaign for Liberty, and the Ayn Rand Center for Individual Rights. FreedomWorks, for example, has provided logistical support and tactical know-how to a network of some 400 activists scattered around the country. In its advisory capacity, its aims have been to push fiscal concerns, not social issues, and to deemphasize personal attacks on Obama, which could be perceived as having racial overtones. "*'Astroturfing' [has been] the critics' preferred term for this phenomenon, with its imputation of a synthetic, top-down structure to contrast with the outward appearance of grassroots independence*."[38] But this hasn't really worked so far:

(1) The Nashville convention was boycotted by several prominent conservative organizations due to its for-profit nature (participants were asked to pay $549 for their ticket) and the fact that Palin was apparently paid $100,000 for her appearance.

(2) The Tea Party Express has earned the scorn of many activists for being too slickly produced.

(3) The Tea Party movement also supported its own, "ideologically purer", candidates in recent local elections. In November 2009, the GOP lost a Senate seat that was taken for granted in upstate

---

netroots politics that he likes (online organizing and fundraising), while dumping the parts that he doesn't (strongly confrontational politics and emphasis on bottom-up decision making). There isn't much room for the netroots and vigorous online partisanship in Obama's plans for the future of the Democratic Party.

[38] Ben McGrath, "The Movement. The Rise of Tea Party Activism", *The New Yorker*, February 1, 2010, http://www.newyorker.com/reporting/2010/02/01/100201fa_fact_mcgrath.

New York. In February 2010, a conservative named Donn Janes opted out of the Republican primary in Tennessee in order to run as “an independent Tea Party candidate”. The same month, the Tea Party movement helped Brown take Ted Kennedy’s Senate seat away from the Democrats in the special election. In Arizona, John McCain was defied by a Tea Party candidate, J. D. Hayworth and even called his fellow candidate Sarah Palin for help in a desperate attempt to rally “tea partiers”. He eventually proceeded to beat Hayworth by a 56 to 32 percent margin in the August 24 primary and Democratic city councilman Rodney Glassman in the general election.

Should the GOP try harder? Some within the party ranks think so, due to the popularity of the movement in the polls. Bill O’Reilly, who had never seemed entirely comfortable with the anarchic impulses of the activist fringe, recently told his new Fox News colleague Sarah Palin that he wouldn’t be surprised to see her lead a Tea Party ticket in 2012. “*Well, there is no Tea Party ticket*,” Palin demurred. “*There could be*,” he said.[39] If a registered Tea Party existed, a recent Rasmussen poll suggested, its popularity would exceed that of the Republicans. Among independent voters, a hypothetical Tea Party candidate would beat a Democrat, too.[40] Therefore, some Republicans argue that their party should channel the discontent to their benefit in order not be consumed by it. Others like David Brooks say it shouldn’t because they don’t want the party to be governed by its extremist fringe[41]. The most important Republican strategists have until now refused to comment on these “spontaneous” protests. Conservative bloggers are similarly ambiguous in their support. While they rejoice in the recent surge in grassroots conservative activism, some of them seem to question the aims of the Tea Party movement. A study of their sociological background helps explain their lack of enthusiasm. Bloggers are members of the educated elite of the country. The vast majority of them are white, male, young[42], and wealthy. Most A-list bloggers have advanced degrees, experience in

---

[39] Bill O’Reilly, “The O’Reilly Factor”, transcript, January 12, 2010, http://www.Foxnews.com/story/0,2933,582924,00.html.

[40] Rasmussen poll, “Tea Party 48%, Obama 44%”, April 15, 2010.

[41] David Brooks, “The Tea Party Teens”, *The New York Times*, January 5, 2010, p. A21.

[42] Most of them are between the ages of 26 and 41.

politics and in political commentary, and are currently employed as journalists or professors. Compared to the majority of the population, they are well-educated. Therefore, the average conservative blogger is not an average citizen and popular depictions of bloggers as individual heroes fighting to get heard seem hopelessly naïve. Likewise, their audience tends to be an elite crowd of political junkies who have almost non-stop access to a computer and large amounts of time to surf the Internet for breaking news. In short: political consultants and journalists. These people are not inspired by populist feelings. Unlike Tea Party activists, they do not see ordinary people as a noble group and the elite class as self-serving. Their aim is to "*influence the influencers.*"

Given these elements, it is fairly difficult to predict whether the Tea Party movement will lead to a larger Republican online mobilization similar to the one that brought Obama to power.

Aurélie Godet

Université Michel de Montaigne Bordeaux 3

Campagne virtuelle et élection réelle, quel rôle a joué l'outil Internet dans l'élection présidentielle de Barack Obama ?

Il y a cinquante ans de cela, les débats télévisés entre les candidats à la fonction suprême firent leur entrée dans le rituel de l'élection présidentielle américaine. Celui entre Richard Nixon et John Fitzgerald Kennedy, le premier de l'histoire des élections américaines, fut décisif. Par son sourire ravageur, ses paroles choisies et son visage hâlé, le jeune candidat à la présidence des États-Unis d'Amérique séduisit de nombreux électeurs. Aussi, contre toute attente, le républicain Richard Nixon, ancien militaire, vice-président en 1955, et président par intérim à trois reprises, fut évincé par le candidat du parti démocrate qui incarnait la jeunesse, le changement et l'optimisme. Ce portrait n'est pas sans rappeler celui du président Barack Obama dont le slogan « *Yes We Can* », scandé lors des élections, faisait écho à son envie de changement et de renouveau. Tout comme John F. Kennedy, Barack Obama sut tirer profit des médias pour attirer les électeurs et notamment les plus jeunes, quelque peu réfractaires à l'idée d'aller voter. Certes, les outils ont changé, désormais les politiques sont davantage tournés vers l'Internet parce qu'il est peu coûteux et très efficace, mais le but est le même : rallier un maximum d'électeurs. En effet, aujourd'hui, les candidats à la présidentielle américaine font face à des électeurs pour qui la Toile constitue l'une des principales voies d'information. Barack Obama a beaucoup misé sur l'outil Internet pour attirer les jeunes de 18 à 29 ans qui représentent près de 43 millions d'Américains, soit 20% du corps électoral. Pages *web*, blogs, sites de visionnage et réseaux sociaux, le candidat était partout. Avec ses 7 millions d'amis répertoriés sur *Facebook* et les milliers de visites journalières de ses blogs et pages *web*, Barack Obama semble avoir atteint son objectif et trouvé dans cet outil un allié. Mais peut-on réellement considérer que l'e-campagne de ce candidat a été décisive dans son élection ? L'outil Internet a-t-il véritablement influencé les jeunes électeurs ? C'est ce que nous tâcherons d'élucider.

1. Barack Obama fait de l'Internet le vecteur privilégié des campagnes modernes

Cet épisode audiovisuel entre Nixon et Kennedy, a démontré que savoir profiter des avantages d'un nouveau média peut s'avérer crucial pour gagner une campagne électorale. Aussi, lorsque l'outil Internet a fait son apparition, de nombreux politiques ont cherché comment il pourrait leur être utile. Ce fut le cas de Howard Dean[1], le rival malheureux de John Kerry pour l'investiture du parti démocrate en 2004 qui, le premier, dans son parti, crut que grâce à ce nouveau média, il pourrait augmenter sa cote de popularité[2]. Son échec démontre cependant que la plus intelligente des e-campagnes ne remplacera jamais un programme fort, proche des attentes de la population, mais qu'elle peut être un véritable atout, comme l'explique Arianna Huffington[3], la fondatrice du *Huffington Post*, le blog de « *Citizen Journalism* » le plus puissant des États-Unis : "*Were it not for the Internet, Barack Obama*

---

[1]Howard Brush Dean III, ancien chef du comité national du Parti démocrate de 2005 à 2009 et candidat aux primaires démocrates de l'élection présidentielle de 2004, fut le favori des militants avant le début des débats. Il marqua tout particulièrement les esprits en raison de sa critique de la politique internationale du président George W. Bush et de l'incapacité des Démocrates à s'opposer à l'administration Bush. Ces propos particulièrement virulents et le fait d'avoir été pionnier dans l'utilisation de l'outil Internet pour propager ses idées politiques lors d'une élection présidentielle lui permirent de fidéliser un grand nombre de militants. Aujourd'hui Howard Dean est une référence pour beaucoup de politologues américains en matière d'utilisation de l'Internet en politique. L'agence *Blue State Digital* qui joua un rôle primordial dans la campagne Internet de Howard Dean, s'occupa également de la campagne présidentielle de Barack Obama en 2008.

[2] Zephyr Teachout, Thomas Streeter, *Mousepads, Shoe Leather, and Hope: Lessons from the Howard Dean Campaign for the Future of Internet Politics*, Boulder, CO: Paradigm Publishers, 2007, p. 15.

[3] Propos recueillis lors du sommet du Web 2.0 de 2008. Claire Cain Miller, « How Obama's Internet Campaign Changed Politics », *The New York Times*, 7 novembre, 2008.

would not be president. Were it not for the Internet, Barack Obama would not have been the nominee"[4].

En effet, alors que certains experts associent la victoire de Barack Obama à sa couleur de peau, d'autres considèrent sa capacité à manier l'outil Internet comme un autre facteur dominant de son élection.

Dès le début de sa campagne, Barack Obama fut convaincu de la capacité des nouvelles technologies à influencer le processus démocratique. Voici ce qu'il déclara lors d'un communiqué en 2007 : « *Depuis que j'ai commencé à m'impliquer dans l'action civique, j'ai réalisé que le vrai changement vient d'en bas, et il n'y a pas d'outil plus puissant pour l'organisation grass-root que l'Internet* [5]».

Peut-on en conséquence voir en Barack Obama un e-président ? En tout cas c'est ce que semble affirmer Joe Trippi, ancien directeur de campagne d'Howard Dean, si l'on se fie à ce qu'il a déclaré, en novembre 2008, lors du sommet du Web 2.0 à San Francisco[6] : "*Just like Kennedy brought in the television presidency, I think we're about to see the first wired, connected, networked presidency,*"[7]. En ce sens, Barack Obama, tout comme Kennedy, il y a cinquante ans de cela, révolutionna le monde politique en y introduisant une nouvelle forme de communication entre candidats et électeurs potentiels. En 2008, pour lui, l'élection présidentielle ne pouvait être qu'une e-élection[8]. Espace de

[4] « *Sans Internet, BO n'aurait pas été élu président, sans Internet, il n'aurait pas même été élu lors des primaires démocrates* ».

[5] Propos recueillis et traduits dans l'article « Election USA : un fondateur de Facebook derrière la stratégie Internet d'Obama », publié le 9 juillet 2008 sur www. ITespresso.fr, auteur inconnu.

[6] Le sommet du Web 2.0 est un événement annuel qui rassemble les chefs d'entreprises, les grands penseurs et les technologues innovants qui font de l'Internet ce qu'il est aujourd'hui.

[7] « *Tout comme Kennedy a introduit une présidence télévisée, Obama sera le premier président en réseau* » Traduction française proposée par Fabrice Epelboin dans son article « Politique et Internet, un premier bilan de l'élection d'Obama », *Web 2.0*, 27 novembre 2008, http://fr.readwriteweb.com/2008/11/27/entrevues/politique-internet-premier-bilan-election-obama/

[8] Ceci est patent lorsque l'on examine l'équipe de campagne choisie par le candidat Obama. En effet, Barack Obama s'entoura de Chris Hughes, l'un des co-fondateurs du réseau social *Facebook* et de Joe Rospars, surnommé « le monsieur campagne-web » par Christophe Gueugneau, journaliste pour *Le Nouvel Observateur*. A la tête d'une équipe de 150 personnes dont Sam Graham-Felsen, responsable des blogs de la campagne, et d'un un budget de 15 millions de dollars, les deux spécialistes de

discussion libre par excellence, la Toile est un outil de ralliement et un vecteur idéal de la démocratie. Consulter les pages *web* pour s'informer et communiquer sur les élections présidentielles devient un acte citoyen. Selon un sondage effectué sur un échantillon de 2251 adultes Américains (dont 1008 jeunes de moins de 30 ans) par le *Pew Internet and American Life Project* entre le 08 avril et le 11 mai 2008, 46% des Américains utilisèrent les sites Internet, leur email ou encore les SMS pour obtenir des informations sur la campagne présidentielle, partager leurs opinions ou pour mobiliser les autres internautes (famille, amis et inconnus). Les chiffres parlent d'eux-mêmes : les candidats à la présidentielle américaine ont dû, plus que jamais, composer avec des électeurs – en particulier les jeunes Américains – pour qui le Net a constitué l'une des principales sources d'information, loin devant les journaux, les magazines et la radio. En effet, depuis les élections de 2000, le pourcentage d'Américains qui s'en remettent à l'Internet comme source principale d'information a plus que doublé, passant de 11 à 26%. C'est pourquoi, les hommes politiques et leurs conseillers ont fait de ce média la pierre angulaire de leurs campagnes électorales, d'autant qu'il semble présenter de nombreux avantages.

En tant que media de l'interactivité, il permet de prendre le pouls de l'opinion publique en temps réel, ce qui offre aux partis et aux hommes politiques une chance unique de mieux cerner les préoccupations de leurs administrés et d'affiner leur message en conséquence. C'est aussi et surtout un moyen simple et peu onéreux de toucher instantanément un électorat jeune et informé, qui peut exercer une influence positive auprès de son entourage. A titre d'exemple, selon les chiffres de *TechCrunch*[9], la campagne Internet de Barack Obama aurait coûté $7.97 millions, tandis qu'un passage d'une demi-heure à la télévision coûte $4 millions.

Mais l'intérêt du *web* n'est pas seulement d'ordre économique, c'est également un moyen d'obtenir des voix et de récolter des fonds pour une campagne électorale. Dans ce domaine, la campagne de Barack Obama fait figure d'exemple. Là encore, parce que le candidat était convaincu que le vrai changement vient d'en bas, ses appels aux dons ciblèrent tout

---

l'Internet réussirent à faire de l'élection présidentielle de 2008 une e-élection. Gueugeneau, Christophe. « Déjeuner avec la web-campagne d'Obama », *Le Nouvel Observateur*, 3 juin 2010, http://tempsreels.blogs.nouvelobs.com/tag/joe+rospars.

[9] Célèbre blog américain portant sur l'actualité du Web 2.0.

particulièrement l'Américain moyen. C'est ainsi qu'il récolta plus de $160 millions de fonds, grâce au cumul de petites sommes ne dépassant pas $ 200.

Bien que l'utilisation de l'Internet ne soit pas encore décisive dans l'aboutissement d'une campagne, notamment parce que les internautes ne forment qu'une frange privilégiée des électeurs (environ 68 millions d'Américains), on assiste aujourd'hui à une déferlante de blogs écrits par des hommes politiques ; le but étant d'établir une nouvelle relation entre candidats et internautes, c'est un moyen de créer un lien, certes virtuel, mais important aux yeux des électeurs. Le candidat n'est plus inaccessible. Les internautes peuvent lui poser des questions via son site Internet ou son blog et se sentir, ainsi, plus proches à la fois de ses idées et de sa personne.

2. La campagne virtuelle de Barack Obama

Le but de cette campagne virtuelle fut de sensibiliser un maximum de personnes, de tous âges, en utilisant différents supports sur l'Internet selon le public visé, le premier étant le site officiel du candidat. Il permit d'informer les internautes et les électeurs sur ses idées politiques et son programme. Celui de Barack Obama peut intriguer par sa présentation car sa page *web* semble avoir oscillée entre le site officiel et le blog. En effet, il ne s'agissait pas à proprement parler d'un blog, puisque des *podcasts* étaient postés en lieu et place des habituels billets. Pour simplifier, les textes faisaient place à des bandes audio, même si l'objectif était le même que celui de ses adversaires : promouvoir les idées et les propositions du candidat. Le recours aux *podcasts* montre un candidat sachant parfaitement utiliser cette nouvelle technologie et maîtrisant les diverses possibilités offertes par le *web*. Barack Obama envoyait ainsi un message clair aux électeurs : celui d'un candidat à la présidence, moderne, capable de s'adapter à la progression du monde qui l'entoure et désireux d'instaurer le changement. Le fait même de présenter son site Internet d'une manière beaucoup plus novatrice que celui d'Hillary Clinton ou encore celui de John McCain en fit le candidat privilégié des jeunes. Il s'agissait d'une stratégie électorale ou devrait-on dire e-électorale. Parce que son but est avant tout informatif, ce genre de site cible en général les plus de trente ans, or le site de Barack Obama dérogeait à la règle en ajoutant un aspect ludique que les plus jeunes ne manquèrent pas d'apprécier. En cela, le candidat se refusait d'ignorer les électeurs de moins de trente ans. En effet, dès le début de sa course pour la Maison-Blanche, il avait compris qu'un manque d'intérêt envers la jeune génération le conduirait à une fin malheureuse. C'est la raison pour laquelle il n'hésita pas à faire appel à des spécialistes pour diriger sa campagne Internet[10]. Le choix de Chris Hughes fut loin d'être une coïncidence puisque ce jeune homme talentueux, alors âgé de 24 ans, n'est autre que le co-fondateur de *Facebook*, le réseau social le plus visité par les jeunes internautes. Aujourd'hui, deux tiers des internautes de moins de trente ans ont un profil sur au moins un réseau social et la moitié d'entre eux utilisent ces réseaux afin de partager des informations sur la politique et les campagnes électorales. Barack Obama fut le premier candidat à voir dans *Facebook* un moyen de toucher les plus jeunes et ainsi devenir leur candidat préféré car il avait beau être plus âgé que la plupart des utilisateurs, il avait pris conscience du potentiel de ce réseau social pour communiquer et rassembler des fonds pour sa campagne Par conséquent, Barack Obama et son équipe ne se sont pas contentés de créer un profil sur *Facebook*, ils ont également investis les sites *YouTube, MySpace*, *Twitter*, *Flickr*, *Digg*, *BlackPlanet*, *LinkedIn*, *AsianAve*, *MiGente*, *Glee* et bien d'autres[11].

Afin d'attirer un maximum d'électeurs, le défi de Chris Hughes fut donc d'appliquer les principes des sites de réseaux sociaux comme *Facebook* ou *MySpace* à une communauté bien plus large. Sur *MyBarackObama.com* par exemple, le site officiel du candidat, les supporters purent faire partie du groupe de soutien local, organiser des événements, souscrire à une *newsletter*, et bien sûr, contribuer financièrement. Chris Hughes a absolument tout géré sur les sites de réseaux sociaux, des vidéos diffusées sur les pages *web* en passant par les SMS envoyés aux électeurs. *Facebook*, conscient de son impact sur la campagne présidentielle, a même lancé son propre forum pour encourager les débats d'opinion en ligne. Il s'est également associé à l'une des principales chaînes de télévision, ABC, pour la couverture médiatique des événements politiques et les forums. Les résultats

---

[10] Voir note 8, *supra*.

[11] Voir le témoignage de Rahaf Harfoush qui a brièvement fait partie de l'équipe de campagne d'Obama à ses débuts, *Yes We Did. An Inside Look at How Social Media Built the Obama Brand*, Berkeley, CA: New Riders Press, 2009, p. 5.

probants obtenus par Barack Obama sur les différents réseaux sociaux ont suscité l'intérêt des autres candidats. De ce fait, ce fut la première fois dans toute l'histoire des USA que tous les candidats à la présidentielle cherchèrent à se rapprocher des électeurs via des réseaux sociaux tels que *MySpace* et *Facebook*. Un événement qui a valu à cette élection le surnom d'« élection *Facebook* »[12].

Ces sites de réseaux sociaux permettent aux candidats et à leur équipe d'établir un lien direct avec les électeurs mais aussi de disséminer des informations ou de réfuter les attaques d'autres candidats. Inversement, ils permettent également aux non-supporters d'ouvrir des forums contre le candidat en question. Pendant les deux années qui ont précédé l'élection d'Obama, *Facebook* est devenu le territoire virtuel du candidat. Durant les primaires, Obama y était très populaire tandis qu'Hillary Clinton se débattait contre un mouvement appelé « *Stop Hillary Clinton* ». Dès lors, la différence entre les deux candidats se fit sentir : tandis que la page *Facebook* d'Obama affichait 250000 membres, celle d'Hillary Clinton n'en comptait que 3200. L'élaboration du profil est capitale car celui-ci est le premier contact entre le candidat et le jeune électeur potentiel. Barack Obama a su en tirer profit ; son adversaire John McCain, moins au fait de l'importance des nouvelles technologies dans cette campagne, en a subi les lourdes conséquences. Ainsi, si l'on compare leurs profils respectifs sur le site *Facebook*, on constate que l'utilisation des réseaux sociaux semble n'avoir aucun secret pour Obama. En dépit de son âge, il a l'étoffe d'un grand *Facebooker*. Sur sa page personnelle, qui est annoncée par son slogan « *Our Moment is Now* », Obama, comme n'importe quel autre utilisateur, donne le nom de ses chanteurs et musiciens préférés tels que Miles Davis, Stevie Wonder, et Bob Dylan. Il fait la liste de ses passe-temps favoris comme le basketball, lire et s'occuper de ses filles. Il n'hésite pas, d'ailleurs, à utiliser des abréviations dont les jeunes usent et abusent sur le *web* : « *loafing w/kids* ». Là encore, il s'agit d'une stratégie pour montrer que Barack Obama est accessible : c'est un

[12] Matthew Fraser, Sumitra Dutta, « Barack Obama and the Facebook Election », *US News and World Report*, 19 novembre 2008 http://www.usnews.com/opinions/articles/ 2008/11/19/barack-obama-and-the-facebook-election. Sur l'utilisation des médias dans la campagne 2008, voir aussi : Rafah Harfoush, *op. cit.*, chapitre 11 et Kate Kensky, Bruce W. Hardy, Katheleen H. Jamieson, *The Obama Victory: How Media, Money, and Message Shaped the 2008 Election*, New York: Oxford University Press, 2010.

candidat qui comprend les jeunes et utilise leur code et leur langage. En effet, près d'un jeune sur dix de moins de trente ans (8%) avoue avoir demandé à être l'ami de leur candidat préféré tandis que seulement 3% des plus de trente ans ont fait la même demande. À titre de comparaison, John McCain, soixante-douze ans lors de la campagne électorale, mentionne la pêche comme l'un de ses passe-temps favoris, ce qui peut être populaire auprès de certains internautes, mais pas vraiment « branché ». Au vu de ces profils, les chiffres ont parlé. Obama avait plus de 2 millions de supporters sur *Facebook* au 9 octobre 2008 tandis que McCain n'en avait que 600 000. Sur *MySpace*, un autre site de réseau social, Obama comptait 700000 supporters tandis que McCain n'en avait que 190000 au 14 octobre 2008.

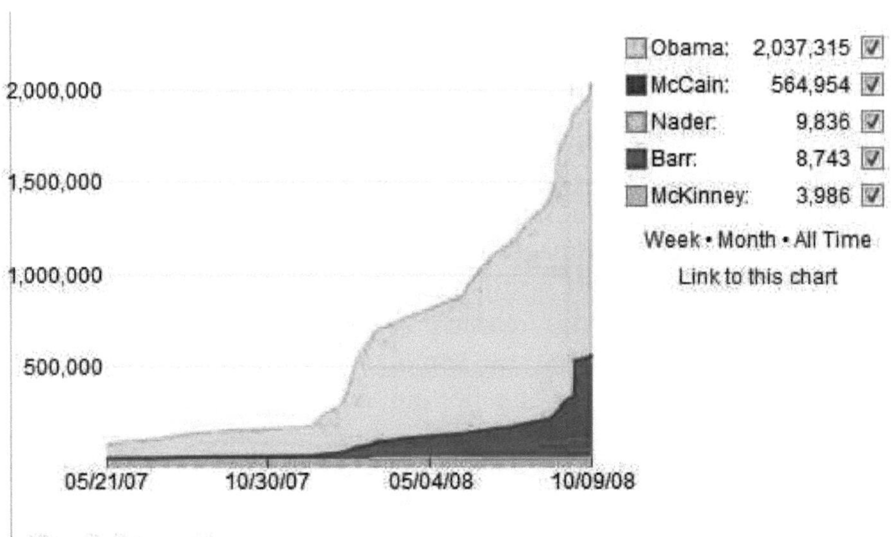

www.vicastel.net/.../06/facebook-supporters.jpg

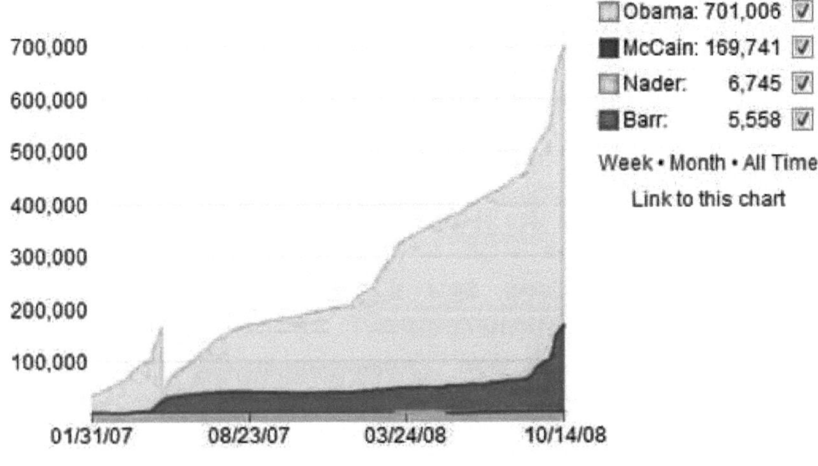

MySpace friends www.taorama.net/images/dems.gif

Ces deux graphiques démontrent qu'un candidat sachant manier l'outil Internet semble bel et bien faire la différence auprès des internautes et ce, parce que, son utilisation change la vision que ceux-ci se font de la politique. En effet, la Toile modifie la dynamique des relations entre les électeurs et les candidats. Puisqu'il n'y a pas de barrière sur des sites tels que *Facebook* et *MySpace*, tout le monde peut s'exprimer et participer. Au cours de la campagne présidentielle de 2008, 12% des 18-29 ans ont posté leurs commentaires politiques sur un groupe en ligne, sur des blogs ou des sites Internet[13]. Par conséquent, on peut en déduire que l'e-politique est avant tout un moyen d'attirer un public jeune qui se retrouve sur la Toile pour regarder les vidéos des débats politiques, les discours des candidats et se mobiliser pour inciter les gens à voter, tandis que les Américains plus âgés sont plus enclins à s'informer grâce aux sources d'informations traditionnelles, notamment les programmes télévisés sur les élections et la presse écrite. C'est ainsi que de nombreux supporters d'Obama, dont les jeunes de moins de 30 ans, ont décidé de

---

[13] Sondage effectué par le *Pew Internet and American Life Project* entre le 08 avril 2008 et le 11 mai 2008. Aaron Smith, « The Internet and the 2008 Election », *Pew Internet and American Life Project*, 15 juin 2008. http://www.pewinternet.org/Reports/2009/6--The-Internets-Role-in-Campaign-2008/3--The-Internet-as-a-Source-of-Polical-News/2--Online-news-audience.aspx.

s'investir dans la campagne présidentielle non seulement en consultant les sites en sa faveur mais également en créant, eux-mêmes, des sites, des blogs, des forums et des vidéos. Il semblerait que l'engouement de Barack Obama pour l'Internet ait fait naître chez ces internautes une conscience politique.

3. L'engagement e-politique des jeunes Américains

Selon le sondage effectué par le *Pew Internet and American Life Project*, 22% des 18-29 ans affirment qu'ils ne se seraient pas intéressés à la campagne présidentielle s'il n'y avait pas eu l'Internet et 42% d'entre eux admettent s'informer sur la campagne par ce biais. A titre de comparaison, en janvier 2004, seul 20% des jeunes Américains disaient s'informer régulièrement sur la Toile. Les supporters de Barack Obama furent tout particulièrement actifs dans la recherche d'informations sur leur candidat préféré et dans leur engagement e-politique. A cet effet, 74% d'entre eux utilisèrent l'Internet alors que ce fut seulement le cas pour 57% des supporters d'Hillary Clinton et 56% de ceux de John McCain. Ses supporters supplantèrent également ceux de ses adversaires à propos de l'usage de la vidéo, des sites de réseaux sociaux et autres activités concernant la campagne virtuelle. Par exemple, ils ont extrait plus de 1800 vidéos du site *YouTube* qu'ils ont ensuite téléchargées sur la chaîne *BarackObama.com* qui comptait un peu plus de 15000 inscrits. Celle-ci a reçu plus de 18 millions de visites lors de la campagne présidentielle. John McCain, quant à lui, il n'est apparu que sur 330 vidéos de *YouTube* sur *JohnMcCain.com.* Ce site officiel ne comptait que 28000 inscrits en 2008 et n'a attiré que 2 millions de visiteurs. D'une manière générale, les électeurs d'Obama, en comparaison avec ceux de McCain, ont été plus enclins à[14]:

- Partager des opinions politiques (21% contre 16%).
- S'inscrire sur un site pour recevoir les dernières informations sur l'élection présidentielle (18% contre 9%).

---

[14] Sondage effectué en novembre et décembre 2008 auprès de 637 électeurs de Barack Obama et 579 électeurs de John McCain par le *Pew Internet and American Life Project.*

- Donner des fonds pour un candidat ou un parti politique (15% contre 6%).
- Recevoir des courriels d'alerte concernant la campagne présidentielle (12% contre 8%).
- S'inscrire via Internet pour des activités de volontariat en faveur de leur candidat préféré (11% contre 4%).

Grâce à l'Internet, les électeurs ne sont plus seulement spectateurs de l'élection présidentielle, ils en sont les acteurs : ils participent réellement à la campagne. De nombreuses vidéos d'amateurs ont circulé pour promouvoir le programme des candidats. La vidéo est l'un des supports qui attirent le plus d'internautes car les images, bien souvent, parlent d'elles-mêmes. Environ six jeunes de moins de trente ans sur dix ont visualisé au moins une vidéo sur la campagne électorale. Ce qui leur plait beaucoup, ce sont les données non-filtrées : vidéos, débats, discours, déplacements. Les candidats ont été ainsi confrontés à une « *Youtubification* de la politique », selon les dires de Gavin Newsom[15], le maire démocrate de San Francisco, c'est-à-dire à la mise en ligne de vidéos les concernant, qu'elles soient positives ou pernicieuses pour leur campagne. On se souvient de l'intervention malheureuse du révérend Wright qui a bien failli coûter à Obama sa victoire à l'investiture. L'intérêt de ces vidéos est de pouvoir se faire sa propre idée du candidat et de son programme puisque selon Joe Trippi : "*This medium demands authenticity, and television for the most part demanded fake*"[16].

Sur la plupart des vidéos diffusées sur *YouTube*, les candidats ne paradent pas, ils ne jouent pas. Contrairement à la télévision où l'on répète avant que les projecteurs ne soient braqués sur soi, l'Internet fait dans l'instantané et donc dans l'authenticité et c'est ce que semblent rechercher les Américains, notamment les plus jeunes. Mais l'homme politique n'est pas forcément présent sur ces vidéos, parfois il s'agit simplement d'électeurs criant haut et fort leur soutien envers leur candidat préféré. C'est le cas de la jeune femme, quelque peu dénudée, dansant pour Barack Obama dans une vidéo intitulée « *Crush on*

---

[15] Propos utilisé par Gavin Newsom lors du Sommet du Web 2.0 à San Francisco en 2008.

[16] Propos de Joe Trippi lors du Sommet du Web 2.0 à San Francisco en 2008 « Ce média demande de l'authenticité, alors que la télévision demande, en grande partie, du spectacle ».

Obama » qui compte, à ce jour, près de 18 millions de visionnages. De la même manière, les célébrités s'investissent auprès de leur candidat de prédilection. Sorte de tradition aux États-Unis, les acteurs et chanteurs n'hésitent pas à s'afficher auprès du candidat dans l'espoir d'influencer le vote d'électeurs encore indécis. En 2008, les célébrités en faveur de Barack Obama ont quelque peu innové en proposant un clip vidéo diffusé sur MTV et *YouTube*. Il s'agissait du discours d'investiture du candidat « *Yes We Can* » mis en musique par William, le chanteur des Black Eyed Peas, un groupe très apprécié des jeunes Américains, et chanté par de nombreuses célébrités dont les acteurs des séries à succès *CSI* et *Grey's Anatomy*, principalement regardées par un jeune public. Obama apparaît dans le clip à l'aide d'un montage vidéo qui permet de le mêler aux célébrités. Il est assimilé à une pop star. Très vite, cette vidéo, qui fut un succès, fit le tour du monde. À ce jour, elle compte plus de soixante millions de visionnages. Il semble bien que ces vidéos, comme les réseaux sociaux, aient joué un rôle déterminant dans l'implication des jeunes Américains[17]. La campagne Internet de Barack Obama a conquis de nombreux électeurs qui se sont informés et engagés politiquement via le Net. Aujourd'hui, nous savons que sa victoire est due principalement au soutien des jeunes Américains. Très tôt dans sa campagne, les sondeurs politiques observèrent qu'Obama bouleversait les intentions de vote de cette partie de l'électorat. Cette tendance s'est confirmée puisqu'il a obtenu les suffrages de près de 70% des Américains de moins de 25 ans, le pourcentage le plus important jamais atteint par un candidat depuis 1976[18].

Néanmoins, on ne saurait attribuer la victoire d'un candidat au simple fait de l'utilisation de l'outil Internet. L'élection de 2004 en est la preuve : bien que les jeunes se soient présentés aux urnes en grand nombre, sur les 125 millions de bulletins seuls 20,9 millions provenaient de jeunes de moins de trente ans. Demander à un candidat d'être votre ami sur un site de réseau social ne veut pas forcément dire que l'on va voter pour lui. En revanche, manier l'outil Internet comme Barack Obama a su le faire lors de l'élection de 2008 s'est avéré être un véritable atout pour ce candidat. Tout d'abord parce que le support choisi était en corrélation avec son programme – tous les deux modernes

[17] Voir Rahaf Harfoush, *op. cit.*, chapitre 12.
[18] Voir Matthew Fraser, Sumitra Dutta, *op. cit.*

et novateurs – mais aussi et surtout parce que Barack Obama a pris très tôt conscience, à la différence de ses adversaires, que c'était un moyen de rassembler les citoyens et de les mobiliser en vue de son élection à la présidence. Ceci n'est pas sans rappeler le président Kennedy qui s'était servi de la télévision dans le même but.

A ce titre, Marshall McLuhan dans son livre *Pour comprendre les médias*[19], disait de Kennedy qu'il avait trouvé naturel de faire participer le public aux fonctions de la présidence grâce à la télévision car cette dernière fait ressortir les attributs corporatifs de la fonction. En 2008, le média qui a su rassembler bon nombre d'Américains est l'Internet et c'est ce qui semble avoir valu à Barack Obama le titre de premier occupant de la Maison-Blanche à avoir gagné une élection présidentielle sur le *web*[20]. Aujourd'hui le nouveau président continue d'utiliser la Toile pour diffuser ses idées, c'est le cas avec le site de la Maison-Blanche et celui intitulé *Change.gov*, un site de réseau social et de discussion citoyenne. La participation y est importante et beaucoup y voit les prémisses d'une e-démocratie américaine, une e-démocratie qui risque de changer inexorablement le visage de la politique selon les dires de Joe Trippi[21] :

> *Avec autant de personnes derrière lui, connectées, le pouvoir du président par rapport au congrès va changer. Nous allons voir une présidence plus forte et un congrès plus faible, parce que c'est un président avec un peuple,*

---

[19] Marshall McLuhan, *Pour comprendre les médias*, Paris : Editions Seuil, 1968, seconde édition, 1977, traduction française d'*Understanding the Media. The Extensions of Man*, New York: McGrow-Hill, 1964. « Par la télévision, Kennedy a trouvé tout naturel de faire participer le public aux fonctions de la présidence, tant comme machine administrative que comme image. La télévision fait ressortir les attributs corporatifs de la fonction », p. 381.

[20] Claire Cain Miller, « How Obama's Internet Campaign Changed Politics », *The New York Times*, 7 novembre, 2008, http://bits.blogs.nytimes.com/2008/11/07/how-obamas-internet-campaign-changed-politics/.

[21] Propos recueillis et traduits par Fabrice Epelboin dans son article « Politique et Internet, un premier bilan de l'élection d'Obama » dans *Web 2.0*, 27 novembre 2008, http://fr.readwriteweb.com/2008/11/27/entrevues/politique-internet-premier-bilan-election-obama/ Joe Trippi est l'auteur de *The Revolution Will Not Be Televised*, New York: HarperCollins, 2004.

et ils sont des millions. Le congrès devra suivre l'agenda du président et sera sous pression : il aura non seulement à affronter le président, mais également les réseaux sociaux qui le supportent.

Aurélie Blot

Université Paris Ouest Nanterre La Défense

Developing Democratic Debate: A Case Study of American Political Blogs and the Mainstream Print Media in the Run-up to the 2008 Presidential Election

The American presidential election of 2008 pitted Democratic Illinois senator Barack Obama and Delaware senator Joe Biden against Republican Arizona senator John McCain and Alaskan governor Sarah Palin. History would be made no matter the outcome: a Democratic win would put the first African-American president in the White House, and a Republican win would mean the country's oldest elected president and first female vice-president. During the presidential campaign, the United States was in the midst of a financial crisis and still actively involved in two major international wars. The electorate was divided along ideological lines; believing that the future success of the country depended on the outcome of the election, each side tried to persuade independent voters to their point of view.

The 2008 presidential campaign was also historic because of the role played by the Internet, and more specifically blogs, as a means of communication between candidates, the public, and the media. Until the creation of the Internet, the public was relegated to being a passive audience, and the mainstream media took on the role of informing the electorate about the candidates and their political positions. The creation of blogs has given rise to a different way for the electorate to inform itself and, at the same time, to become a more active participant in the media landscape.

In their report entitled "State of the News Media 2009", Tom Rosenstiel and Bill Kovach analyzed the coverage of the 2008 presidential election by traditional and new media. They argued that "*a more nuanced understanding of the media network is that the old and the new media were interdependent and often complementary (...) the two media were hardly in competition. They informed each other.*"[1] Rosenstiel and Kovach asserted that blogs provide additional services that the mainstream media are unable or unwilling to provide.

Presidential campaigns are always a hotbed of political journalism, as citizens seek information about the candidates in order to make their choices. This case study will test to what extent the relationship between blogs and newspapers was complementary: was it a mutual relationship or was the division of labor more unequal? Ten high-profile political blogs and three major American newspapers were selected. Blogs were chosen by cross-referencing the political blogs from two well-respected lists of the most popular blogs in 2008: Technorati's Top 100[2] and the Truth Laid Bear Ecosystem.[3] Basing the selection on these two lists ensured political blogs with an extensive audience. Newspapers were selected from a list of the top 100 newspapers in the United States in 2008.[4] In the days leading up to Election Day, 88% of registered voters were following the presidential campaign closely according to *the Pew Research Center*, so that period is the focus of this study.[5] Blog posts and newspaper articles published between midnight on November 1, 2008, and 11:59pm on Election Day, November 4, were chosen for analysis. First, I will provide a brief description of the rise of blogs in the United States. That will be followed by a quantitative analysis of first the political blogs and then the newspapers chosen for this study. Finally, I will compare the content of the political blogs and the newspapers in order to determine the relationship between political blogs and the mainstream print media.

---

[1] Bill Kovach and Tom Rosenstiel, "Lessons of the Election", *State of the News Media 2009,* Pew Project for Excellence in Journalism, http://www.stateofthemedia.org/2009/narrative_special_lessonsoftheelection.php?cat=1&media=12.

[2] "Blogger Central: Top 100 Blogs", *Technorati*, 30 April 2008, http://replay.wayback machine. org/20080430232440/http://www.technorati.com/pop/blogs/.

[3] "The Truth Laid Bear Ecosystem", *The Truth Laid Bear*, 22 August 2008, http://web.archive.org/web/20080822085400/http://truthlaidbear.com/ecosystem.php.

[4] "2008 Top Newspapers, Blogs, and Consumer Magazines", *BurrellesLuce*, 2008, http://www.burrellesluce.com/top100/2008_Top_100List.pdf.

[5] "Election Weekend News Interest Hits 20-Year High", *Pew Research Center for the People and the Press*, 6 November 2008, http://people-press.org/report/469/election-news-interest.

1. A Brief Survey of the Creation and Development of Blogs in the United States

Blogs were created by computer programmers at the end of the 20th century, before the rise of search engines such as Google, in order to share links to interesting websites.[6] The newest information was placed at the top, pushing the old content further down the page.[7] Because these pages represented the log of each individual's navigation through the Internet, they were named "web logs", which was later shortened to "blogs". The vast community of blogs is commonly referred to as the blogosphere, and blog authors are referred to as bloggers.

When blogs were first created, bloggers had to have the technological know-how to design and maintain them; thus it is not surprising that the first blogs focused primarily on technology. In 1998, there were only a few sites that would be identified today as blogs.[8] The following year, there were an estimated fifty blogs, and blogging tools were created, allowing anyone to create and publish a blog online, often for free. As a consequence of no longer needing in-depth technical knowledge to have a blog, anyone with a passion could become a blogger and publicly share his knowledge. The number of topics expanded exponentially, as did the number of blogs; in 2003, there were an estimated 2.4 million to 4.1 million blogs in existence.[9] Blog-analysis site Technorati counted over 70 million blogs in April 2007[10] and over 133 million blogs worldwide in 2008.[11] These estimates are unfortunately the most recent figures; as

[6] Rebecca Blood, "Introduction", in *We've Got Blog: How Weblogs Are Changing Our Culture*, Cambridge, MA: Perseus Publishing, 2002, p. x.
[7] Rebecca Blood, "Introduction", in *We've Got Blog: How Weblogs Are Changing Our Culture*, Cambridge, MA: Perseus Publishing, 2002, p. ix.
[8] Kathy E. Gill, "How can we measure the influence of the blogosphere?" http://faculty.washington.edu/kegill/pub/gill_blogosphere_www2004.pdf, p. 2.
[9] Daniel W. Drezner and Henry Farrell, "Web of Influence", *Foreign Policy*, November/December 2004, http://foreignpolicy.com/story/cms.php?story_id=2007&print=1.
[10] David Sifry, "The State of the Live Web", *Sifry's Alerts* 2007, http://www.sifry.com/alerts/archives/000493.html, as quoted in Jill Walker Rettberg, *Blogging (Digital Media and Society)*, Cambridge, UK: Polity Press, 2008, p. 30.
[11] Douglas Quenqua, "Blogs Falling in an Empty Forest", *The New York Times*, 5 June 2009, http://www.nytimes.com/2009/06/07/fashion/07blogs.html.

the number of blogs skyrocketed, it has become increasingly difficult to evaluate the size of the blogosphere. Because it is easy and virtually free to create a blog, many people create one, only to abandon it later. At the same time, it is virtually impossible to maintain a complete central blog directory, given the rate of blog creation and the time required.

Blogs are categorized into two distinct groups: personal blogs and filter blogs. Personal blogs are essentially public personal diaries in which the author recounts the events which occur in his life.[12] Filter blogs focus on a particular subject, such as politics, and link to websites in order to direct readers to interesting material. Filter blogs allow humans to sift through and amplify content from innumerable sources. In spite of an enormous number of personal blogs, it is filter blogs that garner the largest audience and are the more widely read form.[13] The subject of a filter blog is usually broad enough to interest a larger number of readers than a personal blog. Filter blogs are also considered the more influential kind of blogs because filter bloggers back up their commentaries by posting links to relevant information.[14] Personal blogs, on the other hand, tend to have a more focused demographic, and thus fewer readers.

In order to encourage readers to visit often, a blogger must update his blog on a regular, if not daily, basis. This type of commitment requires a certain level of dedication. Given the fervent passion often associated with modern politics in the United States, it is unsurprising that politics is one of the main subjects of American blogs: a July 2006 Pew Internet Research Survey of American bloggers found that approximately 11% focus mainly on politics.[15] America's two-party political system fosters a strong spirit of competition, with each side trying to outdo the other. The constant back-and-forth between political parties and candidates

---

[12] James Branum, "The Blogging Phenomenon: An Overview and Theoretical Consideration", *Southwest Texas State University* December 2001, http://www.ajy.net/jmb/blogphenomenon.htm.

[13] Michael Tyworth, "An Exploratory Analysis of Weblogs", 2004, http://www.fraters libertas.com/MJT_FINAL.pdf, p. 2.

[14] Gene Edward Veith and Lynn Vincent, "Year of the blog", *World Magazine*, 4 December 2004, http://www.worldmag.com/articles/10018.

[15] Jill Walker Rettberg, *Blogging (Digital Media and Society)*, Cambridge, UK: Polity Press, 2008, p. 16.

provides a steady stream of information on which the media and bloggers can comment.

Until the creation of the Internet, the American media landscape was primarily uni-directional: the public had no choice but to remain passive and accept the information provided. The mainstream media had control of all means of public broadcasting, such as newspapers, radio, and television. Thanks to the arrival of blogs, the public has become an active participant in the information cycle. While it is true that most blogs have a very small audience,[16] some of the top-rated political blogs equal, and sometimes even outperform, traditional media when it comes to audience: Andrew Sullivan reported that his political blog, Daily Dish, received "*over 23 million pageviews from 14 million visits*"[17] in October 2008, which means approximately 450,000 per day. There were only nine American newspapers with higher 2008 daily circulation rates.[18]

When examined together, political bloggers and professional journalists form a media community to which people can turn for information. Whereas previously the public had no choice but to consume the information provided by the mainstream media, blogs allow their audience the chance to react publicly to it. Over the past decade, blogging has evolved into an integral part of the political media landscape. As blogging has become more accepted, its role in the media community has changed.

In 2004, as the number of people turning to blogs for information was slowly increasing, the mainstream media tried to discredit bloggers as 'amateur journalists'.[19] Their primary reason was simple: if more and more people used blogs for information, the circulation rates and viewership numbers would drop, thus leading to less revenue from advertisers. This in turn would cause the company financial problems and possible cutbacks. Criticism of bloggers focused on their reliance

---

16 Clay Shirky, "Power Laws, Weblogs, and Inequality", *Clay Shirky's Internet Writings*, 8 February 2003, http://www.shirky.com/writings/powerlaw_weblog.html.

17 Andrew Sullivan, "Home News" *Daily Dish*, 2 November, 2008,http://andresullivan.theatlantic.com/the_daily_dish/2008/11/home-news.html.

18 "2008 Top Newspapers, Blogs, and Consumer Magazines", *BurrellesLuce*, 2008, http://www.burrellesluce.com/top100/2008_Top_100List.pdf.

19 Matt Welch, "The New Amateur Journalists Weigh In", *Columbia Journalism Review,* September/October 2003, http://www.cjr.org/issues/2003/5/blog-welch.asp.

on the information published by the mainstream media. Professional journalists even referred to bloggers as 'parasites'[20] due to their dependence on mainstream media; without professional journalists to sustain them, bloggers would not be able to survive.

Bloggers, however, fought back against the 'amateur journalist' claim, arguing that they had uncovered two political scandals that the mainstream media had originally ignored. First, in December 2002, after Senator Lott made racist comments at a public gathering, bloggers teamed up to uncover Lott's history of racist comments, thus forcing him to step down as a candidate for Senate Majority Leader. In September 2004, CBS News broadcast a report examining President Bush's military service based on documents it had received. A number of blogs questioned the validity of the documents, deciding that certain fonts used had not existed when the documents were said to have been made. CBS News eventually admitted that it had not properly vetted the documents before the broadcast. As a result, a number of CBS executives were fired, and the host of the program, long-time broadcaster Dan Rather, was forced to resign.

2. Quantitative Analysis of 10 A-list Political Blogs

The blogs chosen for this study are, in alphabetical order: The Corner,[21] Crooks and Liars,[22] Daily Dish,[23] DailyKos,[24] Instapundit,[25] Little Green Footballs,[26] Michelle Malkin,[27] Powerline,[28] Talking Points Memo,[29] and Think Progress.[30] In order to avoid confusion, each blog will be referred to by its title instead of the names of its authors.

---

[20] Robert Niles, "Are blogs a 'parasitic' medium?", *The Online Journalism Review*, 2 March 2007, http://www.ojr.org/ojr/stories/070301niles/.
[21] http://corner.nationalreview.com
[22] http://andrewsullivan.theatlantic.com
[23] http://www.dailydish.com
[24] http://www.dailykos.com
[25] http://www.pajamasmedia.com/instapundit/.
[26] http://www.littlegreenfootballs.com
[27] http://www.michellemalkin.com
[28] http://www.powerlineblog.com
[29] http://www.talkingpointsmemo.com
[30] http://www.thinkprogress.org

Before examining their content, it is important to establish the political viewpoint of each blog. Content analysis of a political blog is linked to the political affiliation of the blogger(s) because of the passionate fervor often associated with politics. In order to determine political viewpoint, qualitative analysis of the political content on the blogs over the four days and self-published "about the author(s)" pages of the ten blogs were considered.

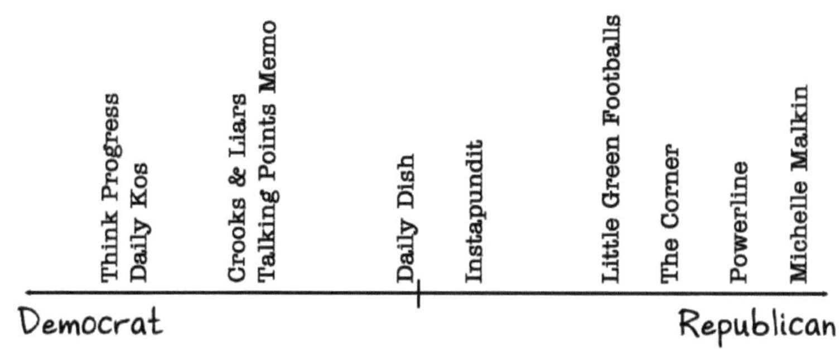

Figure 1 – The political positions of the ten blogs studied

Figure 1 shows the results of that analysis. A blog listed close to the center demonstrated a more moderate political viewpoint than a blog further away from the center. The blogs at the two endpoints of the spectrum showed the most extreme viewpoints of the blogs analyzed. The results show that there was an even split between the number of Democrat and Republican blogs in this study. The least moderate Democratic blogs are Think Progress and DailyKos, whose opinions of McCain and Palin are the most negative. While neither blog attacks the Republican candidates directly, they both highlight negative aspects of the Republican campaign. For example, on November 3, 2008, DailyKos published a post entitled, "McCain Forgets Who Endorsed Him," which describes McCain's difficulty in remembering the names of his endorsers during an interview. A video is included in the post, allowing readers to watch the blunder for themselves.[31] By focusing on McCain's forgetfulness, DailyKos is indirectly highlighting McCain's age. The

[31] Jed Lewison, "McCain Forgets Who Endorsed Him", *DailyKos*, 3 November 2008, http://www.dailykos.com/story/2008/11/3/648228/-McCain-Forgets-Who-Endorsed-Him.

difference in age between McCain, 72, and Obama, 47, at the time of the election made age a relevant factor for voters. Crooks & Liars and Talking Points Memo are more moderate, and Daily Dish is the most moderate of the Democratic blogs. Despite its Democratic leanings, Daily Dish presented a more balanced view of the campaign over the four days, including positive and negative stories about both sides. A post was published on the Daily Dish about McCain's concession speech, calling it "*very classy, very moving, and finally worthy of the man we once thought we knew.*"[32] Knowing that the Democratic candidate had won, *Daily Dish* posted a respectful text about the losing candidate.

On the Republican side, Instapundit was similar to Daily Dish in its moderate nature. Despite its Republican tendencies, the posts published on Instapundit over the four days studied were more informative than persuasive. For example, the post on Instapundit commenting on Obama's acceptance speech called it "*classy.*"[33] The posts about Obama's acceptance speech on Michelle Malkin, on the other hand, were full of negativity. In one post, the blogger revealed that Obama's did not get as many popular votes as previously reported before calling Obama's post-speech 'Yes We Can' chant "*creepy*" and "*cult-ish.*" The same post uses sarcasm, "*Oh, man.*", twice in just a few lines, in order to highlight the blogger's disgust at what she is witnessing.[34] In between the two extremes are the other Republican blogs, Powerline, The Corner, and Little Green Footballs.

In order to encourage readers to check their blogs often, high-profile political bloggers tend to add new content many times, often spacing publication out throughout the day. This claim is supported by the data in this study. Table 1 shows the total number of posts published on each blog.

---

[32] Andrew Sullivan, "McCain's Concession", *Daily Dish*, 4 November 2008, http://andrewsullivan.theatlantic.com/the_daily_dish/2008/11/mccains-concess.html.

[33] Glenn Reynolds, *Instapundit*, 4 November 2008, http://pajamasmedia.com/instapund dit/026749/.

[34] Michelle Malkin, "The One ascends; McCain Concedes", *Michelle Malkin*, 4 November 2008, http://michellemalkin.com/2008/11/04/the-one-ascends/.

Think Progress	39
Michelle Malkin	42
Powerline	44
Little Green Footballs	50
Crooks and Liars	74
Talking Points Memo	122
Instapundit	129
Daily Dish	191
DailyKos	201
The Corner	291

Table 1 – Total number of posts published on each of the 10 blogs studied

At the low end, blogs like Think Progress, Michelle Malkin and Powerline published an average of 10 to 11 new posts per day. At the other end of the scale, The Corner published an average of about 72 articles per day.

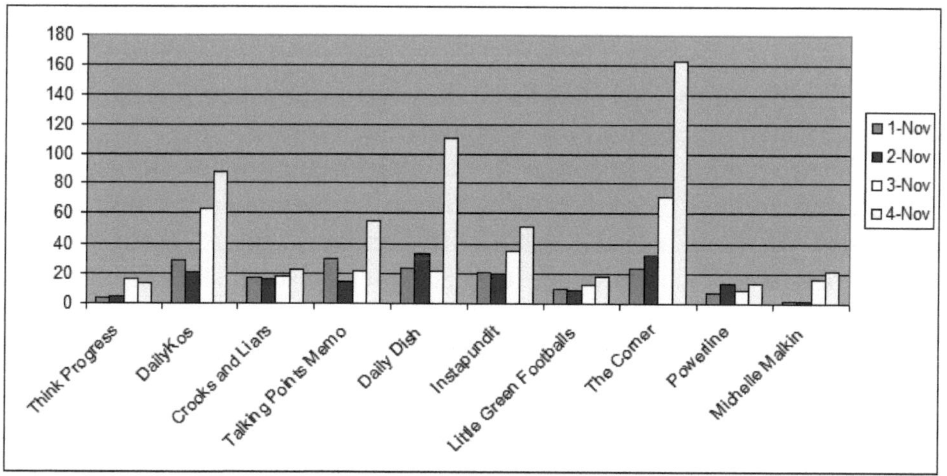

Figure 2– Number of blogs per day

Figure 2 shows a graph of the number of political posts published each day. Arranging the blogs names in the same order as Figure 1, with the extremely Democratic blogs on the far left, the moderate blogs in the center, and the fervent Republican blogs on the right, facilitates a comparative analysis of Republican and Democratic blogs as well.

It is surprising to see that the most extreme viewpoints at both ends of the spectrum published very few posts compared to some of the more moderate viewpoints. Given the zealous passion for politics demonstrated by the bloggers at the extremes, it seems evident that they would publish often in the last few days before the election, in the hope of convincing readers to vote their way. However, that is not the case here: Democratic blog Think Progress published four posts on November 1 and five posts on November 2, and Republican blog Talking Points Memo published only two posts on both November 1 and November 2. On those same days, more moderate blogs Daily Dish and Instapundit each published over 20 posts.

The number of posts published on Election Day, November 4, was greater than the number of posts published on the other days for every blog in this study except one, Think Progress. This can be explained by the fact that on Election Day, blogs provided bits and pieces of information about the election in progress. Bloggers discussed different aspects of the election, such as voter turnout, poll results, and expectations, in addition to publishing reader commentary from around the country. Think Progress published 14 posts on Election Day, but had posted 16 the day before. Nevertheless, compared to the first two days of the study when only four and five posts were published, the number of posts published on Election Day remains much higher.

While frequency is essential to maintain a significant audience, the quality and content of each post is of equal importance because not all posts are created equal. What differentiates blogs from printed newspapers is that each blogger has his or her personal style of blogging. Most American newspapers have adopted a policy of trying to remain as objective as possible, which results in most news stories being essentially the same. Because most blogs are written without editors, they are much more subjective. Bloggers express their opinions, meaning that each blog has a difference voice. For example, the blogger for Instapundit tends to post frequently throughout the day, but each post contains at most a few sentences and a link or two and rarely an image or a video. On the other hand, Talking Points Memo has longer, more detailed posts and includes videos. Being able to embed audio and video into a blog is one of the major differences between print communication and Internet communication.

3. Quantitative Analysis of Three Newspapers

Three newspapers with different circulation figures were chosen in order to test the relationship between blogs and national, regional, and local newspapers. *The New York Times* is one of the United States' most widely-read newspapers, with some analysts calling it a national newspaper.[35] *The Boston Globe* is a more regional newspaper, with distribution focusing on New England.[36] Finally, *The Providence Journal* is a local newspaper centered on Providence and the state of Rhode Island.[37] *The Boston Globe* and *The Providence Journal* were chosen based on accessibility of archives through the public library in my hometown. Choosing three newspapers from the same geographic region – in this case, the Northeast – limits the scope of the study but also constrains the conclusions of this study.

Like blogs, the size of a newspaper's audience, its circulation, is important. The higher the number of people reading a certain newspaper, the more money that newspaper can make from advertisers and the more money that newspaper can afford to pay journalists.

Table 2 shows the 2008 daily circulation rates of the three newspapers studied. *The New York Times* had over a million daily readers, making it the 3rd largest newspaper in the country. There is a steep drop-off between *The New York Times* and *The Boston Globe* in the number of daily readers, putting *The Boston Globe* in 14th place. *The Providence Journal*, in 76th place, has almost 140,000 daily readers.[38]

---

35 "The State of the News Media 2004", *Project for Excellence in Journalism*, 2004, http://www.stateofthenewsmedia.org, quoted in Hugh Hewitt, *Blog: Understanding the Information Revolution That's Changing Your World*, Nashville, TN: Nelson Books, 2005, p. 81.

36 "Boston Globe", http://www.mondotimes.com/1/world/us/21/1038/2795.

37 "Providence Journal", http://www.mondotimes.com/1/world/us/39/2226/5470.

38 "2008 Top Newspapers, Blogs, and Consumer Magazines", *BurrellesLuce*, 2008, http://www.burrellesluce.com/top100/2008_Top_100List.pdf.

	Daily Circulation
New York Times (3rd)	1,077,256
Boston Globe (14th)	350,605
Providence Journal (76th)	139,055

Table 2 – 2008 Daily Circulation Rates for the 3 newspapers studied

If the link between daily circulation and advertising rates exists, it would imply that a newspaper with higher circulation rates has a more significant budget and, therefore, more journalists on its staff. As a result, the newspaper would be able to publish more articles than a smaller circulation newspaper. To test this assumption, the number of articles focusing on the presidential election in the three newspapers was compared.

	Number of Articles
New York Times	164
Boston Globe	63
Providence Journal	18

Table 3 – Total number of articles published over the four-day period studied which dealt with the 2008 presidential election

Table 3 shows there is a correlation between the number of readers and the number of articles about the upcoming election: over the four-day period, *The New York Times* published the most articles with 164, there was a steep drop to 63 with *The Boston Globe*, and *The Providence Journal* printed just 18 articles.

It is equally important to analyze the number of articles published on each of the days in question. Figure 3 below, shows the distribution of

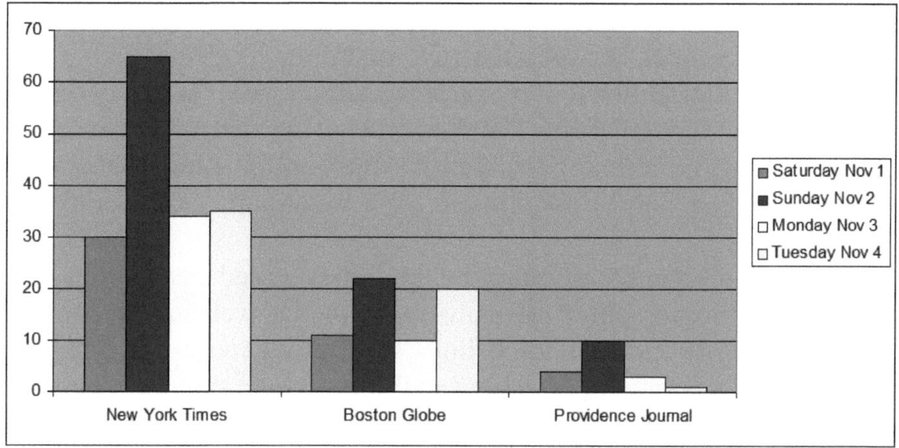

Figure 3 – Number of newspaper articles per day

newspaper articles broken down over the four days. Each newspaper showed an increase in published articles about the election on Sunday, November 2. This can be explained by the fact that newspaper companies publish a longer and more detailed newspaper on Sunday due to a higher circulation. This analysis holds true for all three of the newspapers. One surprising detail in Figure 3 is that *The Providence Journal* only published one article about the election on Tuesday, November 4. Given the historic nature of the election, it seems abnormal that the newspaper did not talk about it in greater detail on Election Day.

4. Comparative Analysis of the Blogs and the Newspapers

Having established a framework for blogs and newspapers, a comparative analysis can now be made. In terms of quantity, the blogs tended to publish more posts than *The Boston Globe* and *The Providence Journal. The New York Times*, however, was more impressive; only three blogs managed to publish more posts than *The New York Times*. The fact that these blogs outperformed two of the three newspapers is not surprising, given that printed newspapers have deadlines and limited space; blogs, on the other hand, can be updated at any time and the content can be as long or as short as desired.

Newspaper articles are usually at least a couple of paragraphs, if not more, whereas quite a few of the blog posts studied consisted of just one or two sentences. Comparing the number of articles printed by newspapers with the number of posts published by bloggers highlights one of the differences between the two mediums: blogs have an ease of publication that traditional newspapers cannot have because of their printed format. Nonetheless, *The New York Times* proved to be on par with the blogs in terms of quantity, thus establishing that money, resources, and a large circulation give newspapers a competitive advantage.

In terms of content, the blogs in this study relied heavily on links, both to other bloggers and to mainstream media websites, in order to support their positions. Providing links to external sources is one of the primordial aspects of a blog. This capability can be compared to using references when writing a research paper; it makes it easier for the reader to access the original source. As a result, the blog's commentary is enhanced because the blogger can assume that the reader already has some understanding of the source in question. The printed format of a newspaper restricts the possibilities of reprinting original sources, especially when it comes to online audio or video files.

Another interesting advantage of blogs that emerged from this study was the interactivity between the bloggers and their readers. From the beginning to the end of Election Day, political bloggers were constantly posting updates to their blogs. On Instapundit, 52 posts were published on Election Day, starting at 2:00am and not stopping until shortly before midnight. DailyKos showed a similar pattern: 88 posts published between 1:00am and 11:50pm. As stated previously, publishing often encourages readers to check the blog more regularly, and it also gives readers a chance to comment. A number of blogs published comments from their readers as individual posts. For example, a large number of the posts on Instapundit and Daily Dish were from readers around the country as to what it was like to vote on Election Day. The digital nature of blogging allows bloggers to update their readers in real-time about events that are taking place at that very moment. This "man on the ground" journalism is possible thanks to the participation of readers who take an active role in emailing the blogger. At 11:08am, the blog Daily Dish published a post entitled, "The View From Your Election: Pennsylvania." The content of this post included a photo and description of how many people were waiting to vote in Pennsylvania at 7:00am on Election Day. The blog post clearly indicates that this information was sent in by a reader.[39] This interactivity cannot exist with printed newspapers because of the constraints of their paper format. While it is extremely likely that the newspapers printed articles about the voter experience the day after the election, the bloggers had the advantage of technology.

Another difference between printed newspapers and blogs is voice. The political articles published by the three newspapers studied all provided similar information, despite the fact that they were written by different reporters in different geographical locations. It is only in editorials that journalists are allowed to express their own ideas. Otherwise, a certain level of objectivity is required. There is little interpretation of events and speeches because of the desire of newspaper editors to print objective stories.

Political blogs, on the other hand, are loaded with opinion and interpretation. The political blogs in this study showed passionate beliefs about the election. Given the partisan nature of blogs, political bloggers tend to be biased towards the candidate(s) or party they support, which leads to a lot of negativity and trying to discredit the opposing candidate instead of extolling the virtues of the candidates they respect and admire. The blog Michelle Malkin, the most extreme Republican blog in the study on Election Day, published a blog post entitled "The One ascends; McCain concedes" at 11:15pm.[40] The title and content of this blog post shows a lot of sarcasm when referring to Democratic candidate Barack Obama, calling him "*The One.*" The image of Obama with a halo above his head seems to represent Obama as the second coming of Christ. While this could be interpreted in a number of different ways, the fact that the blogger was vehemently against Obama's candidacy means that this picture was intended to criticize Obama's self-portrayal as a savior. It is hard to imagine a newspaper printing this type of derogatory commentary.

In order to determine the relationship between blogs and the mainstream media, it was necessary to analyze the links and references from one to the other. As expected, the blogs studied often linked to

[39] Andrew Sullivan, "The View From Your Election: Pennsylvania", *Daily Dish*, 4 November 2008, http://andrewsullivan.theatlantic.com/the_daily_dish/2008/11/the-view-fro-18.html.

[40] Michelle Malkin, "The One ascends; McCain Concedes", *Michelle Malkin*, 4 November 2008, http://michellemalkin.com/2008/11/04/the-one-ascends/.

information published and broadcast by the mainstream media, mostly corporate newspapers and, more recently, television channels. Blogs are reliant on the mainstream media for a lot of their information, as bloggers are rarely paid for their work and therefore cannot afford to do their own investigative journalism. Newspapers have the means to pay reporters to do the research, and once the articles are published, both in print and online, blogs can link to the online versions of the newspapers. For example, a November 2, 2008, post on Daily Dish linked to and quoted an article from *The Sunday Times* of London about the "*wave of optimism behind Obama.*"[41] Think Progress published an article entitled "Think Fast" on November 3, 2008 in which *The New York Times* is quoted and linked to as well.[42] While outside the scope of this study, it is important to note that television also played a significant role for blogs. Thanks to the increasing popularity and access to streaming video, blogs can link to and analyze video clips like they have been doing for years with printed and online newspapers.

This relationship highlights just how dependent blogs are on the mainstream media, but the relationship is not just one-way. News reporters can use high-profile political blogs to gauge the public's interest in certain subjects. Blogging advocates have argued that mainstream media reporters read blogs.[43] In this relatively small sample, the newspapers made a few references to bloggers. In addition to a few quick references to blogs in different articles over the four days studied, *The New York Times* published an article entitled "The '08 Campaign: Sea Change for Politics as We Know It" on November 4. [44] This article examines the changing political landscape and the role played by the Internet and blogs. *The Boston Globe* made four general references to blogs and bloggers, with one reference on November 4 to specific blogs

[41] Andrew Sullivan, "A President, Not A Messiah." *Daily Dish*, 2 November 2008, http://andrewsullivan.theatlantic.com/the_daily_dish/2008/11/a-president-not.html.
[42] "Think Fast: November 3 2008", *Think Progress*, 3 November 2008, http://think progress.org/2008/11/03/thinkfast-november-3-2008/.
[43] Mark Glaser, "Distinction Between Bloggers, Journalists Blurring More Than Ever", *Mediashift (PBS)*, 28 February 2008, http://www.pbs.org/mediashift/ 2008/02/distinct ion-between-bloggers-journalists-blurring-more-than-ever059.html.
[44] Adam Nagourney, "The '08 Campaign: Sea Change for Politics as We Know It." *The New York Times*, 4 November 2008, p. 1.

that readers could turn to online for information.[45] Although *The Providence Journal* provided only two brief and mostly general references to blogs, these references show that the newspaper reporters were, at the very least, aware of the existence of political blogs. At the same time, the newspapers in this study did not directly quote any specific blogs. One possible explanation is that blogs are the intermediary between the public and the mainstream media. By publishing links to and commentary about mainstream media stories, bloggers bring attention to the stories they consider important. Due to this intermediary role, blogs are not necessarily referenced if another mainstream media outlet picks up the story, as the story can be traced back to its original thanks to the links provided on the blog.

This study has demonstrated the validity of Rosenstiel and Kovach's claim that high-profile political blogs complemented the coverage of the presidential election provided by newspapers in the last four days of the 2008 presidential election. The analysis showed that political blogs can match or even outdo newspapers in terms of sheer quantity. In terms of quality, both traditional newspapers and blogs bring their own advantages to political journalism: traditional newspapers have the financial resources to do their own investigative reporting whereas a majority of blogs are dependent on the information provided by the mainstream media. Blogs, however, have a speed of publication that allows constant updates and real-time, "man on the ground" coverage of important events like the 2008 presidential election. The question about the quality of such coverage remains to be seen. Thanks to their digital nature, blogs can be extremely interactive, with many blogs posting comments and emails from readers as part of their commentary. Blogs are also relatively transparent when it comes to political bias: whereas most journalists try to maintain a certain neutrality when discussing politics, political blogs revel in partisanship and competition.

This study is in no way complete. Because of the different levels of newspaper circulation, the coverage provided by the newspapers cannot be compared; for that reason, expanding the selection to other

---

[45] Tom Haines, "3 Ways to Survive Tonight", *The Boston Globe*, 4 November, 2008, p. 10.

newspapers of similar circulation figures would balance out the study. Given the size of the United States, only a few newspapers are considered national, which implies that the location of a newspaper is important. In order to expand this study, it might be important to select a broader geographical range of newspapers. Nonetheless, it is an important first step to understanding the relationship between political blogs and mainstream media. Having demonstrated that newspapers and blogs are complementary on a small scale, the next step would be to analyze the information provided by political blogs and the mainstream media in order to determine to what extent this new media landscape is affecting politics.

Erica Johnson

Université Paris Est Créteil.

Protéger les valeurs fondatrices de la démocratie américaine à l'ère du numérique

Protéger la liberté d'expression et l'accès à l'information sur l'Internet. Enjeux et défis

Pour la première fois en 1996 le Congrès à majorité républicaine chercha, à réglementer l'accès à certains documents sur l'Internet et vota le 1er février le *Telecommunications Act*, amendant le *Communications Act* de 1934[1]. Si son principal objectif était de déréguler le marché des télécommunications, le Titre V, intitulé « obscénité et violence », incluait les dispositions du *Communications Decency Act*, adopté l'année précédente afin de protéger les mineurs et pénalisait la diffusion de ceux dont le contenu serait jugé « indécent » ou « vraiment choquant » (*patently offensive*) par la *Federal Communications Commission* (FCC), comme c'était déjà le cas pour la télévision et la radio. Le premier amendement protégeant la liberté d'expression interdit toute réglementation du contenu d'un message ; l'*American Civil Liberty Union*, dès la signature de la loi par le président Bill Clinton le 7 février, intenta une action et obtint, à la suite d'une injonction prise par la Cour fédérale du District

[1] Confirmant les dispositions prises dans le *Radio Act* de 1927, cette loi réglementait l'attribution des fréquences et des licences d'exploitation. Elle créa la *Federal Communications Commission* (FCC), composée de membres nommés par le président, et lui confia la coordination des télécommunications. On peut s'étonner que cette loi n'ait pas été invalidée, comme le furent d'autres lois du *New Deal*. Le Congrès fonda son autorité sur les pouvoirs que la Clause du commerce lui confère et la Cour, dans l'arrêt *NBC Co. v FCC*, 319 U.S. 190, 1943 décida que la loi donnait à cette Commission le pouvoir de réglementer les réseaux. Lorsque la télévision commerciale se développa, à partir de 1948, la FCC contrôla l'attribution des licences jusqu'en 1952. Voir Elisabeth Boulot, « Les médias et l'information : le cadre juridique », *Les médias et l'information aux Etats-Unis depuis 1945*, Suzanne Durruty et Jean-Paul Gabillet (dir.), Paris : Editions du Temps, 1997, p. 7-21.

Est de Pennsylvanie, que soit suspendue temporairement l'application de ces dispositions jugées trop vagues[2].

La première partie de cet article expose les motifs qui ont conduit la Cour fédérale de district à invalider certaines dispositions de la section 502 et la décision de la Cour suprême qui a confirmé leur inconstitutionnalité. La seconde examine, avec le recul du temps, l'impact de cette décision sur le développement de ce nouveau média. A-t-il favorisé l'échange des idées et le partage des savoirs ? La dernière partie considère les menaces qui pèsent aujourd'hui sur la « neutralité de l'Internet ».

1. Quel statut juridique pour l'Internet en tant que média : *ACLU v. Reno* ?

Afin de déterminer si les mesures votées par le Congrès ne violaient pas le premier amendement, la Cour fédérale de district explique dans les 123 paragraphes de son arrêt relatant les faits et les questions soulevées au cours des cinq jours d'audience, les spécificités de l'Internet et ses différences majeures avec les deux medias soumis aux règles édictées par la FCC[3] : le fait qu'il permet des échanges ou le partage de documents à l'échelle mondiale, son caractère décentralisé, l'absence d'une administration qui pourrait exercer un contrôle sur l'information transmise, la multiplicité des moyens d'accès, des modes de communications et des documents consultables ainsi que son interactivité – le récepteur d'un message pouvant en retour s'adresser à un ou plusieurs internautes. Elle en conclut qu'il s'agit d'un média entièrement nouveau et unique en son genre auquel les critères établis par la Cour suprême pour affirmer la constitutionnalité des formes de censure imposées sur les ondes ou à la télévision ne peuvent s'appliquer : le ou les récepteurs d'un message ne peuvent être assimilés au public « captif » d'une radio ou d'une chaîne de télévision à une heure de grande écoute[4]. Au cours des débats furent mis en lumière les

[2] *ACLU v. Reno,* 929 F. Supp. 824 (E.D. Pa. 1996), http://www.ciec.org/decision_PA/decision_text.html.

[3] Les réseaux câblés ont un statut mixte (*Cable Communications Policy Act,* 1984 et *Cable Television Consumer Protection Act,* 1992).

[4] *ACLU v. Reno,* § 88. « *Communications over the Internet do not "invade" an individual's home or appear on one's computer screen unbidden. Users seldom*

problèmes suivants : opérer la vérification de l'âge et de l'identité d'un internaute était difficile et l'identification par carte de crédit seulement envisageable sur les sites commerciaux[5]. Il apparut aussi que des logiciels de contrôle parental efficaces existaient, contrairement à ce qu'affirmaient les avocats du gouvernement. Les témoignages d'associations qui se joignirent à la plainte de l'ACLU[6] et d'un certain nombre de fournisseurs d'accès démontrèrent que les termes de la loi étaient trop vagues[7] et que le gouvernement n'avait pas apporté la preuve que l'application des dispositions portant fortement atteinte à la

---

encounter content "by accident." A document's title or a description of the document will usually appear before the document itself takes the step needed to view it, and in many cases the user will receive detailed information about a site's content before he or she need take the step to access the document. Almost all sexually explicit images are preceded by warnings as to the content. Even the Government's witness, Agent Howard Schmidt, Director of the Air Force Office of Special Investigation, testified that the "odds are slim" that a user would come across a sexually explicit site by accident ».

[5] Il est interdit aux moins de treize ans de révéler leur identité sur l'Internet (*Children Online Privacy Protection Act*, 1998). Tout récemment, lors du e-G8, Mark Zuckerberg indiquait que *Facebook* ne pouvait pas s'assurer que certains adolescents de moins de 13 ans – auxquels le site est interdit – n'étaient pas membres, tout en souhaitant que cette restriction légale soit supprimée. L'accès à des films pornographiques sur le réseau câblé aux Etats-Unis et aux numéros de téléphones « roses » (*dial-a-porn*) a été autorisé aux adultes à condition qu'ils utilisent une carte de crédit.

[6] Il faut préciser qu'à la plainte de l'ACLU s'étaient jointes des associations de lutte contre le SIDA et de prévention contre les agressions sexuelles. Une plainte avait été ensuite déposée par les bibliothèques publiques, les libraires et les fournisseurs d'accès à l'Internet (*American Library Association v. Department of Justice*). Si les mesures prévues par le CDA avaient été appliquées, les demandeurs auraient dû cesser de diffuser un grand nombre d'informations sous peine de lourdes sanctions. Les deux affaires furent examinées et jugées conjointement. Voir les articles de Paul M. Smith et de John B. Morris, avocats des parties, dans Joseph Russomanno, Ed., *Defending the First. Commentary on First Amendment Issues and Cases*, Mahwah, NJ: Lawrence Erlbaum Associates, Publishers, 2005, p.163-201.

[7] Le terme « *indecent* » n'est pas défini dans le texte de la loi et aucune différence n'est faite avec ce qui est considéré comme *« patently offensive »*, alors que cette distinction a été effectuée par la Cour suprême dans l'arrêt *Miller v. California* (413 U.S. 15) en 1973 et que les contrevenants encourent des sanctions pénales. De plus, le principe selon lequel les autorités locales élaborent leurs propres critères en matière de décence (*community standards*) semble peu compatible avec les dispositions du CDA qui cherchent à créer une norme nationale, (opinion du juge Buckwalter, partie B).

liberté d'expression des adultes, permettrait de protéger efficacement les moins de 18 ans[8]. Les trois juges fédéraux qui statuèrent sur cette affaire en première instance, décidèrent de prolonger la non-application des articles contestés jusqu'à ce que la Cour suprême rende son jugement.

Chacun d'entre eux développa ses arguments dans une opinion séparée. La juge Dolores Sloviter déclara que le premier amendement protège « l'un des droits les plus chers », celui de « choisir les documents auxquels nous avons accès » et se dit peu convaincue par les arguments du ministère de la Justice[9]. Elle affirma que c'était aux tribunaux fédéraux de défendre la liberté d'expression pour les « générations futures ». Le juge Buckwalter, quant à lui, rappela que les restrictions apportées à l'exercice de ce droit ne sont justifiées que dans un nombre très limité de cas[10], et que c'est au législateur de les définir avec le plus grand soin, surtout lorsqu'une loi prévoit des sanctions pénales. La législation en vigueur lui parut suffisante pour protéger les mineurs, même dans le cas d'une diffusion sur l'Internet de documents jugés « indécents ». Il argua que l'analogie faite par le gouvernement entre l'Internet, la radio et la télévision pour justifier cette réglementation, afin d'assurer la décence dans les communications, était infondée et que la jurisprudence établie dans l'arrêt *FCC v. Pacifica Foundation*, rendu par la Cour suprême en 1978[11], était inappropriée

---

[8] Opinion de la juge Sloviter, parties D. *The Nature of the Government's Interest*, E. *The Reach of the Statute* et F. *Whether CDA Is Narrowly Tailored*?

[9] «*Whether Congress' decision was a wise one is not at issue here. It was unquestionably a decision that placed the CDA in serious conflict with our most cherished protection – the right to choose the material to which we would have access*».

[10] Les publications obscènes ou pornographiques ne sont pas protégées par le premier amendement. Les lois des Etats interdisent la vente ou l'accès de ces publications aux mineurs.

[11] Cette décision maintenait la condamnation d'une station de radio de l'Etat de New York pour la diffusion de propos considérés comme obscènes au beau milieu de l'après-midi. Le juge Stevens, auteur de l'opinion de la Cour y déclarait : « *The broadcast media have established a uniquely pervasive presence in the lives of Americans. Patently offensive, indecent material presented over the airwaves confronts the citizen, not only in public, but also in the privacy of the home, where the individual's right to be left alone plainly outweighs the First Amendment rights of an intruder. Because the broadcast audience is constantly tuning in and out, prior warnings cannot completely protect the listener or viewer from unexpected program content. To say that one may avoid further offense by turning off the radio when he*

pour défendre les dispositions de la loi, un point de vue partagé par les deux autres juges, en particulier à cause des sanctions pénales encourues et de défenses inapplicables, en pratique, à cette nouvelle technologie. Pour sa part, le juge Stewart Dalzell dénonça avec vigueur les mesures prévues par le CDA à cause des effets négatifs qu'elles ne manqueraient pas d'avoir sur les adultes utilisant l'Internet, en les incitant à une forme d'autocensure, par peur d'être l'objet de poursuites[12]. Après avoir brossé le tableau d'un paysage audiovisuel soumis au contrôle d'une commission gouvernementale alors que la presse bénéficiait d'une grande liberté, au nom du droit des citoyens à l'information, il défendit le principe que ce nouveau média devait être affranchi de toute censure de son contenu par l'Etat, à l'exception des formes d'expression déjà prohibées afin de protéger les mineurs, car il favorise, encore plus que la presse écrite, l'échange d'idées entre les citoyens de toutes origines, même si parfois celui-ci est à la limite de la « cacophonie » et que les propos tenus peuvent être considérés par certains comme « vulgaires » ou « indécents »[13].

---

hears indecent language is like saying that the remedy for an assault is to run away after the first blow. One may hang up on an indecent phone call, but that option does not give the caller a constitutional immunity or avoid a harm that has already taken place », 438 U.S. 726, 749. Cette citation démontre que cet arrêt ne peut s'appliquer à l'Internet car l'internaute choisit de se connecter à un site et d'ouvrir un document.

[12] « *The CDA's wholesale disruption on the Internet will necessarily affect adult participation in the medium. As some speakers leave or refuse to enter the medium, and others bowdlerize their speech or erect the barriers that the Act envisions, and still others remove bulletin boards, Web sites, and newsgroups, adults will face a shrinking ability to participate in the medium. Since much of the communication on the Internet is participatory, i.e., is a form of dialogue, a decrease in the number of speakers, speech fora, and permissible topics will diminish the worldwide dialogue that is the strength and signal achievement of the medium* ». Cette citation se trouve dans la partie 3 de son opinion intitulée : *The Effect of the CDA on the Novel Characteristics of Internet Communication.*

[13] Voici la conclusion de l'opinion du juge Dalzell : « *True it is that many find some of the speech on the Internet to be offensive, and amid the din of cyberspace many hear discordant voices that they regard as indecent. The absence of governmental regulation of Internet content has unquestionably produced a kind of chaos, but as one of plaintiffs' experts put it with such resonance at the hearing: "What achieved success was the very chaos that the Internet is. The strength of the Internet is that chaos". Just as the strength of the Internet is chaos, so the strength of our liberty depends upon the*

Un an plus tard la Cour suprême, sous la plume du juge Stevens, confirma les attendus du jugement de la Cour fédérale de district. Elle invalida les deux articles contestés du *Communications Decency Act* et décida – l'Internet étant à cette époque un média où la communication passait essentiellement par l'écriture – que celui-ci jouirait des mêmes protections que la presse, laissant au législateur la responsabilité de modifier les lois existantes afin de protéger les mineurs, sans violer le premier amendement ni entraver le libre échange des idées[14] et aux parents celle d'installer un système de contrôle parental afin de protéger leurs enfants, la Cour fédérale de district les ayant jugés efficaces[15].

---

chaos and cacophony of the unfettered speech the First Amendment protects. For these reasons, I without hesitation hold that the CDA is unconstitutional on its face ».

[14] « *The dramatic expansion of this new marketplace of ideas contradicts the factual basis of this contention. The record demonstrates that the growth of the Internet has been and continues to be phenomenal. As a matter of constitutional tradition, in the absence of evidence to the contrary, we presume that governmental regulation of the content of speech is more likely to interfere with the free exchange of ideas than to encourage it. The interest in encouraging freedom of expression in a democratic society outweighs any theoretical but unproven benefit of censorship. For the foregoing reasons, the judgment of the district court is affirmed.* » *ACLU v. Reno*, 521 U.S. 847 1997, http://caselaw.lp.findlaw.com/cgi-bin/getcase.pl?court=us&navby=case&vol=00 0&invol=96-511. 7 juges sur 9 se sont ralliés à l'opinion rédigée par le juge Stevens. La juge O'Connor a choisi de s'exprimer séparément. Si elle soutient l'invalidation partielle du CDA, elle est en faveur de la création d'un espace sur l'Internet réservé aux adultes lorsque les avancées technologiques le permettront ; elle cite en référence l'article de Lawrence Lessig « Reading the Constitution », *Emory Law Journal*, n° 45, 1996, p. 869-910, en dépit du fait que l'auteur soit très réservé à propos de cette idée et conseille à la Cour suprême de ne pas trancher cette affaire : « *The changes we confront should force us to reconsider the values that the Framers gave us, yet we are not yet well situated to do such rethinking. We need a diversity of views with many judgements by many state and federal judges. It is this diversity that will generate an understanding sufficient for the courts to judge upon. And it is this diversity that will help democrats rethink what is at issue* », p. 908. Le *Chief Justice* Rehnquist s'est rallié à l'opinion de la juge O'Connor. A propos de cette décision, voir l'analyse de Douglas M. Fraleigh dans Richard A. Parker, Ed., *Free Speech on Trial: Communication Perspectives on Landmark Supreme Court Decisions*, Tuscaloosa, AL: University of Alabama Press, 2003, p. 298-312.

[15] En 1998, Le Congrès vota le *Children Online Protection Act* qui, au cours des dix années qui suivirent, fut l'objet d'une bataille judicaire qui prit fin en 2009 lorsque la Cour suprême refusa de réexaminer la décision de la Cour d'appel du 3ème circuit suspendant une nouvelle fois l'application de cette loi. Paul Smith conclut : « *The way to the future is training parents to do a better job and training children to protect*

2. L'impact de la partielle invalidation du CDA

Sans aucun doute la décision de la Cour suprême fut une victoire pour les défenseurs de la liberté d'expression. Attachée à préserver les idéaux républicains des fondateurs de la nation, elle a soustrait au contrôle de la FCC ce nouveau média qui lui apparaissait fondamentalement différent des autres moyens de communications électroniques. En conséquence, la jurisprudence élaborée depuis le début du vingtième siècle pour protéger la presse et la liberté d'expression a été appliquée à l'Internet : en particulier l'absence de censure à priori (*prior restraint*) des contenus[16], le droit de formuler des critiques relatives à la conduite des personnages publics sans être poursuivi pour diffamation[17], et celui de défendre des idées divergentes ou controversées. Le juge Dalzell soulignait « les effets démocratiques » des communications sur l'Internet qui permettent à « un citoyen dont les moyens sont limités de parler des questions importantes pour lui à un public à l'échelle mondiale »[18], mais aussi de s'informer, de débattre, d'exprimer des points de vues différents, impopulaires ou vulgaires dans certains cas. Il faisait référence à l'arrêt *Miami Herald Publishing v. Tornillo* où la Cour défendit le rôle essentiel de la presse dans la discussion des affaires publiques, citant ces paroles de Jefferson : « La où la presse est libre et les êtres humains savent lire, tout va bien »[19]. Il soulignait aussi les méfaits de la concentration des médias écrits et audiovisuels entre les

---

themselves and respect limits on where they will go on the Web (...) It is not a perfect solution, but technology in this instance will have the final say. », « The First Amendment in The Internet Age », dans Joseph Russomanno, *op. cit.*, p. 183.

[16] *Near v. Minnesota*, 238 U.S. 697 (1931).

[17] *New York Times v. Sullivan*, 376 U.S. 254 (1964).

[18] « *The plaintiffs in these actions correctly describe the « democratizing » effects of Internet communication: individual citizens of limited means can speak to a worldwide audience on issues of concern to them.* » *ACLU v. Reno*, *op. cit.*

[19] Cet arrêt, fut décidé à la période du scandale du Watergate, en juin 1974, peu de temps avant que la Cour n'ordonne au Président Nixon de remettre les cassettes manquantes. Dans ce contexte, la référence aux propos de Jefferson a, en conséquence, une résonnance toute particulière : « *[W]here the press is free and every man is able to read, all is safe* », 418 U.S. 241, 260. Le juge Dazell mentionnait également l'arrêt *Turner Broadcasting Systems v. FCC,* 512 U.S. 622, 1994 concernant le transport par câble de la télévision hertzienne. Cette obligation de transport (*must carry provision*) figurant dans la loi de 1992, voir note 3 *supra*, fut établie dans l'arrêt *Turner* en 1997, au nom de la défense de la liberté d'expression (520 U.S. 180).

mains de quelques sociétés et voyait dans l'émergence de ce nouveau média, une manière d'établir un accès à une plus grande diversité de sources d'information.

Un autre article du CDA, moins connu du grand public, a cependant joué un rôle essentiel afin de sauvegarder la liberté de parole sur l'Internet. Il s'agit de la section 230 qui prévoit que les fournisseurs d'accès ne peuvent pas être tenus responsables du contenu des documents ou des messages postés sur le Net par une tierce personne. L'immunité dont ils jouissent ne les a, en conséquence, pas incité à contrôler ce que leur clients mettent en ligne[20].

Grâce aux avancées technologiques, l'accès à l'Internet a connu une croissance exponentielle et a beaucoup évolué depuis 1997. Comme le soulignent Jay D. Bolter et Richard Grusin[21], il a une influence significative sur le traitement et la présentation de l'information par les médias audiovisuels et par la presse écrite. Les chaînes de télévision, comme un bon nombre de journaux, ont crée un site en ligne qui offre à ceux qui le consultent une interactivité dont leur forme conventionnelle est dépourvue. Ils n'hésitent pas à publier sur ces sites les commentaires des internautes ni à s'appuyer sur des vidéos transmises par ceux-ci dans les situations où les journalistes ne peuvent collecter des informations. Les reportages sur la révolution de Jasmin dans les pays arabes en est l'illustration la plus récente. De la même manière, l'apparition des blogs et leur importance grandissante en tant que source d'information[22] a affecté la presse écrite, changé la relation entre les journalistes et leurs

---

[20] Cette partie de la loi a fait l'objet de plusieurs litiges devant des tribunaux dans certains Etats, mais sa constitutionnalité a été confirmée. Voir Joseph Russomanno, *Defending the First. Commentaries on the First Amendment Cases*, *op. cit.*, p. 195-196. Cependant, il est aujourd'hui courant que les câblo-opérateurs contrôlent le contenu des documents mis en ligne sur leur réseau.

[21] Voir Jay D. Bolter, Richard Grusin, *Remediation. Understanding the New Media*, Cambridge, MA: MIT Press, 2000, "Mediation and Remediation", p. 1 à 62 ainsi que plusieurs des contributions dans l'ouvrage publié en 2011 par Richard Grusin, David Crowley, Paul Heyer, *Communication in History, Technology, Culture, Society*, Boston, MA: Allyn and Bacon, Pearson.

[22] Voir en particulier l'ouvrage le plus récent de Richard Davis : *Typing Politics. The Role of Blogs in American Politics*, New York: Oxford University Press, 2009. Il compare, dans l'introduction, les blogueurs aux Républicains et aux Fédéralistes défendant leurs idées dans des journaux acquis à leur cause et argue : « *(...) political Blogs affect politics through a transactional relationship with other agenda seekers (politicians, groups, political organizations, ect.), journalists and the audience.* », p. 7.

lecteurs. Même si les internautes et les blogueurs ne disposent pas des ressources des grands médias, les recherches faites par certains et les échanges d'informations entre eux ont permis de mettre à jour, en raison de leurs capacités à se mobiliser et à coopérer[23], des vérités que les médias avaient tues, voire dissimulées. Ils ont également modifié les relations entre les états-majors des deux grands partis et leurs membres, les hommes politiques et les électeurs, suscitant l'enthousiasme de certains à propos de leurs effets démocratiques[24], tempéré par le

[23] Yochai Benkler retrace dans *La richesse des réseaux. Marchés et libertés à l'heure du partage social*, Lyon : Presses Universitaires de Lyon, 2006, comment Bev Harris qui s'interrogeait sur la fiabilité des machines à voter Diebold avait pu, grâce à une information recueillie sur son site *web*, avoir accès à des fichiers de cette entreprise, et comment les commentaires faits par les lecteurs du site néo-zélandais *Scoop.com* lui avaient permis de mettre en lumière « un mécanisme capable de truquer les élections », (p. 292). L'auteur explique ensuite la manière dont l'affaire a été finalement révélée au grand public, soulignant que l'Internet permet à la fois de « lancer le débat » et d'effectuer la diffusion d'informations à une grande échelle, ce qui rend une action collective très efficace, concluant : « Il n'y eut pas de pouvoir d'orchestration unique (...) A la place, une série d'actions non coordonnées se renforçant mutuellement, et émanant d'individus, d'environnements et de contextes différents, avec diverses restrictions et capacités d'organisation, permit d'exposer, d'analyser, de diffuser des critiques et d'en apporter les preuves », (p. 298-299). Un autre exemple, celui de l'affaire Sinclair, illustre les différences entre la réponse des grands médias lors de la révélation d'un scandale et les effets qu'elle suscite ou non en comparaison avec la mobilisation des blogueurs qui, dans ce cas précis, surent se concerter afin de trouver la méthode la plus appropriée et ciblèrent – non pas les grands organismes officiels comme la *Federal Electoral Commission* (FEC) et la *Federal Communications Commission* (FCC), muets dans cette affaire – mais les acteurs économiques, c'est à dire les annonceurs locaux de la chaîne de télévision, pour les persuader de participer à un boycott et causer une perte de revenus significative qui contraindrait cette chaîne à ne pas diffuser un programme dont l'objet était d'influer sur la campagne présidentielle de 2004 dans quatre Etats clés en donnant une image négative de John Kerry, à une semaine et demie du scrutin (p. 284-290). On peut aussi mentionner parmi d'autres cas, celui de Cindy Sheehan qui par sa détermination et grâce au soutien d'un groupe de familles de soldats mort en Irak réussit à organiser le « camp Casey », et par le biais de son blog, à rallier des Américains de toutes origines à sa cause et à occuper un terrain près de la résidence d'été du président Bush à Crawford dans le Texas pendant le mois d'août 2005. Cet exemple est cité par Jerome Armstrong et Markos Moulitsas Zùniga, *infra*, p. 172. Arianna Huffington, opposée à la guerre en Irak, lui fit l'honneur de s'exprimer sur son blog quand les progressistes étaient encore rares à s'y risquer.

[24] Voir en particulier Jerome Armstrong, Markos Moulitsas Zùniga, *Crashing the Gate. Grassroots, Netroots and the Rise of People-Powered Politics*, White River Junction,

scepticisme de ceux qui, au contraire, leur reprochent, quand ils défendent des points de vue jugés trop partisans, de jouer un rôle non négligeable dans la polarisation du débat politique aux Etats-Unis[25]. Que l'on se rende aux arguments des uns ou des autres, il n'en demeure pas moins que l'Internet, est devenu en quelques années le média le plus utilisé partout dans le monde pour entrer en contact, créer des réseaux, communiquer, débattre, s'informer et militer. Un phénomène qui s'est encore accentué avec l'apparition des réseaux sociaux. Maintenir la non-censure des propos, des documents échangés ou consultés et le libre accès par les internautes aux documents de leur choix aux Etats-Unis est un gage d'attachement à la défense de la liberté d'expression et un héritage de la jurisprudence de leurs tribunaux relative au premier amendement. Des citoyens décidés à la conserver et des organisations[26] qui ne ménagent pas leurs efforts font preuve de vigilance pour endiguer les tentatives croissantes d'intérêts économiques toujours plus puissants[27] dans le but entraver « la liberté du cyberspace », c'est-à-dire la liberté d'information, d'expression, d'échange des données et la production de « biens communs »[28], mais aussi les craintes de ceux qui voient dans l'Internet un danger pour la sécurité des Etats-Unis.

VT: Chelsea Green Publisher Co., 2006 et Lowell Feld, *Netroots Rising: How a Citizen Army of Bloggers and Online Activists Is Changing American Politics*, Westport, CT: Praeger, 2008.

[25] On citera à titre d'exemple quelques uns d'entre eux : Sean Tunney, Garrett Monaghan, *Webjournalism:// A New Form of Citizenship*, Portland, OR : Sussex Academic Press, 2010, Cass R. Sunstein, *Republic.com 02*, Princeton, NJ: Princeton University Press, 2007, David D. Perlmutter, *Blogwars*, New York: Oxford University Press, 2008 ; les autres se trouvent dans la bibliographie en fin d'ouvrage.

[26] Citons en particulier : *The Electronic Frontier Foundation*, *The Center for Democracy and Technology* , *The Center for Digital Democracy* et *The Beckman Center for Internet and Society* de l'Université d'Havard.

[27] Récemment Comcast a racheté le groupe de télévision et de cinéma NBC Universal, une fusion approuvée par la FCC, 4 voix à 1.

[28] J'emprunte ces expressions à Lawrence Lessig qui en est l'un des plus constants et ardents défenseurs avec Yochai Benkler. Voir *L'Avenir des idées. Le sort des biens communs à l'heure des réseaux numériques*, Lyon : Presses Universitaires de Lyon, 2005, p. 25 et 46, traduction française par Jean-Baptiste Soufron et Alain Bony de *The Future of Ideas*, New York : Random House, 2001. L'économiste américaine Elinor Ostrom fut la première à démontrer que la gestion en commun des ressources peut être une alternative efficace à leur privatisation ou à leur réglementation par un Etat : *Governing the Commons. The Evolution of Institutions for Collective Actions*, New

3. Les menaces qui pèsent sur la liberté d'expression et le libre accès à l'information

En 1996, Le juge Stevens décrivait l'Internet comme un média sans « location géographique particulière, (...) accessible n'importe où dans le monde à toute personne pouvant se connecter ». A la différence d'une radio, d'une chaîne de télévision ou d'un organe de presse, l'Internet en tant que média, n'appartenait à personne et le créateur du *World Wide Web*, Tim Berners-Lee qui le voulait « incontrôlable », explique : « J'avais construit le *Web* de telle sorte qu'il n'y ait aucun lieu centralisé où quelqu'un serait chargé d'enregistrer un nouveau serveur ou d'obtenir la validation des contenus »[29]. Son projet s'inscrivait dans la logique des concepteurs du réseau qui, parce qu'ils privilégiaient une culture de l'échange et la coopération entre égaux avaient favorisé la création d'une infrastructure facilitant la connectivité et son extension continue, l' « intelligence » étant déposée aux bouts, selon le principe du *end to end* et non au cœur du système[30]. Ceci a permis à des utilisateurs, partout dans le monde, de développer toutes sortes d'applications. A partir de cette plateforme neutre, ils ont créé *Wikipedia*, *Google*, *Facebook*, *Skype* et bien d'autres, transformant grâce à leur ingéniosité, cet outil de communication en inventant de nouvelles formes d'interaction entre les individus afin de faciliter l'accès à la connaissance et libérer la parole. Le mouvement du logiciel libre lancé par Robert Stallman, informaticien au MIT, fondateur en 1985 de la *Free Software Foundation*, a suscité l'innovation et la coopération.

Toutefois, le mouvement de massification résultant du succès de l'Internet n'a pas tardé à changé la donne. Dès les années 2000, l'Etat fédéral a décidé de contrôler l'attribution des noms de domaine – une première tentative pour imposer sa conception de la gouvernance sur l'Internet. Un conflit est né entre ceux qui prônent le libre accès aux ressources à travers la notion de « biens communs » afin de développer

---

York: Cambridge University Press, 1990. Elle a reçu le prix Nobel d'économie en 2009.

[29] Tim Berners-Lee, *Weaving the Web/ The Original Design and Ultimate Destiny of the World Wide Web by Its Inventor*, San Francisco, CA : HarperSanFrancisco, 1999, p. 129-130.

[30] Voir Lawrence Lessig, *L'Avenir des idées*, *op. cit.*, p. 45-46.

la création, « l'innovation ascendante »[31] et la liberté d'expression – tels que les défenseurs de l'*open source* – et les fournisseurs d'accès (câblo-opérateurs et compagnies téléphoniques) afin de résister aux forces conjointes de la privatisation du marché et de la régulation par l'Etat dont les efforts conjugués ont affecté l'architecture de l'Internet aux Etats-Unis, c'est-à-dire les trois « couches » de ce système de communication telles que les a décrites Yochai Benkler, professeur de droit à Harvard[32]. Ainsi au niveau de la couche « physique » (*physical layer*) de la communication informatique, ceux qui défendent l'idée d'un spectre libre contestent le pouvoir accordé par l'Etat fédéral à la FCC pour réglementer l'accès aux fréquences radio qu'utilisent les réseaux sans fil et les lignes téléphoniques, en s'opposant à la gestion du spectre des ondes radio uniquement par la délivrance de licences ou par la privatisation, c'est-à-dire la vente au plus offrant[33]. La loi de 1996 prévoyait une ouverture à la concurrence. Les câblo-opérateurs se sont employés, en saisissant les tribunaux, à déjouer les efforts des municipalités afin d'imposer un marché ouvert grâce au pouvoir en

---

[31] Cette expression a été créée par Eric von Hippel, *Democratizing Innovation*, Cambridge, MA: MIT Press, 2005.

[32] Voir Yochai Benkler, « From Consumers to Users: Shifting the Deeper Structures of Regulation towards Sustainable Commons and Users Access », *Federal Communications Law Journal*, vol. 52, n° 3, 1999, p. 562-579.

[33] Dès 1998 Yochai Benkler arguait : « *Providing an appropriate regulatory space for unlicensed wireless operations is the only available option for allowing the development of unowned information infrastructure. Such an unowned component of the infrastructure could provide a communicative space in the digitally networked environment that would be the equivalent of public sidewalks, streets, and roads in our physical environment. Its implications for our individual autonomy and political culture are likely to be significant. In the absence of adequate regulatory space, such open infrastructure may not develop. While the technology for its development exists, and the economic interests to fuel its development are in place, whether such an infrastructural element will in fact develop depends on institutional choices our society will make in the next decade or so. It is the possibility of such a distributed, open infrastructural component, with its social political benefits, together with the lack of a clearly determined mechanism that will lead to its creation absent regulatory action, that provides the most important reason consciously to strive, as a matter of legislative and administrative policy, towards the creation of a well regulated commons in our information infrastructure* », « Overcoming Agoraphobia. Building the Commons of the Digitally Networked Environment », *Harvard Law Journal of Technology*, n° 105, 1-113, 1998, p. 106.

matière d'attribution de licences qui leur était conféré par cette loi[34]. Ils se sont aussi mobilisés pour échapper à toute réglementation par la FCC en contestant le fait qu'ils étaient, en partie, un service de télécommunications. En 2003 cette dernière, contrairement à la Cour fédérale du 9ème circuit lors de la fusion AOL Time Warner, a reconnu que les câblo-opérateurs proposant un accès haut débit « bande large » (*broadband*)[35], à l'instar des compagnies de téléphone locales fournissant un accès DSL (*Digital Service Line*), comme un service d'information et non plus comme un service mixte[36] ce qui l'a, en pratique, privée de toute possibilité de réglementation[37]. C'est ainsi que

---

[34] Cette série de décisions illustre les batailles auxquelles se sont livrés les câblo-opérateurs pour lutter contre toute forme de concurrence. En 2000, Comcast réussit à obtenir l'invalidation d'un arrêté municipal exigeant un accès ouvert aux lignes du câble par un tribunal en Floride : *Comcast Cablevision of Broward County, Inc v. Broward County, Fla.*, 124 F. Supp. 2d 685 (S.D. Fla, 2000), ce dernier ayant conclu que cet arrêté violait le premier amendement parce qu'il imposait un accès forcé contraire aux dispositions du *Cable Act* de 1984, voir, http://www.techlawjournal.com/courts/broward/20001108.asp. Un arrêt similaire fut rendu en Virginie (*MediaOne Group, Inc. v. County of Henrico, Virginia*, 97 F.Supp. 2d 712 (E.D. Va 2000) et, la même année, la Cour d'appel fédérale du 9ème circuit cassa l'arrêt de la Cour de district ayant statué en faveur d'un accès ouvert selon les dispositions prévues dans l'Oregon : *AT&T v. City of Portland*, interprétant de façon très restrictive l'article 253 (a) du *Telecommunications Act* de 1996 : « *No State or local statute or regulation, or other State or local legal requirement, may prohibit or have the effect of prohibiting the ability of any entity to provide any interstate or intrastate telecommunications service* ». En 1999, la Cour d'appel du District of Columbia, avait en effet conclut qu'un Etat peut légiférer pour interdire à une municipalité d'offrir un accès haut débit à ses résidents, *City of Abilene, Texas v. FCC*, 164 F3d 49. http://caselaw.findlaw.com/us-dc-circuit/1312380.html. Cependant en 2004, la Cour suprême a invalidé une décision similaire de la Cour fédérale du 8ème circuit concernant une loi du Missouri comparable à celle de l'Oregon, *Nixon v. Missouri Municipal League*, 541 U.S. 125. L'interprétation de la section 253(a) du *Telecommunications Act*, faite par la Cour d'appel du District de Columbia, était donc erronée. Mais les décisions antérieures ont permis aux câblo-opérateurs d'éliminer la concurrence dans de nombreuses villes et de gagner ainsi des parts de marché.

[35] Cet accès est fourni par un modem à partir du câble qui relie l'abonné aux chaînes de télévision.

[36] C'est-à-dire un service de transport (port de bits) et un service de communication (messagerie et hébergement du *web*).

[37] La Cour suprême s'est rangée à l'avis des experts de la FCC, dans l'arrêt *National Cable and Telecommunications Association v. Brand X Internet Services*, 545 U.S. 967, 2005.

Comcast[38], l'un des plus importants fournisseurs d'Internet haut débit par le câble, a obtenu de la Cour d'appel fédérale de Washington en avril 2010 l'annulation d'un décret de la FCC lui ordonnant de cesser « ses pratiques discriminatoires »[39], au motif que la législation en vigueur[40] ne donne pas expressément autorité à la FCC pour contrôler les réseaux câblés. L'opérateur du câble ayant un droit de propriété avait argué avoir la liberté de décider de bloquer certains accès à ses abonnés.

Au second niveau, celui de la couche « logique », (*logical layer*), les logiciels dont les codes sont fermés et protégés par un système de brevets ou de *copyright* pendant soixante-dix ans (c'est-à-dire de façon quasi illimitée) se sont multipliés ce qui, selon les défenseurs de l'*open code*, est non seulement contraire à la façon dont l'Internet a été conçu mais porte atteinte à la création puisque plus personne ne sera en mesure de décrypter ces codes après une aussi longue période. Ici, c'est un outil juridique qui cautionne une logique marchande et contrecarre la logique non marchande initiale ; mais l'Etat peut aussi favoriser des modifications de cette couche « logique », par exemple pour protéger les mineurs ou la vie privée des citoyens, ou la sécurité nationale comme l'affaire WikiLeaks l'a récemment montré[41].

---

[38] Comcast dont le siège est à Philadelphie, est le premier câblo-opérateur américain. Il fournit un accès aux chaînes de télévision à plus de 2 millions d'Américains, et au téléphone et à l'Internet haut débit à environ 16 millions.

[39] *Comcast Corp. v. FCC*, 600 F3d, 642, United States Court of Appeals for the District of Columbia, 10 avril 2010 : « *It is true that Congress gave the [Commission] broad and adaptable jurisdiction so that it can keep pace with rapidly evolving communications technologies. It is also true that [t]he Internet is such a technology," indeed, "arguably the most important innovation in communications in a generation," Yet notwithstanding the difficult regulatory problem of rapid technological change posed by the communications industry, the allowance of wide latitude in the exercise of delegated powers is not the equivalent of untrammelled freedom to regulate activities over which the statute fails to confer (...) Commission authority. Because the Commission has failed to tie its assertion of ancillary authority over Comcast's Internet service to any statutorily mandated responsibility, we grant the petition for review and vacate the Order* » , p. 36, http://www.cadc.uscourts.gov/internet/opinions.nsf/EA10373FA9C20DEA85257807005BD63F/$file/08-1291-1238302.pdf.

[40] Voir, *supra*, note 3.

[41] Voir Lawrence Lessig, « The Law of the Horse. What Cyberlaw Teaches », *Harvard Law Review*, n° 113, p. 501-546, 1999. Ces mesures ont été jugées conformes à la Constitution. La Cour suprême, dans l'arrêt *U.S. v. American Library Association*, 539 U.S. 194, 2003 a reconnu la validité du *Children's Internet Protection Act.* Les

Enfin, en ce qui concerne la couche des « contenus » (*content layer*), les menaces qui pèsent sur la liberté d'expression et l'accès à l'information sont patentes. La décision de la Cour d'appel du District de Columbia en faveur de Comcast en est un exemple. En effet, l'une des règles de l'Internet est que les paquets de données qui transitent de routeurs en routeurs pour être acheminés depuis le serveur où ils sont stockés jusqu'à leur destination finale doivent tous être traités de la même façon. Or à la suite de protestations et d'actions en justice des clients du câblo-opérateur, la FCC avait ouvert une enquête et découvert que la société empêchait ses abonnés d'accéder aux réseaux *peer-to-peer* et le libre accès à *Skype*.[42] Depuis la décision de la Cour d'appel du District de Columbia, qui peut maintenant lutter contre les règles de diffusion établies par les géants de la communication comme Comcast, notamment les projets dits de « services multi-niveaux » ou de « priorisation » ?

Depuis la fin des années quatre-vingt-dix, afin de protéger leurs intérêts les groupes de médias, et les industries du disque et du cinéma ont pu compter sur le législateur et sur le droit pour renforcer leur pouvoir et leurs profits. Dès 1996, les marques ont été mieux protégées (*Trademark Anti-Dilution Act*). La loi a été révisée, en 2006, à la suite de la décision de la Cour suprême dans l'arrêt *Moseley v. V Secret Catalogue* (573 U.S. 498, 2003) modifiant la charge de la preuve

---

questions de sécurité peuvent aussi conduire le gouvernement à demander une modification des codes comme le montre l'application des dispositions du *Communication Assistance for Law Enforcement Act* voté en 1994, imposées aux fournisseurs d'Internet haut débit et à leur service de téléphonie en 2004 par la FCC, afin de lutter contre le terrorisme. Jonathan Zittrain aborde certaines de ces questions dans le chapitre 9 de *The Future of the Internet and How to Stop It*, New Haven, CT: Yale University Press, 2007.
Voir les mesures prises récemment par le ministère de la Défense en matière de sécurité sur l'Internet, les difficultés rencontrées et les questions juridiques qu'elles soulèvent : http://www.washingtonpost.com/national/major-internet-service-providers-cooperating-with-nsa-on-monitoring-traffic/2011/06/07/AG2dukXH_story_1.html.

[42] A Philadelphie, il y a eu une action collective contre Comcast pour ce motif ; le câblo-opérateur souhaitant mettre un terme aux poursuites a accepté un règlement à l'amiable en juillet 2010 et le versement de 16 millions de dollars aux victimes, sans pour autant reconnaître la moindre responsabilité.

en leur faveur[43]. Puis en 1998, une loi a prolongé le terme des droits d'auteur (*Sonny Bono Copyright Term Extension Act*)[44] et le *Digital Millenium Copyright Act* (DMCA) a renforcé la protection d'un bien sous *copyright* à l'ère du numérique, notamment en interdisant, par le biais de la clause de « non contournement », la création de logiciels de décryptage ou d'autres technologies d'accès à des matériels sous *copyright*. La durée des brevets a été aussi allongée. Enfin, en 2008 le président Bush a signé le *Pro IP Anti Piracy Act*, renforçant les sanctions en cas de piratage de films, de vidéos ou de morceaux de musique. On se souvient que Napster, un service *peer to peer* créé par Shawn Fanning et Sean Parker, pour l'échange de fichiers musicaux avait conduit les grandes maisons de disques à protester et demander la fermeture du service pour violation des droits d'auteur. Elles obtinrent que le logiciel soit retiré après deux ans de procédure, en 2001. Un autre site de partage de dossiers Kazaa, extérieur aux Etats-Unis, a été également l'objet d'une bataille juridique que la *Recording Industry Association of America* (RIAA) a fini par gagner en 2005[45]. En 2009, *Google*, sous la pression de Rupert Murdoch, le puissant patron du groupe de médias *News Corp.* a accepté de limiter l'accès en ligne des internautes aux articles de presse gratuitement. Il a aussi, sous la pression des éditeurs, limité l'extension du projet *Google Books*. Ces lois qui ont pour objet de protéger la propriété intellectuelle sont, pour ceux qui s'y opposent, une utilisation abusive des dispositions prévues par la Constitution et bien loin d'encourager la création, elles poussent

[43] La Cour ayant décidé qu'il fallait apporter la preuve d'une réelle atteinte au nom de la marque. Le Congrès a réduit le degré de la preuve : il suffit, pour le propriétaire de la marque, de prouver qu'il y a eu une « possible » (*likely)* atteinte au nom de celle-ci.

[44] Cette loi a amendé le *Copyright Act* de 1976 qui avait établi qu'une œuvre tombait dans le domaine public 50 ans après la mort de son auteur, en allongeant la durée de 20 ans (soit 70 ans et 120 ans après leur création) pour les œuvres collectives d'entreprise. De plus, les œuvres publiées après 1978 ne tomberont dans le domaine public qu'à l'issue de 95 ans. Cette législation a grandement profité à la compagnie Walt Disney qui risquait de perdre ses droits sur *Mickey Mouse* (créé en 1923). La Cour suprême a reconnu la constitutionnalité de cette loi, en dépit de sa rétroactivité, dans l'arrêt *Eldred v. Ashcroft*, 534 U.S. 186, 2003. Lawrence Lessig et Jonathan Zittrain ont défendu Eric Eldred. Il est essentiel de rappeler que le droit d'auteur ne protège que les œuvres originales, *Feist Publications Inc. v. Rural Telephone Service Co*, 499 U.S. 340, 1991 ce qui n'est pas le cas de l'information contenue dans un annuaire de téléphone, c'est-à-dire des données brutes et par extension les bases de données.

[45] *Metro Goldwyn Meyer v. Grokster*, 545 U.S. 913, 2005.

les sociétés de médias à fusionner avec des groupes de production de télévision et de cinéma, afin de lutter contre la concurrence.

Lawrence Lessig, qui a créé *Creative Commons*, dénonce « l'aveuglément qui affecte l'ensemble de [la] culture politique [aux Etats-Unis] » ; un aveuglement qui consiste à « assimiler la propriété intellectuelle à la propriété tout court », en réduisant considérablement le principe de l'utilisation équitable (*fair use*), dans le but de préserver des intérêts économiques acquis[46], au lieu de chercher « la réponse régulatrice la moins intrusive » [47] au profit de l'innovation. Il compare ces mesures à la mise en place d'un système de « clôtures »[48], tandis que Julie Cohen établit un parallèle entre le recours des législateurs et des juristes d'aujourd'hui aux droits d'auteur et au dépôt de brevets, prévus par la Constitution[49], afin préserver les médias de masse et leur modèle industriel et commercial séparant production et consommation, à utilisation de la liberté de contrat, au début du siècle, pour empêcher l'amélioration des conditions de travail des salariés[50].

Outre les incidences économiques de ces mesures et leurs effets sur l'architecture de l'Internet, il faut également souligner leurs effets pervers sur la liberté d'expression et d'information. Puisqu'elles limitent l'accès libre ou supprime tout accès des internautes à certains documents ou à certains sites, elles sont une forme de censure (*suppression of free speech*). A l'échelle internationale, des

---

[46] Lawrence Lessig, *L'Avenir des idées*, *op. cit.*, p. 293.

[47] *Ibid.*, p. 307.

[48] Par analogie avec le mouvement des *enclosures* en Grande Bretagne au XVIIe siècle, destiné à diviser et remembrer les terres agricoles et supprimer l'*openfield.*

[49] Jefferson défendait le principe que la liberté était fondée sur la propriété individuelle mais partageait le scepticisme de Benjamin Franklin à propos des brevets ; bien qu'il fût inventeur, ce dernier les jugeait immoraux. Quant à Jefferson, dans une lettre à James Madison, il jugeait que « le bénéfice même de monopole pour un temps limité est trop douteux pour être mis face à celui de leur interdiction générale », Lawrence Lessig, *L'Avenir des idées*, p. 255.

[50] Julie E. Cohen, « *Lochner* in Cyberspace. The New Economic Orthodoxy of Rights Management », *Michigan Law Review*, n° 97, 1998, p. 462-563. La Constitution protège la liberté de contrat dans le cinquième amendement. L'article I, section 8, alinéa 8 donne au Congrès le pouvoir « d'encourager le progrès de la science et des arts utiles, en assurant pour une période limitée, aux auteurs et inventeurs, un droit exclusif sur leurs écrits et sur leurs découvertes ».

mesures comparables ont été prises[51], et certains pays tels que la Chine ou l'Iran ont restreint l'accès à l'Internet et créé leur propre intranet, si bien qu'aujourd'hui de grandes disparités géographiques existent d'un pays à l'autre, ce dont Jack Goldsmith et Tim Wu se disaient très préoccupés dès 2006[52]. A l'ère du numérique, le premier amendement, doit sauvegarder aux Etats-Unis, non seulement la capacité des citoyens à participer au processus démocratique par le biais d'un « robuste » échange des idées sur la place publique mais aussi, selon Jack M. Balkin, la participation à l'élaboration d'une culture démocratique où les citoyens sont acteurs autant que récepteurs au lieu d'être condamnés à être les consommateurs passifs des choix culturels opérés par les

---

[51] En 2001, Lawrence Lessig fustigeait les tribunaux américains et le Congrès pour avoir initié le processus de réglementation et dénonçait ses effets pervers, non seulement pour les Etats-Unis mais pour le reste de la planète : « *The law becomes a tool to assure that new innovations don't dispace the old ones – when instead, the aim of copyright and patent law should be, as the Constitution requires to «" promote the progress of science and useful arts". These regulations will not only affect the Americans. The expanding jurisdiction that American courts claim, combined with the push by the World Intellectual Property Organization to enact similar legislation elsewhere, means that the impact of this sort of control will be felt worldwide. There is no "local" when it comes to corruption of the Internet's basic principles. As the changes weaken the open source and free software movements, countries with the most to gain from a free and open platform will lose. Those affected will include nations in the developing world and nations that do not want to cede control to a single private corporation (...) The Internet promised the world – particularly the weakest world – the fastest and most dramatic change to existing barriers to growth. That promise depends on network remaining open to innovation. That openness depends upon policy that better understands the Internet's past.* », « The Internet under Siege », *Foreign Policy*, n° 127, 11/12, 2001, p. 56-65.

[52] Voir la conclusion de Jack Goldsmith et Tim Wu dans *Who Controls the Internet? Illusions of a Borderless World*, New York: Oxford University Press, 2006 : « *It's not just that the nations have the power to shape the Internet's architecture in different ways. It is that the United States, China, and Europe are using their coercive powers to establish different visions of what the Internet might be. In so doing, they will attract other nations to choose among models of control ranging from the United States relatively free open model to China's model of political control. The result is the beginning of a technological version of the cold war, with each side pushing its own wisdom of the Internet future. The failure to understand the many faces and facts of territorial government coercion is fatal to globalisation theory as understood today, and central to understanding the future of the Internet.* », p. 184.

médias[53]. Quelles sont les solutions envisagées pour préserver ce droit fondamental ?

Une solution serait d'inscrire le principe d'un Internet neutre dans la loi. Depuis 2006, plusieurs tentatives ont été faites pour faire voter par le Congrès une loi afin de préserver la « neutralité du Net ». Durant la campagne présidentielle Barack Obama avait fait renaître l'espoir en s'engageant à la défendre. Dans l'année qui a suivi son élection, un projet de loi n'a pas abouti. En janvier 2011, deux sénateurs démocrates Al Franken (Minnesota) et Mary Cantwell (Etat de Washington) ont déposé une nouvelle proposition de loi afin d'interdire les restrictions imposées par les fournisseurs d'accès (*Internet Freedom Broadband Promotion Act*). Quant à la *Federal Trade Commission* (FTC)[54], afin d'obtenir l'annulation de la décision de l'arrêt *Comcast*, elle a engagé Tim Wu, professeur de droit à l'Université Columbia, ardent défenseur de la liberté d'expression sur le Net et de la protection des consommateurs contre les restrictions imposées par les câblo-opérateurs[55]. Selon Yochai Benkler, invité du e-G8, il est aussi,

[53] Jack M. Balkin argue dans « Digital Speech and Democratic Culture: A Theory of Freedom of Expression and Information Society », *New York Law Review*, n° 79, 1, 2004, p. 1-55, qu'une nouvelle interprétation du premier amendement est nécessaire car l'Internet permet à tous les citoyens et non plus uniquement aux élites (politiques, économiques ou culturelles) de participer à l'élaboration d'une culture commune : « *Freedom of expression protects the ability of individuals to participate in the culture in which they live and promotes the development of a culture that is more democratic and participatory.* », p. 4.

[54] Elle a été créée en 1914 par le *Federal Trade Commission Act* pour lutter contre les pratiques anticoncurrentielles des trusts. Aujourd'hui elle protège les droits des consommateurs.

[55] Tim Wu est considéré comme le créateur de l'expression « la neutralité du Net » ; en effet un article qu'il a publié en 2003 s'intitulait : « Network Neutrality, Broadband Discrimination », *Journal of Telecommunications and High Technology Law*, n° 2, p. 141-175. Dans cet article, il défend l'idée que pour maintenir un Internet neutre il faut lutter contre les pratiques discriminatoires des câblo-opérateurs qui limitent ou bloquent l'accès de leurs clients à certains sites ou monnayent l'accès à certaines applications comme les vidéos ou les jeux en ligne. Tim Wu propose dans cet article un projet de loi pour lutter contre cette forme de discrimination à l'égard des consommateurs. Il a publié, en 2010, *Master Switch. The Fall and Rise of Information Empires*, New York: Albert Knopf.

aujourd'hui, urgent de prendre conscience que l'un des enjeux pour maintenir cette neutralité, est de veiller à ce que l'Internet mobile sur les *smartphones* et les tablettes numériques ne l'emporte pas sur le monde du PC. En effet celui-ci « vient d'une tradition des téléphones portables qui fonctionnent sur des réseaux contrôlés appartenant à des compagnies et des outils, des objets contrôlés et des propriétaires. Si l'Internet mobile l'emporte sur le monde du PC et de l'Internet associé, alors l'âge de l'information par lequel nous avons commencé à embrasser la démocratisation va perdre »[56]. Les Démocrates encore majoritaires au Sénat sont-ils conscients du danger et malgré le poids des lobbies et les difficultés économiques, vont-ils se décider à agir ?

Elisabeth Boulot

Université Paris Est Marne-la-Vallée

Voir, la vidéo de la conférence qu'il a donnée au *Berkman Center for Internet and Society* pour présenter son livre : http://cyber.law.harvard.edu/events/luncheon/2011/01/wu, et celle où il expose les thèses qu'il défend : http://www.youtube.com/watch?v=ib1btypiaV4&feature=related.

[56] « Yochai Benkler : « La guerre d'usure entre les vieilles industries et l'Internet », interrogé par Eric Scherer lors du e-G8, le 27 mai 2011 ; entretien retranscrit et traduit par Thierry Lhôte, http://owni.fr/2011/05/27/yochai-benkler-nous-assistons-a-une-guerre-dusure-entre-les-vieilles-industries-et-internet/. La décision de Hewlett Packard, le premier fabricant mondial d'ordinateurs, de se séparer de ses PC du fait de la progression constante des ventes de tablettes, corrobore les craintes exprimées dans cet entretien. Voir : « H.P. Weighs Spinning Off Its PC Unit » *The New York Times*, 18 août 2011, http://www.nytimes.com/2011/08/19/technology/hp-plans-big-shift-toward-business-customers.html?pagewanted=2&_r=1&nl=todaysheadlines&emc=tha26.
Il faut aussi mentionner l'importance de la décision prise par *Google* de racheter Motorola Mobility, « Google's Big Bet on Mobile Future », *The New York Times*, 15 août 2011, http://dealbook.nytimes.com/2011/08/15/googles-big-bet-on-the-mobile-future/?nl=todaysheadlines&emc=tha2.

Le bruit et la fureur : WikiLeaks contre l'administration Obama

L'impact de la révolution numérique sur notre vie privée comme dans le domaine public n'est plus à démontrer, mais s'il le fallait, deux illustrations récentes viennent rappeler le rôle considérable que le développement de l'Internet joue désormais dans la politique des nations et les relations internationales. La première concerne le rôle crucial des réseaux sociaux tels que *Facebook* et *Twitter* dans la vague révolutionnaire qui ébranle le Moyen-Orient et une partie du Maghreb depuis décembre 2010. De façon significative, car révélatrice des relations ambivalentes que notre époque entretient avec ces réseaux, les medias ont relevé l'effet de « contagion », véhiculé par les réseaux Internet au niveau national et régional. La deuxième, qui a d'ailleurs précédé la révolution de Jasmin tunisienne et pourrait bien en être à l'origine, est l'affaire WikiLeaks et les réactions de l'administration Obama, dont il sera question ici.

Ces réactions ont été étonnamment violentes de la part d'une nation qui a vu naître l'Internet et qui érige la liberté d'expression en valeur suprême. Que Sarah Palin ose comparer Julian Assange à Al-Qaida et le présenter comme « un agent anti-américain qui a du sang sur les mains » passe encore, il est de notoriété publique que l'égérie des *Tea partiers* ne s'encombre pas de nuances. Mais des propos similaires ont aussi été tenus au plus haut sommet de l'Etat fédéral américain : le Vice-président Biden a défini le leader charismatique de WikiLeaks comme un « terroriste high-tech » ayant « comploté avec un militaire des Etats-Unis pour mettre la main sur des documents secrets » et qui mérite pour cela le châtiment le plus sévère possible ; le président de la Commission parlementaire pour la sécurité intérieure, Peter King, souhaite que WikiLeaks soit inscrite sur la liste des organisations terroristes tandis que Joe Lieberman, très influent sénateur, membre de plusieurs commissions sénatoriales, a publiquement demandé au président Obama de « faire disparaître » WikiLeaks par tous les moyens possibles.[1] Si aucun homme politique n'a explicitement réclamé la peine de mort pour Assange, ce châtiment n'est pas exclu s'il était inculpé pour espionnage et ses avocats ont publiquement exprimé leur crainte après qu'un membre du Congrès, Mike Rogers, s'y soit déclaré favorable en ce qui concerne l'informateur de WikiLeaks, Bradley Manning. Les conditions de détention de ce dernier ont par ailleurs soulevé beaucoup de critiques, et causé la démission du porte-parole du département de la Défense, qui était en désaccord avec sa hiérarchie sur ce point.[2] De façon troublante, ce climat remet au goût du jour le spectre du maccarthysme parce qu'il évoque le procès des époux Rosenberg, condamnés à la peine capitale en 1953 pour espionnage, en pleine hystérie anti-communiste[3]. Les partisans d'Assange ont d'ailleurs enfoncé le clou en faisant remarquer qu'il était traité dans les Etats-Unis d'Obama – prix Nobel de la paix – comme les dissidents le sont en Chine, et que le gouvernement américain persécutait tout autant ceux qui osaient dévoiler une vérité dérangeante pour le pouvoir en place[4] .

---

[1] Pour ce qui est de Sarah Palin, les propos ont été tenus sur sa page *Facebook* le 29 novembre 2010 et ont été largement commentés par la presse nationale et internationale les jours suivants (voir par exemple *Le Monde* du 1/12/2010, p. 5). Ceux de Joe Biden ont été exprimés sur NBC le 19 décembre 2010 dans l'émission « *Meet the Press* ». Enfin, les propos de Peter King et Joe Lieberman datent de fin novembre 2010 et ont notamment été rapportés par Declean McCullagh, « Congressman Wants WikiLeaks Listed as Terrorist Group », *CNET News*, 28 novembre 2010, accessible en ligne à: http://news.cnet.com/8301-13578_3-20023941-38.html.

[2] Philip Crowley a en effet démissionné trois jours après avoir critiqué les mesures prises par le Pentagone à l'égard de Manning, voir « Official Exits State Dept. After Jabs at Pentagon », *The New York Times*, le 13 mars 2011.

[3] En effet, on peut faire un parallèle entre l'hystérie anti-communiste qui dominait alors la classe politique américaine et condamnait d'avance les époux Rosenberg, et la crispation anti-terroriste, quasi obsessionnelle chez certains, qui font de Manning et Assange des ennemis à abattre ou en tout cas à neutraliser par tous les moyens. Sur l'affaire Rosenberg, voir André Kaspi, *Les Américains*, Paris : Editions du Seuil, 2002, tome 2, p. 428.

[4] Voir par exemple Chris Floyd, « The Arrest of Julian Assange », *Counterpunch*, 7 décembre 2010, téléchargeable à : http://groups.google.com/group/InfoAccessNow/browse_thread/thread/723dea0546595165.

.

Si nous ajoutons à ce tableau la volonté de la Secrétaire d'Etat Hillary Clinton de faire des Etats-Unis le parangon de la transparence et de « la liberté de se connecter », la politique de l'administration Obama paraît peu lisible, voire peu cohérente. Est-il possible de réconcilier ces différents aspects contradictoires ? C'est ce que nous nous efforcerons de faire dans cet article, en démêlant les fils de l'écheveau pour prendre la mesure de la complexité de la question et de sa résonance particulière dans la culture et le subconscient collectif américains. Pour cela, il faudra d'abord situer la relation que les Etats-Unis entretiennent avec le secret d'état dans une perspective historique longue en remontant aux origines de la République fédérale, pour ensuite se pencher sur le contexte contemporain pour mieux appréhender le dilemme spécifique à l'administration Obama.

1. Les données de l'affaire WikiLeaks et les réactions politiques : *Much Ado About Nothing ?*

Mais d'abord, restons dans le présent et examinons les faits et les réactions politiques qu'ils ont suscitées. C'est surtout le *cablegate* de novembre 2010, c'est-à-dire la diffusion de télégrammes diplomatiques américains, qui a fait connaître WikiLeaks dans le monde entier, et attiré les foudres de l'administration Obama. Auparavant, et toujours en 2010, WikiLeaks avait par trois fois déjà diffusé des documents secrets américains : en avril, fut publiée une vidéo du raid aérien américain du 12 juillet 2007 en Irak, qui s'était soldé par la mort de 18 civils, dont deux photographes de l'agence Reuters ; en juillet, plus de 90 000 documents sur la guerre en Afghanistan avaient été divulgués, en collaboration avec de grands quotidiens européens et américains. Puis en octobre, ce sont près de 400 000 documents relatifs à la guerre en Irak qui furent mis à disposition de la presse.

Une différence importante sépare cependant les trois premières divulgations de celle du *cablegate* : la particularité de ce dernier est d'avoir dévoilé des câbles diplomatiques entre le département d'Etat et les ambassades américaines du monde entier. Il ne s'agissait pas de documents compromettants dévoilant des pratiques ou des faits inavouables, telles que le grand nombre de victimes collatérales des guerres d'Irak et d'Afghanistan, abondamment illustrés par les précédentes révélations. Ces dernières n'en étaient que plus dommageables, car elles sont clairement désavouées par l'opinion publique et sont donc susceptibles d'entamer sa tolérance vis-à-vis des guerres actuellement menées par les Etats-Unis. La grande majorité des quelques 250 000 télégrammes reflètent l'activité normale des diplomates américains, qui est bien sûr de promouvoir les intérêts de leur pays tels qu'ils sont définis par le gouvernement fédéral. Comme l'a notamment remarqué Timothy Garton Ash, « ce qui ressort de tous ces échanges diplomatiques, c'est à quel point les questions liées à la sécurité et au contre-terrorisme ont imprégné le moindre aspect de la politique étrangère américaine depuis une décennie »[5]. Un de ces télégrammes a, il est vrai à juste titre, fait grand bruit : celui qui fut adressé à la mission américaine à l'ONU par le département d'Etat contenant des consignes précises pour obtenir des informations personnelles sur leurs homologues, y compris ceux des pays alliés[6]. A n'en pas douter, il s'agit-là d'un aspect tout aussi embarrassant pour la secrétaire d'Etat que troublant pour les Américains et le reste du monde. Toutefois, il représente l'exception qui confirme la règle, et sur le fond, s'apparente à un secret de Polichinelle tant la porosité entre diplomatie et espionnage fait partie de la tradition diplomatique. Plus généralement, les commentaires parfois peu amènes des diplomates américains sur les responsables politiques n'ont rien d'exceptionnels dans le monde diplomatique, comme Hillary Clinton l'a souligné à sa manière, en rapportant que certains de ses homologues ont réagi à ses excuses en disant qu'ils auraient tout autant à en formuler si elle connaissait la teneur de leurs propres dépêches[7]. On peut enfin relativiser la valeur réelle des fuites en faisant remarquer qu'aucun des milliers de documents n'étaient « top secret », la plupart étant classés « confidentiels » – soit le dernier des trois niveaux de classement utilisés par le gouvernement américain – certains n'étant pas « classifiés » du tout[8]. C'est d'ailleurs ce

---

[5] Cette citation provient de son article « Les documents secrets révélés par Wikileaks relèvent de l'intérêt général. Au final, les ambassadeurs américains n'ont pas grand-chose à se reprocher », *Le Monde*, 2 décembre 2010, p. 25.

[6] Sur ce point, voir par exemple *Le Monde* du 30/11/2010, p. 15.

[7] Hillary Clinton a en effet précisé qu'un de ses homologues lui avait dit : « Bon, pas de souci. Si vous saviez ce qu'on dit de vous ». Voir : « La diplomatie américaine minore l'impact des fuites », *Le Monde*, 1 décembre 2010, p. 5.

[8] *Ibid.* Le gouvernement fédéral américain a retenu trois principaux niveaux de classement des documents officiels : top secret, secret et confidentiel.

qui explique que quelque trois millions de fonctionnaires fédéraux, dont Bradley Manning, avaient accès à ces documents via l'Internet militaire[9].

Le plus gênant est que ces informations, qui n'étaient destinées à être déclassifiées que dans quelques années, le soient maintenant car la très grande majorité (90% des télégrammes) concerne les années 2004-2010. C'est ce que reprochent surtout les autorités à WikiLeaks, en insistant sur le manque de responsabilité dont Julian Assange aurait fait preuve en divulguant des informations pouvant mettre des personnes en danger. Or, les faits montrent plutôt le contraire, puisque loin d'avoir été mis en ligne directement et sans précaution, les documents ont été initialement mis à disposition de cinq grands quotidiens unanimement reconnus pour leur sérieux (*The New York Times*, *The Guardian*, *El Pais*, *Der Spiegel* et *Le Monde*) et qui ont d'ailleurs collaboré de façon inédite pour décider des thèmes retenus et pour établir des listes communes de noms ne devant pas être révélés[10]. Ces journaux, soit quelques cent vingt journalistes, ont non seulement opéré un traitement de l'information brute pour protéger les personnes, mais ont, de plus, préalablement prévenu Washington de la publication des articles. Si l'on ajoute que WikiLeaks a aussi décidé, en accord avec les quotidiens, de ne pas diffuser la totalité des 250 000 câbles et « mémos » (circulaires) diplomatiques mais seulement ceux ayant servi à la rédaction des articles, on comprend mal le procès en irresponsabilité qui lui est fait. A ce jour, il n'est nullement avéré que la divulgation ait mis des personnes en danger, ni d'ailleurs que l'intérêt national ou la sécurité des Etats-Unis aient été affectés de façon tangible.

Si victime il y a, c'est bien la diplomatie, ou du moins la confidentialité sur laquelle elle repose, d'une part entre les diplomates et leurs interlocuteurs dans les pays où ils sont en poste, d'autre part entre ces mêmes diplomates et le département d'Etat américain. Sur ce point,

---

[9] A la suite des attentats du 11 septembre, qui avait illustré les conséquences du manque de coopération entre les différents services de sécurité et autres ministères fédéraux, un dispositif de partage électronique des informations « secret défense » entre le Pentagone et le département d'Etat avait été mis en place. C'est ainsi que les trois millions de personnes ayant accès à l'Internet militaire avaient également accès aux câbles diplomatiques, voir : « Une cellule anti-WikiLeaks à Washington », *Le Monde*, 4 décembre 2010.

[10] Par la suite, les documents ont été transmis à d'autres médias européens : *Aftenposten* (Norvège), *20 Minutes* (France), *Die Welt* (Allemagne), *Svenska Dagbladet* (Suède), *Politiken* (Danemark), et *Der Standaard* (Belgique).

les diplomates américains ont unanimement réagi dans la presse en déclarant qu'ils ne travailleraient plus jamais comme avant. On peut également parler d'une victime collatérale dans le camp américain, qui est le dispositif de partage des informations entre le département d'Etat et le Pentagone, et plus largement sans doute la coopération entre les différentes institutions gouvernementales des Etats-Unis. Dans les jours qui suivirent les révélations, l'administration Obama a mis en place une « cellule anti-WikiLeaks » au Conseil national de sécurité, suspendu l'accès à la base de données du département d'Etat (*Net Centric Diplomacy*) où sont stockés les télégrammes diplomatiques, interdit aux ambassades de distribuer les dépêches sur l'Internet militaire du Pentagone, et chargé Russell Travers – appartenant au Centre national contre le terrorisme – de diriger les réformes de structures nécessaires pour empêcher de nouvelles fuites[11].

Ces mesures bien compréhensibles ont cependant été complétées par une campagne de diabolisation de Julian Assange qui est par contre plus étonnante. Comme pour mieux le priver de la protection du premier amendement et préparer le terrain à son éventuelle extradition, celui qui était jusqu'à récemment porte-parole du département d'Etat, Philip Crowley, l'a dès le début dépeint comme un anarchiste, un voleur d'informations classifiées, un dangereux imposteur se faisant passer à tort pour un journaliste[12]. Les déclarations des membres du gouvernement et des leaders du Congrès – issus des deux partis – ont eu tendance à le présenter comme l'ennemi public N°1, une sorte de Ben Laden en col blanc complotant avec les ennemis des Etats-Unis qui devait être neutralisé par tous les moyens, y compris juridiques et financiers. Bien que Hillary Clinton s'en défende, la décision initiale d'Amazon, Paypal, Mastercard, Visa et de diverses banques de bloquer

---

[11] Voir « Une cellule anti-WikiLeaks à Washington », *Le Monde* du 4 décembre 2010. Pour plus d'informations sur la cellule anti-WikiLeaks, baptisée *Interagency Policy Committee for Wikileaks*, voir « U.S. Panel to Study Damage of Leaks », *The Washington Post*, le 2 décembre 2010, disponible en ligne : http://www.financialpost.com/related/topics/panel+study+damage+leaks/3916667/story.html.

[12] En ce qui concerne les propos de Crowley, voir « Une cellule anti-WikiLeaks à Washington », *ibid.* Plus de détails sur les velléités d'extradition peuvent être obtenues dans Ewen MacAskill, « US Lawyers Explore Extradition Routes for Julian Assange », *The Guardian,* 16 décembre 2010, accessible en ligne à : http://www.guardian.co.uk/media/2010/dec/16/julian-assange-extradition-us.

les comptes de WikiLeaks est à l'évidence liée à la chasse aux sorcières orchestrée par l'administration Obama, et qui comme il a déjà été dit, n'est pas sans évoquer la période maccarthyste[13]. Curieusement, les réactions les plus mesurées furent celles du secrétaire à la Défense, Robert Gates, qui a estimé que les conséquences des révélations pour la politique étrangère américaine étaient assez « limitées »[14]. Ce point de vue mesuré tranche avec la rhétorique offensive du département d'Etat, mais ils se rejoignent néanmoins dans une stratégie commune, qui est de discréditer l'adversaire. Consciente que la guerre se situait surtout sur le terrain de la communication, l'administration Obama a en effet contre-attaqué en niant que les fuites aient une valeur réelle. La politique étrangère est définie à Washington par le président, pas par les ambassadeurs, a insisté la Secrétaire d'Etat, et les câbles diplomatiques représentent des fragments de points de vue isolés et partiels qui n'ont que peu d'intérêt pour le public. Mais si tel est le cas, si les révélations n'ont que des conséquences limitées sur la diplomatie américaine, et un intérêt plus limitée encore pour le public, comment expliquer l'offensive générale d'un gouvernement qui s'est par ailleurs publiquement engagé en faveur de la transparence ? Une explication possible réside dans le caractère incontrôlable de l'Internet, qui rend les responsables politiques américains d'autant plus nerveux que les Etats-Unis sont au centre d'un échiquier international lui-même devenu très imprévisible, ce qui fait de la diplomatie un des rares leviers de contrôle dans un monde désormais incertain et anarchique.

---

[13] Pour plus de détails sur le boycott de Wikileaks par ces compagnies, voir notamment « Paypal Cuts Access for Donations » sur le site de la BBC : http://www.bbc.co.uk/news/world-us-canada-11917891 et « WikiLeaks traqué » sur le site de Reporters sans frontières : http://www.bbc.co.uk/news/world-us -canada-11917891.

[14] « Les conséquences pour la politique étrangère américaine ? Je pense qu'elles sont très limitées » a déclaré Gates dans une conférence de presse fin novembre 2010, notamment accessible à: http://smallwarsjournal.com/blog/2010/11/quotable-secretary-gates-on-wi/. Il faut néanmoins nuancer le détachement du Pentagone en rappelant que ses services de contre-espionnage avaient, dès 2008, réalisé une étude sur WikiLeaks (d'ailleurs révélée par WikiLeaks en 2010 !) concluant que le site représentait une « menace potentielle pour l'armée », voir : « le plan de l'armée américaine contre WikiLeaks publié par … WikiLeaks », *Le Monde*, 18 mars 2010, accessible en ligne à: http://www.lemonde.fr/technologies/article/2010/03/18/le-plan-de-l-armee-americaine-contre-wikileaks-publie-sur-wikileaks_1320923_651865.html.

2. Le secret d'état dans la tradition américaine : un héritage ambivalent

Mais la logique interne à ce paradoxe et la raison d'une certaine disproportion des réactions se trouvent surtout dans les rapports historiquement ambivalents des Etats-Unis avec le secret d'état et la diplomatie traditionnelle. A beaucoup d'égards, Julian Assange a mis le doigt sur un sujet très sensible dans la tradition politique et la culture américaines, qui en tant que tel provoque des réactions épidermiques. L'indépendance des colonies britanniques, et dans une moindre mesure la création de la République fédérale américaine, furent en effet placées sous le signe de l'exceptionnalisme supposé de l'Amérique dont l'expression privilégiée était l'opposition à la diplomatie traditionnelle européenne. L'ambition des *leaders* de la Révolution était notamment d'avoir des relations transparentes et franches avec les autres Etats de la planète, pour la très grande majorité monarchiques, comme pour mieux afficher leur différence. La franchise était alors perçue, au même titre que le désintéressement et le sens du devoir, comme une des ses vertus nécessaires à la survie d'une république. La légende selon laquelle George Washington, le héros de la Révolution et premier président américain, n'a jamais menti dans sa vie, illustre bien cet état d'esprit, alors très répandu, faisant de la franchise et de la transparence des éléments constitutifs de l'identité américaine dont Washington était le parangon. Comme le montre l'affirmation de Benjamin Franklin, représentant des Etats-Unis à Paris de 1776 à 1785, les premiers diplomates américains souhaitaient que les relations de leur pays avec le reste du monde reflètent cette différence vertueuse : « J'ai longtemps observé la maxime de ne m'occuper d'aucune affaire dont je puisse rougir en la rendant publique, et de ne rien faire que les espions ne puissent pas voir »[15].

Pourquoi une telle opposition à la diplomatie européenne et à son emblème, le secret d'état, qui étaient alors conçues en Europe comme

[15] Franklin rédigea ces lignes dans une correspondance à un ami, pour décrire son activité diplomatique à Paris, où il partit peu de temps après la Déclaration d'indépendance pour négocier un traité d'alliance avec la France. La citation, traduite par nos soins, est tirée de Davis McCullough, *John Adams*, New York: Simon & Schuster, 2011, p. 201.

une science honorable[16] ? En premier lieu parce qu'ils sont les symboles des monarchies donc de la métropole honnie par les révolutionnaires américains. Mais il ne s'agit pas seulement d'un réflexe patriote dicté par le ressentiment envers la couronne britannique. Il y a aussi une dimension à la fois plus universaliste et plus idéologique, fondée sur l'idée que la politique étrangère de l'Europe ne reflète que les intérêts des gouvernants, qui sont opposés à ceux des peuples. Or ces derniers ne veulent pas la guerre, et si la diplomatie reflétait l'opinion publique, l'Europe et le monde seraient en paix. Pour beaucoup de révolutionnaires, l'indépendance des treize colonies représentait une alternative républicaine au modèle monarchique et l'avènement potentiel si ce n'est d'un monde, du moins d'une Amérique pacifiée, à condition d'en finir avec la vieille diplomatie européenne. Cette ambition est, par exemple, exprimée dans *Common Sense*, le fameux pamphlet de Thomas Paine qui joua un rôle capital dans l'adhésion populaire à l'objectif d'indépendance. Pour lui, rester dans le giron impérial, signifiait demeurer prisonnier de l'état de guerre européen[17]. Paine partait du principe, élevé au rang de vérité par Montesquieu, que « l'esprit de la monarchie est la guerre et l'agrandissement ; l'esprit de la république est la paix et la modération »[18]. Dans ce même pamphlet, Paine propose même d'en finir avec la diplomatie : « Notre projet, c'est le commerce, qui, bien considéré, nous assurera la paix et l'amitié de toute l'Europe » écrit-il. Les relations entre les Etats-Unis et le reste du monde seraient ainsi fondées sur le libre-échange, et éventuellement sur les traités de commerce, mais en aucun cas sur les alliances et la raison d'état[19]. Cette dernière reflétait le primat des questions de sécurité et de politique étrangère dont ne voulaient absolument pas les Américains : ce primat sous-entendait en effet une armée permanente, un exécutif fort et des droits individuels proportionnellement limités. Il reposait aussi sur

---

[16] Sur le XVIIIe siècle en tant qu'âge d'or de la diplomatie européenne, voir par exemple Felix Gilbert, *To the Farewell Address*, Princeton, NJ: Princeton University Press, 1961, chapitre IV, p. 76-114.

[17] Thomas Paine, « Common Sense ». *Selected Work*, New York: Modern Library, 1945.

[18] Cette célèbre citation est de Montesquieu, dans *L'esprit des lois*, Livre IX, chapitre 2.

[19] Pour une analyse de la tradition européenne de la raison d'état, voir l'ouvrage classique de Friedrich Meinecke, *L'Idée de la raison d'Etat dans l'histoire des temps modernes,* Genève : Droz, 1973.

l'existence d'une éthique politique distincte de la moralité commune, sur l'idée que la politique étrangère constituait un domaine réservé et autonome obéissant à ses propres lois, et enfin que les intérêts de l'Etat étaient supérieurs à ceux de la société civile. Tout cela était très exactement l'inverse de l'idéologie dominante américaine de la période révolutionnaire, dont la conception des *radical whigs* constituait la matrice et qui accordait la primauté aux affaires intérieures. Pour Paine, comme pour les autres représentants américains des *Whigs* radicaux, le gouvernement idéal avait pour seuls buts de pourvoir au bonheur des citoyens et de protéger leur liberté :

> *Our true situation appears to me to be this – a new extensive Country containing within itself the materials for forming a Government capable of extending to its citizens all the blessings of civil and religious liberty, capable of making them happy at home. This is the great end of republican Establishments. We mistake the object of our government, if we hope or wish that it is to make us respectable abroad.*[20]

Comme Robert Tucker et David Hendrickson l'ont souligné dans leur *Empire of Liberty*, Thomas Jefferson fut le concepteur d'une diplomatie nouvelle dont les objectifs étaient plus ambitieux encore que ceux des Etats européens tout en écartant les moyens traditionnellement retenus pour les atteindre, à savoir les alliances, la raison d'état et les négociations secrètes.[21] Pour Jefferson, la sécurité d'une république dépendait surtout de la confiance des citoyens dans leur gouvernement et dans leur volonté de la défendre en cas de besoin. Point de primat des

---

[20] « Notre situation réelle me semble être celle-ci : un pays nouveau et étendu, présentant toutes les conditions requises à la formation d'un gouvernement capable d'accorder à ses citoyens tous les bienfaits de la liberté civile et religieuse, et susceptible de les rendre heureux dans leur pays. Telle est la grande finalité d'un établissement républicain. Nous nous méprenons sur l'objectif de notre gouvernement si nous pensons qu'il soit de nous rendre respectables à l'étranger », Thomas Pinkney, cité par Max Farrand, *The Records of the Federal Convention of 1787*, New Haven, CT: Yale University Press, 1937, Tome 1, p. 402. Pour plus de détails sur les idées des *Whigs* radicaux, voir Bernard Baylin, *The Ideological Origins of the American Revolution*, Cambridge, MA: Harvard University Press, 1967 et J.G.A. Pocock, *The Machiavellian Moment. Florentine Political Thought and the Atlantic Republic Tradition*, Princeton, NJ: Princeton University Press, 1975.

[21] Robert Tucker, David Hendrickson, *Empire of Liberty. The Statecraft of Thomas Jefferson*, New York: Oxford University Press, 1990.

questions de sécurité ou de politique étrangère, l'expansion territoriale et l'édification d'un « empire de la liberté » étant pour lui un moyen de protéger et de promouvoir la liberté et le bonheur « intérieur » des citoyens de la république fédérale. Le système fédéral permettait de réconcilier expansion et droits individuels, dans la mesure où ceux des territoires annexés seraient égaux à ceux des autres citoyens et qu'ils s'auto-gouverneraient. La tradition de la raison d'état et son dualisme éthique, postulant que la politique avait ses propres lois, devait céder la place « à un seul et unique système éthique valable pour les hommes comme pour les nations, consistant à être reconnaissant, fidèle à ses engagements en toutes circonstances, à être ouvert et généreux, et à promouvoir sur le long terme les intérêts de chacun des deux »[22].

Il faut certes nuancer la portée de cette idéologie fondatrice des Etats-Unis hostile à la diplomatie traditionnelle et au secret, dont l'emprise n'a été ni totale ni durable. Le « traité modèle » élaboré par John Adams sous l'influence de Paine, que Franklin avait emporté à Paris dans l'espoir de conclure un accord purement commercial avec la France en échange d'une aide militaire contre l'Angleterre, dut finalement être complété par un traité d'alliance tout à fait conforme aux pratiques diplomatiques en vigueur en Europe[23]. Jefferson était très au fait des rivalités et des subtilités diplomatiques européennes, ainsi que des exigences de l'équilibre des puissances, et en tira le plus grand parti pour avancer les intérêts des Etats-Unis[24]. Plus généralement, dans la mesure où elle visait principalement à étendre le territoire national, sa politique en tant que président des Etats-Unis était tout à fait conforme à la maxime bien connue de la raison d'état européenne, selon laquelle tout état doit tendre vers l'expansion. Mais surtout, il faut tenir compte du déclin de l'idéologie radicale *whig* et du tournant de 1787 qui, à beaucoup d'égards, a sonné le glas des ambitions politiques réformatrices des Américains et réorienté leur théorie ainsi que les institutions politiques dans un sens beaucoup plus européen. Le débat décisif pour l'avenir des Etats-Unis qui se tint lors de la Convention de Philadelphie

---

[22] Jefferson cité par Robert Tucker et David Hendrickson, *ibid*, p. 15.

[23] Voir Felix Gilbert, *To the Farewell Address*, *op. cit.*, p. 48-56.

[24] Pour plus de détails, voir Norman Graebner, *Foundations of American Foreign Policy. A Realist Appraisal from Franklin to McKinley*, Wilmington, Delaware: Scholarly Resources, 1985, p. 47-76.

vit la victoire de ceux qui ne croyaient pas ou plus assez dans l'exceptionnalisme américain pour supposer que les Etats-Unis puissent ignorer ce qui, en Europe, passait pour l'alpha et l'oméga de la politique d'un état, à commencer par la diplomatie et la nécessaire concentration du pouvoir[25]. En se dotant d'un exécutif « énergique », selon l'expression d'Alexander Hamilton, les Etats-Unis ont en effet adopté la tradition machiavélienne et greffé sur les institutions fédérales un élément monarchique[26]. La création d'un exécutif fédéral indépendant reflétait une inflexion décisive vers la reconnaissance d'un certain primat des questions de sécurité, et d'une éthique politique propre. De façon significative, c'est à cette période que fut créé un réseau diplomatique américain digne de ce nom, et l'attitude des responsables américains envers la diplomatie changea du tout au tout durant les années qui précédèrent la Convention de Philadelphie – au point que le représentant de la France révolutionnaire fut désagréablement surpris par la pompe et l'ambiance aristocratique qui régnaient dans le milieu diplomatique de Philadelphie en 1791[27]. Loin de vouloir éradiquer la diplomatie traditionnelle, les Américains venaient de se doter de deux attributs emblématiques des puissants Etats européens pour mieux se faire respecter sur la scène internationale – un exécutif indépendant et un corps diplomatique – et reconnaissaient désormais la valeur des doctrines européennes pour la conduite des affaires étatiques, notamment le primat du politique et des questions de sécurité, ainsi que son corollaire obligé : une éthique politique distincte.

La période fondatrice des Etats-Unis, avec ses deux pôles de 1776 et 1787, est donc marquée du sceau de l'ambivalence par rapport à la diplomatie européenne et plus spécifiquement à cet aspect particulier de

---

[25] Pour une analyse du débat sur l'exceptionnalisme américain dans les années 1780, voir Jean-Marie Ruiz, « Should the U.S. Adapt to the World? The First Debate on American Exceptionalism and Its Impact on the Founding of the United States », *Polissema* n° 9, 2009, p. 47-60.

[26] Harvey Mansfield, *Taming the Prince. The Ambivalence of Modern Executive Power*. Baltimore, MD: The Johns Hopkins University Press, 1989. Sur l'adoption de la tradition machiavélienne et le tournant de 1787, voir Gordon Wood, *The Creation of the American Republic, 1776-1787*, Chapel Hill, NC: The University of North Carolina Press, 1969.

[27] Pour plus de détails sur ce point et pour une analyse de l'adoption américaine des pratiques diplomatiques traditionnelles, voir Felix Gilbert, *To the Farewell Address, op. cit.*, p. 76-114.

l'héritage machiavélien qu'est le secret d'état. Cette ambivalence originelle demeure encore aujourd'hui, et a nourri des débats récurrents dans l'histoire américaine sur les relations que les Etats-Unis devaient avoir avec le monde extérieur, et surtout sur la question de savoir s'ils devaient adopter des normes de conduite reflétant leur différence supposée. L'un des plus importants eut lieu au début du vingtième siècle, peu de temps après que les Etats-Unis aient franchi une nouvelle étape dans l'adoption de l'héritage politique européen en se dotant de colonies outre-mer à la suite de la guerre américano-espagnole de 1898. C'est en effet en réaction à ce tournant majeur de la politique étrangère américaine que Wilson entreprit de remodeler les relations internationales et remit au goût du jour l'idée d'une « nouvelle diplomatie » opposée à la « vieille diplomatie » européenne. Son fameux discours au Congrès du 8 janvier 1918, dit des « Quatorze points », dans lequel il énonçait les principes généraux qui guideraient les négociations de paix pour mettre fin à la Première Guerre mondiale, le secret d'état est particulièrement montré du doigt :

> *It will be our wish and purpose that the processes of peace, when they are begun, shall be absolutely open and that they shall involve and permit henceforth no secret understandings of any kind. The day of conquest and aggrandizement is gone by; so is also the day of secret covenants entered into in the interest of particular governments and likely at some unlooked-for moment to upset the peace of the world.*[28]

De fait, le premier des « quatorze points » revient d'ailleurs sur cette question de la transparence, suggérant que pour Wilson – et pour les Etats-Unis, insiste-t-il – elle est la première des conditions pour parvenir à une paix durable : « Des traités de paix négociés au grand jour, après

---

[28] « Notre souhait et notre but est que, une fois le processus de paix entamé, il soit totalement ouvert et qu'il ne comporte ni tolère aucun arrangement secret d'aucune sorte. L'ère des conquêtes et de l'agrandissement est terminée, tout comme l'est celle des accords secrets reflétant l'intérêt de certains gouvernements, susceptibles de troubler la paix au moment où l'on s'y attend le moins ». Woodrow Wilson, discours au Congrès du 8 janvier 1918, notamment téléchargeable à : http://wwi.lib.byu.edu/index.php/President_Wilson%27s_Fourteen_Points.

lesquels plus aucun arrangement international privé ne sera possible, afin que la diplomatie soit désormais menée de façon franche et transparente »[29].

Il est vrai que Wilson lui-même dérogea à la règle quelques mois plus tard, lorsqu'il négocia le traité de Versailles à huis clos avec les chefs de gouvernement français, anglais et italien, à l'écart de l'opinion publique[30]. Mais l'intérêt de ces citations est de prendre toute la mesure du changement intervenu dans le point de vue officiel sur la question du secret d'état. En effet, alors que Wilson partait du principe qu'il ne saurait y avoir de paix durable sans transparence et que cette dernière était par conséquent cruciale, Hillary Clinton présuppose au contraire que la diplomatie a besoin du secret pour être efficace et remplir pleinement son rôle dans la résolution des problèmes internationaux. Par un étrange paradoxe, ce renversement de situation place l'administration Obama en porte-à-faux avec la tradition wilsonienne, et suggère une plus grande affinité avec la tradition politique américaine. Dans un ouvrage publié en 1994, Henry Kissinger définissait précisément la différence entre l'interprétation européenne des relations internationales et celle de Wilson en ces termes :

> *The fundamental difference between the Wilsonian and the European interpretations of the causes of international conflicts is reflected in these words. European-style diplomacy presumes that national interests have a tendency to clash, and views diplomacy as the means for reconciling them; Wilson, on the other hand, considered international discord the result of "clouded thinking", not an expression of a genuine clash of interests.*[31]

---

[29] « Open covenants of peace, openly arrived at, after which there will be no private international understanding of any kind but diplomacy shall proceed always frankly and in the public view. » *Ibid.*, p. 209.

J'emprunte cette remarque à Aurélien Colson, « Fin du secret diplomatique ? », *Le Monde*, 14 décembre 2010, p. 24.

[31] « La différence fondamentale entre l'interprétation wilsonienne et européenne des conflits internationaux est reflétée dans ces mots [l'auteur se réfère à une citation de Wilson]. La diplomatie européenne présume que les intérêts nationaux ont tendance à provoquer des conflits et voit la diplomatie comme un moyen de les réconcilier ; Wilson considère quant à lui que la discorde internationale résulte d'une « pensée obscure », non pas l'expression d'un véritable conflit d'intérêts ». Henry Kissinger, *Diplomacy*, New York: Simon & Schuster, 1994, p. 248.

En déclarant que les publications des télégrammes diplomatiques « ne représentent pas seulement une attaque contre les intérêts diplomatiques américains ... [mais] aussi une attaque contre la communauté internationale », Hillary Clinton suggère d'une part que les Etats-Unis ont renoncé à imposer une « nouvelle diplomatie » distincte de celle de l'Europe, d'autre part que l'essence de la diplomatie et la clé de son succès exigent qu'elle se déroule à l'écart de l'opinion publique[32]. Il s'agit aussi d'une reconnaissance implicite de l'existence d'une éthique propre à la diplomatie, et donc d'une remise en cause d'un principe cardinal de la tradition wilsonienne, qui était elle-même l'expression de valeurs américaines beaucoup plus anciennes remontant à la Révolution et à la tradition jeffersonienne, et ainsi constitutives de l'identité nationale.

3. La métamorphose du Parti démocrate et le syndrome post-Bush : les raisons d'une schizophrénie américaine

Comment expliquer le paradoxe d'un tel décalage entre le Parti démocrate actuel et les traditions jeffersonienne et wilsonienne ? Le contexte, à la fois immédiat et de long terme, y est pour beaucoup. Comme nous l'avons déjà dit, il y a toujours eu une certaine duplicité américaine à l'égard de l'héritage européen et de sa composante machiavélienne, qui a en partie été réhabilitée en 1787. En se dotant d'un exécutif puissant au pouvoir potentiellement discrétionnaire, les Etats-Unis se donnaient les moyens institutionnels de devenir la puissance planétaire qu'ils sont devenus depuis le début du vingtième siècle, sans pour autant reléguer aux oubliettes de l'histoire l'idéologie ou l'esprit de 1776, qui refait périodiquement surface depuis lors. Le mouvement du *Tea Party* représente le visage actuel de cette tendance libertaire, jadis incarnée par les anti-fédéralistes et Jefferson, en dépit de sa longue traversée du désert durant la période de la guerre froide. Etant dominée par les questions de sécurité, cette dernière était en effet peu compatible avec l'anti-étatisme de la tradition jeffersonienne et sa diatribe contre la tradition diplomatique européenne. A partir de 1947, malgré la domination du Parti démocrate, héritier de Jefferson et de Wilson jusqu'en 1968, la politique étrangère américaine s'est au contraire européanisée comme jamais auparavant pour faire face au défi

[32] Cette déclaration, reproduite dans *Le Monde* du 1/12/2010, p. 5, constitue la première réaction officielle de la secrétaire d'Etat à la publication des télégrammes diplomatiques dans la presse fin novembre 2010.

soviétique. Confrontés à un ennemi puissant qu'ils ne pouvaient ni vaincre ni ignorer dans le contexte nouveau d'un monde à la fois globalisé et nucléarisé, les Etats-Unis prêtèrent une oreille attentive aux conseils des nombreux historiens et politologues européens qu'ils avaient accueillis durant la Deuxième Guerre mondiale[33]. Le résultat fut la transposition en Amérique d'une conception des relations internationales typiquement européenne, reflétant l'idée que l'état de guerre qui caractérisait depuis longtemps le Vieux continent était la condition normale des relations inter-étatiques. L'un de ces immigrés, Hans Morgenthau, joua un rôle particulièrement important dans l'essor de ce que les Etats-Unis appelèrent *political realism*, c'est-à-dire une théorie des relations internationales rappelant aux Américains que les relations entre états sont basées sur la puissance et l'intérêt et non pas sur les principes[34]. Or, le réalisme politique postule que l'essence des relations internationales est l'anarchie du fait de l'absence d'un gouvernement mondial, et que dans un tel environnement il est légitime que les états défendent avant tout leurs intérêts nationaux, notamment par la diplomatie et l'équilibre des puissances. Il va sans dire qu'une telle conception des choses était anathème pour les Wilsoniens, et que c'est contre elle que s'étaient élevés les révolutionnaires américains, avant de la réhabiliter quelques années plus tard[35]. Mais elle demeura néanmoins le paradigme dominant durant toute la guerre froide, et trouva son apogée dans la politique menée, de 1968 à 1973, par Richard Nixon et Henry Kissinger qui, plus que tout autres responsables américains se

---

[33] Pour plus d'informations sur le rôle des intellectuels européens dans l'essor des sciences sociales américaines voir Laura Fermi, *Illustrious Immigrants*, Chicago, IL: The University of Chicago Press, 1968, chapitre 11, p. 320-372. Pour plus de détails sur leur rôle dans l'étude des relations internationales comme discipline académique, voir Stanley Hoffmann, « An American Social Science: International Relations », *Daedalus*, Eté 1977, p. 41-59.

[34] Hans Morgenthau est l'auteur de *Politics Among Nations. The Struggle for Power and Peace*, New York: Knopf, 1948, qui fut l'ouvrage de référence pour l'étude des relations internationales de l'après guerre, et l'orienta pour de nombreuses années vers le réalisme politique. En ce qui concerne ce dernier, voir notamment Kenneth Thompson, *Political Realism and the Crisis of World Politics*, Boston, MA: University Press of America, 1982.

[35] Sur l'impact du réalisme politique sur la fondation de la république fédérale américaine, voir Jean-Marie Ruiz, *Une tradition transatlantique. L'Impact du réalisme politique sur la fondation des Etats-Unis et la pensée politique américaine du XIXe siècle*, Chambéry: Editions de l'Université de Savoie, 2010.

sont efforcés de conduire la diplomatie américaine à l'abri de l'opinion publique[36].

Il n'est donc pas étonnant que la longue période de guerre froide en général, et celle de la présidence Nixon en particulier, aient été propices à la légitimation, voire à la valorisation du secret d'état. Celui-ci était l'une des conséquences logiques du primat des questions de sécurité qui prévalait alors aux Etats-Unis comme il avait jadis prévalu en Europe pour des raisons analogues. La normalisation du secret d'état au nom de la sécurité nationale alla d'ailleurs de pair avec le développement d'autres traits caractéristiques de la tradition politique européenne, tel que celui qu'Arthur Schlesinger appela la *présidence impériale*, c'est-à-dire la montée en puissance de l'exécutif, et l'affaiblissement concomitant des fameux « freins et contrepoids » si emblématiques de la tradition américaine[37]. Dans le même temps, comme les *Pentagon papers* le révélèrent en 1971 à propos du Vietnam, les présidents, durant la période de la guerre froide, prirent l'habitude de tromper délibérément l'opinion publique au nom de la sécurité nationale[38]. C'est aussi ce primat que reflète enfin la progressive élaboration de ce que Dwight Eisenhower appela le *national security state*, à savoir une puissante bureaucratie fédérale garante de la sécurité nationale, dont la seule évocation aurait sans aucun doute fait blêmir la plupart des Pères fondateurs[39].

Les excès de l'administration Nixon et son obsession du secret ont mis un terme temporaire à cette tendance. Mais la diplomatie secrète, et son corollaire la présidence impériale, avait encore de beaux jours

[36] On trouvera une analyse de l'influence du réalisme politique sur la politique étrangère américaine de cette période dans Stanley Hoffmann, *Primacy or World Order. American Foreign Policy Since the Cold War*, New York: McGraw-Hill, 1978, p. 33-101.

[37] Arthur Schlesinger, *The Imperial Presidency*, Boston, MA: Houghton Mifflin, 1973.

[38] L'affaire Wikileaks fait d'ailleurs écho à celle des *Pentagon papers*, dans la mesure où ceux-ci furent aussi publiés par le *New York Times* et le *Washington Post* après avoir été dérobés au Pentagone par Daniel Ellsberg. Pour une réaction dans ce sens de ce dernier à l'affaire Wikileaks voir l'entretien diffusé sur son site, téléchargeable à : http://www.democracynow.org/seo/2011/3/18/daniel_ellsberg_on_bradley_mannings_solitary. Pour les documents eux-mêmes, voir *The Pentagon Papers*, Boston, MA: The Beacon Press, 1971.

[39] Pour une analyse synthétique et claire du rôle du secret d'état et des adaptations institutionnelles au primat des questions de sécurité de la guerre froide jusqu'à nos jours, voir Anne Deysine et al., *L'empire de l'exécutif américain, 1933-2006*, Paris : Atlande, 2008, p. 348-374.

devant elle, y compris après la fin de la guerre froide. Reagan l'a remise au goût du jour pour s'affranchir des limites imposées par le Congrès dans la lutte anti-communiste, en s'appuyant notamment sur la doctrine du « privilège de l'exécutif », revendiquant le droit de ne pas livrer des informations au Congrès et aux cours fédérales au nom de la sécurité nationale[40]. Les attentats du 11 septembre 2001 ont ensuite redonné toute sa légitimité à une présidence forte, structurée sur le primat des questions de sécurité et le secret d'état. Tout en évitant de se réclamer explicitement de la doctrine du privilège de l'exécutif, George W. Bush et Dick Cheney se sont efforcés de soustraire le plus d'informations possibles au Congrès, n'hésitant pas à affirmer que « la pression du Congrès sur le processus décisionnel du pouvoir exécutif est incompatible avec la séparation des pouvoirs et menace la liberté individuelle »[41]. La présidence de George W. Bush a suscité beaucoup de réactions, dont celle, indignée et féroce, d'Arthur Schlesinger, et celle de John Dean, un ancien conseiller juridique du Président Nixon, pour qui « George W. Bush et Dick Cheney ont créé la présidence la plus secrète que j'ai connue. Leur secret est bien pire que celui de la période du Watergate »[42].

Pour comprendre la réaction de l'administration Obama à l'affaire WikiLeaks, il faut d'une part prendre en compte le temps long en remontant aux origines de la république fédérale, et d'autre part le contexte particulier de son arrivée au pouvoir, qui exigeait un changement par rapport à son prédécesseur et à ses excès. La prise en compte d'éléments contradictoires liés à ces deux temps permet de saisir

---

[40] La doctrine du « privilège de l'exécutif » a été initialement définie par Eisenhower (*Ibid.*, p. 365-366). En ce qui concerne le regain de la présidence impériale après Nixon, voir Andrew Rudalevige, *The New Imperial Presidency*, Ann Harbor, MI: The University of Michigan Press, 2005.

[41] « *Congressional pressure on executive branch prosecutorial decision making is inconsistent with separation of powers and threatens individual liberty* ». Cette citation provient d'une circulaire datant de décembre 2001, « *Memorandum for the Attorney General* », et est empruntée à Andrew Rudalevige, *The New Imperial Presidency*, *ibid*, p. 186.

[42] « *George W. Bush et Richard Cheney have created the most secretive presidency of my life time. Their secrecy is far worse than during Watergate.* » Cette citation est empruntée à Arthur Schlesinger, *War and the American Presidency*, New York: Norton, 2004. Les réactions de Schlesinger à la présidence de G. W. Bush figurent dans cet ouvrage.

les raisons de l'ambivalence et de la virulence à l'endroit de WikiLeaks, parce que celle-ci réactive des tensions qui, bien que depuis longtemps à l'œuvre dans l'histoire américaine, ont été exacerbées par la présidence controversée de George W. Bush. Ces tensions sont inhérentes à la nécessité de réconcilier la liberté et la sécurité. Dans la mesure où Barack Obama a été élu pour tourner la page peu glorieuse de la période Bush, marquée par l'unilatéralisme et le néo-impérialisme pour ce qui est de la politique étrangère, et sur le plan intérieur par des entorses à l'Etat de droit, il incarne le retour à une présidence plus respectueuse des droits et de la liberté individuelle, du multilatéralisme et de la diplomatie. Cette dernière avait été mise à mal par le peu de cas que George W. Bush faisait des alliés traditionnels des Etats-Unis, par l'idée sous-jacente que la sécurité des Etats-Unis ne pouvait pas être assurée de façon collective, et par le primat accordé à la puissance militaire qui reléguait au second plan la dimension politique de la résolution des conflits. Conscient de la nécessité de revenir à une approche plus multilatéraliste, et moins va-t-en-guerre, Barack Obama se fait le défenseur de la diplomatie et des solutions politiques aux problèmes de sécurité. Le plus étonnant est que cette posture le met en porte-à-faux par rapport à l'héritage démocrate, incarnée par Jefferson et Wilson, qui chacun à sa façon s'étaient opposés à la diplomatie traditionnelle européenne. Ce paradoxe tient en partie à ce que Pierre Hassner a appelé le « wilsonisme botté » du président Bush et des néoconservateurs qui l'ont influencé : « le puits de la tradition wilsonienne » a été comme empoisonné par son association avec la croisade néoconservatrice, de telle sorte qu'Obama s'en dissocie aujourd'hui pour se rapprocher d'une approche plus « réaliste » des relations internationales, alors que celle-ci était plus traditionnellement associée aux Républicains[43]. Le glissement du réalisme vers le Parti démocrate était d'ailleurs assez patent lors de la campagne pour les élections présidentielles de 2008, et il n'est donc pas étonnant que le candidat démocrate incarne aujourd'hui cette approche[44]. Or, comme

[43] Pierre Hassner, « L'empire de la force ou la force de l'empire ? », *Cahiers de Chaillot*, n° 54, 2002. Sur le néoconservatisme on se réfèrera à l'ouvrage de Justin Vaïsse, *Histoire du néoconservatisme aux Etats-Unis*, Paris : Odile Jacob, 2008.

[44] A titre d'illustration, on se reportera aux articles publiés dans la revue *Foreign Affairs* par différents candidats, notamment Barack Obama, "Renewing American Leadership", *Foreign Affairs*, vol. 86, n° 4, July/August 2007 et Hillary Clinton,

nous l'avons vu, le réalisme conçoit la politique étrangère comme un art compliqué qui doit être réservé aux spécialistes, en dehors de toute pression de l'opinion publique.

L'ambivalence des Démocrates et du gouvernement Obama par rapport à WikiLeaks tient aussi à leur volonté d'apparaître malgré tout comme les défenseurs des libertés fondamentales, notamment la liberté d'accès à l'information dont l'Internet est le symbole, et ce qu'Hillary Clinton appelle la « liberté de naviguer ». Depuis son arrivée au pouvoir, l'administration Obama a en effet affiché sa volonté de transparence, en mettant en avant son projet dit *Open Government Initiative*, et en faisant des nouvelles technologies de l'information la nouvelle arme des pays démocratiques contre les régimes dictatoriaux[45]. Pour ce qui est du volet « extérieur » de cette posture, elle n'est pas tant une réaction à son prédécesseur – qui lui aussi utilisait volontiers la rhétorique de la liberté – qu'une volonté d'utiliser l'Internet à des fins de propagande et d'en faire une arme dirigée contre les pays antagonistes des Etats-Unis comme la Chine, et l'Iran, où le libre accès à l'information n'existe pas. En ce sens, l'administration Obama peut à la fois se saisir de l'Internet pour promouvoir l'intérêt des Etats-Unis tout en empruntant une rhétorique wilsonienne de croisade en faveur de la démocratie.

Dans l'ensemble, ce qui frappe néanmoins le plus dans les réactions officielles à l'affaire WikiLeaks est la difficulté de réconcilier les différents aspects antagonistes d'un héritage et d'une problématique complexes. Les arguments utilisés pour défendre le libre accès à

"Security and Opportunity for the Twenty-first Century", *Foreign Affairs*, vol. 86, n° 6, November/December 2007.

[45] Voir le discours d'Hillary Clinton au Newseum de Washington, « Remarks on Internet Freedom », le 21 janvier 2001, accessible en ligne à : http://www.state.gov/secretary/rm/2010/01/135519.htm. H. Clinton y déclare notamment : « *Some countries have erected some electronic barriers that prevent their people from accessing portions of the world's networks (...) They have violated the privacy of citizens who engage on non-violent political speech. These actions contravene the Universal Declaration on Human Rights, which tells that all people have the right 'to seek, receive and impart information and ideas through any media and regardless of frontiers* ». Pour ce qui est du projet *Open Government Initiative*, voir le discours prononcé par B. Obama le jour de sa prise de fonction, diffusé sous l'appellation « *Memorandum on Transparency and Open Government* », accessible en ligne à : http://www.whitehouse.gov/the_press_office/TransparencyandOpenGovernment/.

l'information en Chine ne sont-ils pas aussi pertinents pour la société américaine ? Une démocratie authentique peut-elle se passer de *whistleblowers*, dont la finalité reste, quels que soient les progrès technologiques et les modifications apportées dans les termes du débat sur la transparence, de veiller à ce qu'un gouvernement démocratiquement élu n'outrepasse pas ses pouvoirs ? En ces temps de présidence impériale, la question mérite plus que jamais d'être posée, aux Etats-Unis non moins qu'ailleurs.

Jean-Marie Ruiz

Université de Savoie

L'Impact des *netroots* sur le débat politique et la démocratie américaine : à la fois positif et pernicieux

Tout observateur avisé de la société américaine a pu constater à quel point la campagne présidentielle de 2008 a été à la fois dominée et profondément façonnée par l'Internet. Greg Mitchell, auteur de l'ouvrage : *Why Obama Won? The Making of a President 2008*[1], pouvait ainsi déclarer qu'elle a « changé les règles du jeu pour toujours »[2]. Le 4 novembre 2009, le *New York Times* lui même reconnaissait le formidable impact de ce média dans un éditorial intitulé : *The 2008 Campaign: Sea Change for Politics as We Know It*[3]. De fait, il est incontestable que l'usage qui a été fait de la Toile par les candidats mais également le rôle prééminent joué par les *netroots* ont modifié le rapport que le peuple noue avec ses dirigeants. Cette évolution, qui apparaît de prime abord tout à fait positive, en ce qu'elle offre une tribune à tout citoyen lambda, présente toutefois certains effets pervers qui, poussés à l'extrême, pourraient se révéler pernicieux pour la qualité du débat politique et, au bout du compte, pour la démocratie.

Nous nous attacherons dans un premier temps à analyser la genèse et l'évolution des *netroots*. Il nous faudra ensuite mettre en lumière en quoi ce mouvement participe sans conteste de la vitalité du débat démocratique. Enfin il conviendra d'examiner les dangers qui guettent si aucun garde-fou n'est mis en place : de la tyrannie de la transparence au

[1] Greg Mitchell, *Why Obama Won? The Making of a President 2008*, New York: BookSurgePublishing, 2009.
[2] Greg Mitchell, « The Revolution in Online Politics – and What Happens Next », *Huffingtonpost.com*, 4 février 2009.
[3] Adam Nagourney, «The 2008 Campaign: Sea Change for Politics as We Know It », *The New York Times*, 3 novembre 2008.

populisme le plus débridé, tous les dérapages semblent permis, ce qui pourrait se révéler corrosif pour la démocratie elle-même.

1. Origine et développement des *netroots*

Les tout premiers blogs politiques sont apparus à la fin des années quatre-vingt-dix ; mais ils commencent véritablement à s'imposer dans le paysage médiatique américain lors du premier mandat de George W. Bush. La décision de la Cour suprême de mettre fin au recomptage des voix en Floride lors de l'élection controversée de 2000 mais également le suivisme de l'élite démocrate vis-à-vis de l'administration Bush, au moment du vote de la guerre en Irak en mars 2003, eurent un rôle de catalyseur. De nombreux blogs progressistes fleurirent en effet dans leur sillage, critiquant violemment les caciques du Parti démocrate, accusés d'accepter docilement une victoire jugée indue et de s'égarer dans des compromissions inacceptables. Blogueurs de la première heure, Markos Moulitsas Zùniga et Jerome Armstrong furent considérés comme le fer de lance du mouvement. Le premier, parce qu'il créa *DailyKos* en mai 2002, devenu l'un des sites les plus consultés et les plus influents de la blogosphère, le second, car il utilisa le terme *netroots* pour la première fois sur son site *myDD* à peu près à la même période. Jerome Armstrong est, en effet, le premier à mettre un nom sur le phénomène, au moment où son blog prend ouvertement parti pour le candidat Howard Dean dans la course aux primaires démocrates[4]. Il sera d'ailleurs engagé quelques mois plus tard comme consultant politique par l'ancien gouverneur du Vermont. De spectateurs passifs du délitement d'un Parti démocrate dont ils estiment qu'il a depuis trop longtemps renié ses valeurs fondamentales – notamment en adoptant la stratégie de triangulation chère à Bill Clinton – les blogueurs se muent en véritables acteurs du changement. L'ambition première de ces pionniers de la blogosphère est d'utiliser les nouvelles technologies et en particulier l'Internet, afin de fédérer les sympathisants de base qui ne se sentent plus représentés par l'*establishment* démocrate, pour en finir en quelque sorte avec la hiérarchie pyramidale qui régit la prise de décision :

> *Those of us who became energized ever since Bush and his circle of friends took over in 2000 – the netroots, the grassroots, the progressive base of*

[4] Jerome Armstrong, « Netroots for Dean in 2004 », *MyDD*, 18 décembre 2002.

> *America – must act now to take back our party and our country (...) Technology has opened up the previously closed realm of activist politics to riffraff like us. Whether the stagnant establishment wants it or not, the new progressive populist movement will reclaim the Democratic Party as the party of the people.*[5]

Si les blogueurs souhaitent faire pression sur l'élite et donner à la base la possibilité de se faire entendre, leur objectif est également d'affaiblir les lobbies traditionnels du Parti démocrate, accusés d'être obnubilés par la défense d'une seule et unique cause, qui prime sur toute autre considération[6]. Le néologisme *netroots* qui se référait initialement aux blogs progressistes englobe désormais tout type de mouvement de démocratie participative qui a recours aux nouvelles technologies, même s'il faut noter que pour se différencier de leurs homologues de gauche, les militants républicains font de plus en plus allusion au terme *rightroots*. Par extension, l'expression s'applique aux réseaux sociaux qui abritent des forums de démocratie participative tels *FaceBook* ou *MySpace*, mais également aux sites comme *YouTube* ou *Twitter* qui permettent de visionner des vidéos en ligne.

Depuis le début des années 2000, les *netroots* ont connu une croissance fulgurante. On estime à environ 133 millions le nombre de blogs aux Etats-Unis[7], même si un très grand nombre d'entre eux ont une audience confidentielle. Entre les campagnes présidentielles de 2004 et de 2008, le pourcentage d'Américains qui ont dit s'informer uniquement grâce à la Toile est passé de 21% à 36%. Par ailleurs, selon un sondage effectué par le *Pew Research Center* en mars 2010, 61% des Américains surfent quotidiennement sur l'Internet pour s'informer[8]. Les jeunes âgés de 18 à 29 ans sont les plus friands de ces sites[9]. Et si la

---

[5] Jerome Armstrong, Markos Moulitsas Zùniga, *Crashing the Gate. Netroots, Grassroots and the Rise of People-Powered Politics*, White River Junction, VT: Chelsea Green, 2006, p. 2-3.

[6] *Ibid.*, p. 30.

[7] « Blogging in 2010: What You Need to Know », *enginejournal.com*, http://www.searchenginejournal.com/blogging-in-2010-what-you-need-to-know/18886/.

[8] The State of the News Media 2010, Project for Excellence in Journalism, Audience Behavior, *www.stateofthemedia.org/2010/.*

[9] Larry J. Sabato, *The Year of Obama: How Barack Obama Won the White House?* New York: Longman, 2010, p. 182-183.

télévision reste le média de prédilection pour la majorité des Américains, la Toile arrive désormais en deuxième position devant la presse écrite. Les sites qui appartiennent aux grands médias sont toujours les plus consultés (CNN en tête) mais le *Drudge Report*, *DailyKos* et le *Huffington Post* ne sont pas loin de les détrôner en raison du temps que les internautes passent sur leur blog respectif. En fait si les blogueurs qui officient pour les sites progressistes les plus influents continuent de revendiquer leur fonction de journalistes citoyens, ils ne peuvent toutefois plus être considérés comme de simples amateurs, non seulement parce que ce sont tous des blogueurs à plein temps mais aussi parce qu'ils ont engagé des reporters qui sont rémunérés grâce aux espaces publicitaires et aux contributions des internautes.

Le recours grandissant de la population américaine à l'Internet, la multiplication exponentielle du nombre de lecteurs de blogs mais également la formidable puissance de feu qu'a représenté la Toile pour lever des fonds, ont propulsé le mouvement au rang d'acteur incontournable du débat politique américain. Et si la campagne présidentielle de 2008 a en quelque sorte consacré le mouvement, l'élection de 2004, mais également les législatives de 2006, ont constitué des étapes majeures dans leur ascension. L'influence des *netroots* a notamment été perceptible dans la manière dont les médias traditionnels ainsi que les hommes politiques ont changé d'attitude à son endroit. A partir de 2004, les grands médias ont cessé de les traiter avec mépris et les caciques des deux partis ont ravalé leurs rancœurs et se sont départis de leur morgue à l'égard d'un mouvement qui commençait à prendre un poids qu'il leur devenait difficile d'ignorer. Ainsi lors de l'élection présidentielle de 2004, les Républicains comme les Démocrates ont invité des blogueurs à couvrir leurs conventions nationales, en les accréditant comme s'ils étaient de vrais journalistes. Par ailleurs, après la défaite de John Kerry en novembre 2004, dans un acte de remise en cause assez exemplaire, les membres les plus influents du Parti démocrate ont sollicité les conseils des blogueurs les plus en vue. C'est toutefois l'élection de Howard Dean, l'homme politique favori des blogueurs libéraux à la présidence du *National Democratic Committee* en janvier 2005, qui les a fait passer du statut d'agitateurs gauchistes à celui d'acteurs proéminents de la grande coalition démocrate[10]. Lors du *YearlyKos*, la première convention sur les *netroots* organisée par Markos Moulitsas Zùniga en mai 2005, des personnalités politiques de premier plan ont pris la parole[11]. Depuis, la convention a été rebaptisée *Netroots Nation* et l'événement est devenu un passage obligé pour toute personnalité démocrate qui caresse l'idée d'un destin politique national[12]. Au lendemain des élections au Congrès en novembre 2006, Harry Reid, le tout nouveau chef de la majorité démocrate au Sénat, reconnaissait sans ambages le rôle primordial joué par la blogosphère dans la victoire écrasante du parti de l'âne : « *Without the netroots, Democrats would not be in the position we are in today* »[13]. De fait, elle a montré qu'elle pouvait faire bouger les lignes et avoir un impact sur l'issue des élections. Cela a notamment été le cas dans le Connecticut où les *netroots* avaient soutenu Ned Lamont, le candidat démocrate aux primaires sénatoriales contre le sénateur démocrate en poste Joe Lieberman, accusé d'être trop complaisant à l'égard de l'administration Bush. Arrivé derrière Ned Lamont lors des primaires, Joe Lieberman avait toutefois conservé son siège de sénateur en se présentant comme indépendant à l'élection générale. Les blogueurs ont, par ailleurs, orchestré une campagne de dénonciation contre le sénateur républicain de Virginie George Allen, qui lors d'un meeting de campagne, avait traité de « macaque » (*macaca*) un stagiaire d'origine indienne officiant pour son adversaire démocrate[14]. La vidéo qui avait été postée sur *YouTube*, avant d'être diffusée en boucle sur les grandes chaînes nationales, avait provoqué l'indignation et avait sans conteste contribué à la défaite du sénateur. Bien d'autres personnalités sont à ajouter à leur tableau de chasse. En fait si le *Drudge Report*, classé proche de la droite néoconservatrice a connu son heure de gloire en divulguant l'affaire Monica Lewinsky le 17 janvier 1998, cette tendance

---

[10] Lakshmi Chaudhry, « Can Blogs Revolutionize Progressive Politics? », *inthesetimes.com*, 6 février 2006.

[11] Ari Melber, « Politicos Court Netroots at Yearly Kos », *The Nation.com,* 26 juin 2006.

[12] Adam Nagourney, « Gathering Highlights Power of the Blog », *The New York Times*, 10 juin 2006.

[13] Eric Boehlert, *Bloggers on the Bus: How the Internet Changed Politics and the Press*, New York: Free Press, 2009.

[14] Tim Craig, Michaël D. Shear, « Allen Quip Provokes Outrage, Apology », *The Washington Post*, 15 août 2006.

à révéler des faits avant les grands médias s'est considérablement accrue au fil des ans, pour atteindre un certain paroxysme lors de la campagne de 2008. Encouragés par les blogueurs à traquer le moindre faux-pas, des anonymes qui n'avaient aucune formation en journalisme ont enregistré les propos controversés tenus par certains candidats lors de conversations informelles. Ces vidéos ont alimenté les nouvelles du soir et ont orienté le débat national. Car une fois que le *scoop* était posté sur un blog, il était repris par les *networks* télévisuels et par la presse écrite avant d'être exploité comme publicité négative par les équipes de campagne[15]. Par ailleurs si les relations entre le candidat Obama et les *netroots* ont parfois été tendues, une fois élu, le président démocrate a donné une vraie légitimité à la blogosphère, notamment en autorisant Sam Stein – un reporter qui officie exclusivement pour le *HuffingtonPost* – à lui poser des questions lors de sa première conférence de presse à la Maison-Blanche[16]. Enfin, preuve supplémentaire s'il en fallait de leur influence grandissante, le *Huffington Post* a été classé comme le blog le plus puissant au monde par l'hebdomadaire britannique *The Observer* en mars 2008, et comme le meilleur blog politique par le magazine *Time* en 2009. Le « *HuffPo* » est, par ailleurs, le seul blog politique non affilié à un autre média à avoir été classé parmi les sites les plus consultés en 2010. Il arrive, en effet, en 11e position dans une étude menée conjointement par *le Project for Excellence in Journalism* et le *Pew Internet and American Life Project* 2010.

En fait, les Républicains qui avaient été à l'avant-garde dans les années quatre-vingt-dix pour utiliser les médias comme véritables armes de propagande, notamment avec des présentateurs vedettes de la droite néoconservatrice tels Bill O'Reilly ou Rush Limbaugh, n'étaient jusqu'à très récemment pas parvenu à utiliser les nouvelles technologies avec la même maîtrise que les Démocrates. Le décalage fut manifeste lors de la campagne de 2008 où les Républicains, et particulièrement John McCain, s'avérèrent incapables d'exploiter l'Internet à leur avantage[17]. Ce n'est qu'après la défaite que de jeunes militants conservateurs se sont

---

[15] Virginie Picquet, *L'Image du président de John Kennedy à Barack Obama*, Paris : Ophrys, 2010, p. 338-339.

[16] Belinda Luscombe, « The Huffpo gets to Question Obama – Making History », *Time*, 10 février 2009.

[17] Jonathan Martin, « GOP Losing the New Media War », *Politico.com*, 24 juillet 2008.

organisés afin de tenter de reconquérir la base du parti grâce aux nouvelles technologies. Pour ce faire, ils ont créé un blog baptisé *rebuildtheparty.com* qui en a appelé à toutes les bonnes volontés pour créer une force *righroots* qui puisse faire gagner les Républicains aux élections de mi-mandat de novembre 2010, puis à l'élection présidentielle de 2012. A l'extrême droite du parti républicain, le *Tea Party movement* s'est également imposé comme une force incontournable notamment à travers des sites comme *Resistnet.com* ou *RedState.com*. Depuis, le fossé entre *netroots* et *righroots* s'est considérablement réduit et la blogosphère de droite constitue une épine dans le pied de Barack Obama[18]. Elle a notamment joué un rôle majeur dans la perte de popularité du président démocrate lors du débat sur la réforme de l'assurance maladie. Les *netroots*, qui pesaient initialement sur le débat à la marge, se sont donc progressivement imposés comme une force incontournable dans le paysage politique américain. Faut-il voir dans ce phénomène un progrès pour la démocratie ?

2. Les *netroots* : un gain pour la démocratie ?

Plusieurs éléments permettent sans conteste de répondre par l'affirmative. D'abord, la blogosphère offre un formidable espace de liberté qui insuffle une nouvelle dynamique démocratique : tout un chacun peut non seulement avoir un accès direct à des informations originales mais également débattre en dehors des cadres institutionnalisés. Les internautes de tout poil s'invitent à un débat dont les termes avaient tendance à n'être fixés que par un groupe restreint d'intellectuels et de décideurs, une minorité issue du sérail, habituée à délibérer dans l'huis-clos feutré d'institutions élitistes. Le citoyen ordinaire – si tant est qu'il se donne la peine de prendre la parole – a désormais le pouvoir d'initier le débat et parfois même d'influer sur le cours des événements :

> *In the past, much of the political agenda has been set by elites – senior party officials, elected representatives, and a congeries of policy wonks and public intellectuals stationed in think tanks, universities, issue groups, and political journals (...) This is changing. Elites are losing some of their*

[18] Patrick Ruffini, « Rising Rightroots and Declining Netroots Now at Parity (or Better) », *TheNext Right.com*, 27 septembre 2009.

agenda-setting power as a much wider set of actors begins to influence the terms of public argument. A sea change is taking place in American politics. Debates that used to be the preserve of a small, self-perpetuating group of pundits, pollsters, and policymakers are now being opened up to a much wider group.[19]

Par ailleurs, les blogs donnent la possibilité à des personnes qui ne font pas partie de l'*establishment* journalistique de faire entendre une voix qui est moins formatée que celle défendue par la ligne éditoriale des médias traditionnels. De fait, tout journaliste en herbe peut donner son opinion et les lecteurs citoyens sont invités à faire avancer la discussion en apportant leurs contributions. Les commentaires des uns nourrissent, en quelque sorte, la réflexion des autres.

Blogs are not only more open than traditional media; they are a better basis for argument. Newspapers, magazines, and broadcast media involve one-way communication from the originator of the content to the readers or audience. To be sure, there are letters to the editor, but blogs are more fundamentally dialogic. Bloggers are engaged in continual debate with each other. Many blogs also have comments sections, allowing non-bloggers to join the conversation. The result is a much more freewheeling, egalitarian form of communication than traditional media, one in which the distinction between author and reader is sometimes blurred to the point of near-irrelevance.[20]

Les *netroots*, et ce n'est pas leur moindre mérite, ont d'ailleurs à leur actif d'avoir propulsé sur le devant de la scène politico-médiatique des personnalités dont le destin politique national semblait au départ assez improbable. Howard Dean en est sans doute l'exemple le plus emblématique. Il n'aurait jamais pu passer, en quelques mois, du statut d'obscur gouverneur du Vermont à celui de vainqueur potentiel des primaires démocrates, sans le formidable relais qu'a représenté l'Internet. Avec le site *Meetup.com*, créé par son équipe de campagne, mais également *AmericansforDean.com*, mis au point par certains de ses sympathisants férus de nouvelles technologies, il a bénéficié d'un réseau social en ligne qui lui a permis de s'enquérir de l'avis des militants, de

---

[19] *Ibid.*

[20] Henry Farrel, « Bloggers and Parties: Can the Netroots Reshape American Democracy? », http://bostonreview.net, septembre/octobre 2006.

fédérer ses soutiens et de lever des sommes substantielles pour financer sa campagne. Par ailleurs si les remarquables qualités de Barack Obama ont compté pour beaucoup dans sa fulgurante ascension, l'utilisation experte des nouvelles technologies s'est également révélée un atout de poids. Le candidat démocrate s'est non seulement inspiré des techniques mises en place par Howard Dean mais il les a perfectionnées. Pour ce faire, il s'est entouré d'une armée de conseillers très au fait des nouvelles technologies dont Chris Hughes, l'un des cofondateurs de *Facebook.* Ce spécialiste des réseaux sociaux a utilisé la plupart des outils qui ont fait le succès de son site pour créer *MyBarackObama.com.* Cette stratégie a permis à Obama de recruter les sympathisants et d'organiser le militantisme : 13 millions d'Américains ont donné leur adresse Internet de manière à recevoir des informations en provenance de l'équipe de campagne. Il a ensuite activé ce réseau pour motiver les troupes à aller voter ; ainsi la veille et le jour de l'élection, des courriels ont été envoyés aux militants avec les noms de 5 personnes à appeler afin de s'assurer qu'elles se rendraient bien aux urnes. 2 millions d'Américains ont souhaité recevoir, en primeur par texto, les informations relatives à la campagne. Barack Obama avait également près de 3 millions d'amis sur *Facebook*[21]. A titre de comparaison, Howard Dean n'en comptait que 600 000 en 2004. Le candidat Obama a, de surcroît, posté 1820 vidéos sur *YouTube*. Ce recours massif aux nouvelles technologies a joué un rôle non négligeable dans le fait que de nombreux Américains, en particulier parmi les catégories les plus abstentionnistes de la population c'est à dire les jeunes et les minorités, sont allés voter pour la première fois de leur vie[22].

Un autre aspect éminemment positif des *netroots* réside dans le fait qu'ils permettent de nouvelles fonctions de vigilance et de jugement qui bousculent l'ordre établi. Car, contrairement aux médias traditionnels dont l'indépendance s'est progressivement émoussée à mesure qu'ils sont tombés aux mains d'une poignée de gigantesques corporations, les blogueurs ne sont soumis à des pressions d'aucune sorte et ils revendiquent haut et fort subjectivité et liberté de ton. Le décalage entre la manière dont l'épisode Trent Lott fut couvert par la blogosphère et par

---

[21] Larry J. Sabato, *op. cit.*, p. 197.

[22] « Surge in Minority Voting Pushed Obama Over the Top », http://www.projectvote.org.

les *mainstream media* a été de ce point de vue particulièrement édifiant. Le 5 décembre 2002, à l'occasion de la cérémonie anniversaire des 100 ans de l'ancien sénateur Strom Thurmond, Trent Lott, alors chef de la majorité républicaine au Sénat, lui rendit un hommage appuyé en tenant des propos qui semblaient faire l'apologie de la ségrégation raciale[23]. Aucun grand média ne jugea ces propos dignes d'être rapportés, à l'exclusion d'Edward O' Keefe, un jeune reporter qui les évoqua dans son blog d'ABC, *The Note*, le lendemain. Alors que l'information n'était reprise par aucun grand média, les blogueurs des sites progressistes, Joshua Marshall de *TalkingPointsMemo* (TPM) en tête, mais également les blogueurs conservateurs Andrew Sullivan et David Frum, dénoncèrent, avec virulence, les propos teintés de nostalgie ségrégationniste de Trent Lott. Virginia Postrel qui écrit pour le blog progressiste *The Scene* n'y alla pas par quatre chemins : « *Out, Out Damned Lott : Trent Lott must go. He's a disgrace to the South, to the Republican Party, to the U.S. Senate, and to the United States of America* »[24]. Dans les jours qui suivirent, alors que la blogosphère réclamait à corps et à cri la démission du chef de la majorité républicaine, le même silence assourdissant prévalait au sein des grandes rédactions. Devant la polémique qui commençait à prendre des proportions difficilement contrôlables[25], Trent Lott présenta ses excuses et ce n'est qu'à ce moment là – soit quatre jours après la parution de l'information dans le blog d'ABC – que les grands médias s'emparèrent du sujet[26]. Dans le blog *Media Notes*, qu'il rédige pour le *Washington Post*, l'éditorialiste Howard Kurtz s'offusqua de cet intérêt tardif avec un titre interrogateur : « *Why So Late On Lott?* ». Dans *Time Magazine* Dan Goodgame et Karen Tumulty saluèrent, quant à eux, le rôle décisif joué par la blogosphère dans la médiatisation de cette affaire : « *The papers did not make note of his comments until days after he had made them. But the stillness was broken by the hum of Internet "bloggers" who were*

[23] Ed O' Keefe, *The Note*, ABC News, 6 décembre 2002.

[24] Virginia Postrel, *The Scene*, 7 décembre 2002, http://www.dynamist.com/weblog/archives/2002/dec02.html.

[25] Mark Glaser, « Trent Lott Gets Bloggered: Weblogs Credited for Lott Brouhaha », *Online Journalism Review*, 17 décembre 2002.

[26] Joel David Bloom, « The Blogosphere: How a Once Humble Medium Came to Drive Elite Media Discourse and Influence Public Policy and Elections », *All Academic*, 27 août 2003.

posting their outrage and compiling rap sheets of Lott's earlier comments » [27]. Acculé, Trent Lott démissionna de ses fonctions de chef de la majorité républicaine au Sénat le 20 décembre 2002, soit 14 jours après le début de la polémique.

La blogosphère a également exercé un rôle de contre pouvoir implacable dans ce qui constitue indéniablement son plus haut fait d'arme, à savoir l'enquête qui a conduit à la démission de l'*Attorney General* Alberto Gonzales. Là encore, le site TPM fut à la pointe du combat en s'intéressant à des faits qui n'avaient pas été jugés dignes d'être exploités par les grands médias. En alliant le journalisme d'enquête et l'appel à ses lecteurs pour qu'ils lui fassent part des informations locales qu'ils détenaient, Joshua Marshall permit de faire éclater un des scandales majeurs qui a entaché l'administration de George W. Bush. Le créateur et blogueur en chef de *TalkingPointsMemo* fut, en effet, le premier à soupçonner Alberto Gonzales de se livrer à un vigoureux « nettoyage » du corps des procureurs généraux jugés hostiles à l'administration. Il flaira, en fait, l'affaire à la lecture d'articles tirés de quotidiens locaux faisant état de la révocation de juges fédéraux. Bien qu'il ne disposât que de très peu d'indices, il posta, néanmoins, les quelques faits qu'il avait en sa possession et exhorta ses lecteurs à aller chercher des informations dans la presse régionale. Cette interactivité absolue dans la recherche de la vérité s'est révélée particulièrement fructueuse : de nombreux internautes, aux quatre coins du pays, ont envoyé des informations que les blogueurs de TPM ont recoupées entre elles et qui ont permis de mettre au jour l'existence un schéma identique dans les procédures de licenciement des neuf juges. Voyant qu'un faisceau d'indices concordants tendait à démontrer que l'*Attorney General* avait été le grand ordonnateur d'une politisation de la justice américaine, les grands médias s'emparèrent à leur tour de l'affaire, précipitant du même coup la chute d'Alberto Gonzales qui présenta sa démission le 27 août 2007. Jay Garney, journaliste à *Time Magazine*, qui avait initialement raillé Joshua Marshall pour sa propension à voir le complot partout[28], a par la suite été forcé de reconnaître que les blogueurs de TPM avaient fait preuve d'une ténacité exemplaire. Joshua

---

[27] Dan Goodgame, Karen Tumulty, « Tripped Up by History », *Time Magazine*, 23 décembre 2002.

[28] Paul Mc Leary, « How Talking Points Memo Beat the Big Boys on the US Attorney Story », *Columbia Journalism Review*, 15 mars 2007.

Marshall se vit décerner le prix George Polk 2007 du journalisme en récompense de sa pugnacité dans la recherche de la vérité[29]. Cette distinction a apporté un peu plus d'eau au moulin de ceux qui voient dans le phénomène *netroots* un formidable gain pour la démocratie. Car si la blogosphère a davantage un rôle de renforcement des positions déjà existantes que d'information ouverte[30], ces deux épisodes illustrent de manière éclatante qu'elle peut aussi être en première ligne pour dénoncer les égarements et autres abus de pouvoir des puissants.

Enfin, un autre élément à mettre au crédit des *netroots* est le fait qu'ils ont révolutionné la manière dont les campagnes électorales sont financées. En exploitant à leur profit la grande réforme du financement de la vie politique votée en 2002, ils ont réduit la mainmise des lobbies. Les blogueurs ont, en effet, immédiatement compris l'intérêt que représentait pour eux cette nouvelle législation et ils ont utilisé leur influence pour convaincre des millions d'internautes de contribuer, souvent pour la première fois de leur vie, aux campagnes de certains candidats démocrates. Ainsi en interdisant aux partis de récolter de l'argent provenant de dons non réglementés (*soft money*) qui atteignaient des sommes colossales et en favorisant les dons de « *hard money* », réglementés et limités initialement à 2000, puis à 2300 dollars à partir de 2006, la loi McCain Feingold a ouvert l'ère du « *small donor* »[31]. Howard Dean a été précurseur en la matière, car il a été le premier candidat au sein de son parti, à démontrer la viabilité d'un système de financement fondé sur la blogosphère. Les blogueurs, Jerome Amstrong en tête puisqu'il était chargé de gérer le site de campagne du candidat Dean, ont encouragé des millions d'internautes à faire des dons et ce aussi modestes fussent-ils. Pendant les primaires démocrates de 2004, l'ex gouverneur du Vermont obtint 41 millions de dollars quasi exclusivement grâce à la Toile, la contribution moyenne étant de moins

---

[29] Noam Cohen, « Blogger, Sans Pajama, Rakes Much and a Prize », *The New York Times*, 25 février 2008.

[30] Anne Deysine (dir.), *Etats-Unis : Une nouvelle donne*, Paris : La Documentation Française, 2010, p. 26.

[31] Françoise Coste, « 'The Whole Blogosphere Is Watching' ou la prise d'assaut du Parti démocrate par la blogosphère libérale », *Revue de recherche en civilisation américaine* (en ligne), http:rrca.revues.org/index 160.html. Depuis, la Cour suprême a invalidé une partie des dispositions prévues par le *Bipartisan Campaign Reform Act* de 2002 dans l'arrêt *Citizens United v. FEC* en 2010 ; voir, Anne Deysine (dir.), *supra*, p. 77-82.

de 100 dollars. John Kerry leva également un tiers de son budget de campagne en ligne, soit 57 millions de dollars. Mais là encore, Barack Obama fit exploser tous les records puisque près de 3 millions d'internautes lui ont permis de récolter la somme vertigineuse de 500 millions de dollars[32]. La multiplication des petites sommes a bel et bien conforté la maxime selon laquelle les petits ruisseaux font les grandes rivières[33]. Outre le fait que la levée de fonds sur l'Internet limite l'influence des groupes d'intérêt, ce qui constitue déjà en soi une avancée incontestable, elle implique véritablement les sympathisants de base qui se voient dotés du pouvoir d'influer sur le résultat d'une élection, ne serait-ce qu'en propulsant sur le devant de la scène politico-médiatique une personnalité qui n'aurait pas pu émerger comme candidat crédible, faute de financement suffisant.

Depuis 2004, le site *ActBlue*, créé avec le soutien actif des *netroots* progressistes, donne la possibilité aux internautes de faire des dons aux candidats démocrates afin de les aider à financer leur campagne. Depuis sa création, le site a permis de récolter près de 170 millions de dollars. Les *righroots* ont créé un site comparable, baptisé *Slatecard*, dans son sillage[34]. D'aucuns déploreront, néanmoins, le fait que les sommes colossales récoltées sur l'Internet aient poussé Barack Obama à renier une de ses promesses de campagne en refusant de faire appel au financement public. Cette décision n'a toutefois pas ébranlé outre mesure la blogosphère de gauche qui a vu dans ce phénomène la première étape d'un processus qui devrait conduire à la refonte du Parti démocrate et à sa reprise en main par les citoyens ordinaires.

3. Des dérives inquiétantes

Après avoir mis en évidence le bénéfice démocratique que constituent les *netroots*, il convient d'analyser en quoi ils présentent également certains effets délétères pour la qualité du débat politique. Un des

---

[32] José Antonio Vargas, « Obama Raised Half a Billion Online », *The Washington Post*, 20 novembre 2008.

[33] Rick Hasen, « Small Donors Grow into a Big Political Force », *The Washington Post*, 2 mai 2004.

[34] Micah, L. Sifry, « Right-roots vs Net-roots: Whose Online Donor Base is Bigger? », http///techpresident.com/blog-entry/right-roots-vs-net-roots-whose-online-donor-base-bigger, 5 mars 2010.

problèmes que pose la blogosphère réside dans le fait qu'elle aggrave la polarisation de la société américaine en raison de sa tonalité très partisane. De fait qu'ils soient progressistes ou conservateurs, les blogueurs rejettent toute forme de compromis et adoptent des positions qui sont souvent tranchées, voire parfois sectaires. Alors que les grands médias de l'*establishment* offrent généralement une tribune à tous les acteurs du débat public et mettent un point d'honneur à présenter les informations de manière factuelle, en faisant une distinction nette entre les articles – qui présentent les faits – et les éditoriaux – qui expriment une opinion, laquelle n'engage que leurs auteurs – les blogueurs revendiquent l'utilisation de leurs blogs comme outils de propagande politique et assument totalement leur soif de victoire partisane. Ils reconnaissent d'ailleurs volontiers que leur intention n'est pas de convaincre les indécis ou de débattre avec leurs adversaires, mais de mobiliser leur camp afin de remporter des victoires politiques. En outre, l'immense majorité des lecteurs de blogs consultent des sites qui affichent des convictions idéologiques identiques aux leurs. Le problème est que, si chacun sélectionne son information en fonction de ce qu'il a envie de lire et si nul n'est plus exposé à des opinions susceptibles de contredire les siennes, l'intolérance grandit. Alors que le paysage politique américain est déjà excessivement fragmenté, ce phénomène tend à radicaliser les positions et à creuser les antagonismes, comme le montrent les conclusions d'une étude réalisée par les politologues Eric Lawrence, Henry Farrell et John Sides :

> *Deliberation entails a dialogue between opposing views, but blog authors tend to link to their ideological kindred and blog readers gravitate to blogs that reinforce their existing viewpoints. Both sides of the ideological spectrum inhabit largely cloistered cocoons of cognitive consonance, thereby creating little opportunity for a substantive exchange across partisan or ideological lines (...) Discourse in the political blogosphere is more compatible with accounts that emphasize the importance of clashes of interest, sharp disagreement and conflict in deliberation.*[35]

[35] Eric Lawrence, Henry Farrell, John Sides, « Self-Segregation or Deliberation? Blog Readership, Participation, and Polarization in American Politics », *Perspectives on Politics*, n° 1, mars 2010, p.152.

A cela s'ajoute l'obsession de transparence d'une société qui a érigé le droit de tout savoir sur les personnalités connues, les hommes politiques y compris, en modèle éclatant de société démocratique. D'une certaine façon, la quête du *scoop*, de la vidéo qui va piéger ou déstabiliser l'adversaire, s'avère un moyen comme un autre d'influer sur l'issue des élections. La stratégie selon laquelle la fin justifie les moyens est érigée en principe absolu. Cette exploitation tous azimuts des failles des personnalités politiques n'est certes pas nouvelle, mais les effets sont décuplés du fait des possibilités infinies qu'offre la Toile. N'importe quel anonyme peut filmer une personnalité à son insu et envoyer quasi en temps réel des images ou des propos qui vont créer le scandale. N'importe quel internaute peut poster une vidéo virale de manière opportune, révéler un fait – même sorti d'un passé lointain – pour tenter de saper les chances de victoire ou salir la réputation d'une personnalité politique. La plus petite maladresse, le moindre dérapage verbal se propagent à la vitesse de l'éclair et l'élu impliqué apparaît alors dans sa trivialité la plus navrante. Le risque est que le candidat qui veut avoir des chances d'être élu contrôle son message au point de s'en tenir à un discours totalement aseptisé :

> *Le pouvoir de surveillance que constitue l'Internet peut conduire les acteurs politiques à surprotéger leurs actions. On le voit déjà lors des campagnes électorales : les candidats, sachant que leurs moindres actes ou déclarations peuvent être désormais captés et diffusés sur Twitter ou YouTube, ont de plus en plus tendance à corseter leur communication.*[36]

Une telle prime au discours formaté est-elle vraiment un progrès pour la démocratie ? Une personnalité publique qui brigue ou détient un mandat électif n'a-t-elle pas le droit à ses moments d'intimité ? Cette forme particulièrement agressive de journalisme, cet empiètement systématique sur la sphère privée dont la classe dirigeante porte une part non négligeable de responsabilité et cette transparence absolue à laquelle on veut astreindre les politiques, revêtent un caractère totalitaire. De plus, à force de flatter les instincts les plus vils d'une population friande de tout

---

[36] Thierry Vedel, « La généralisation d'Internet engendre des effets pervers», *Le Monde*, 3 décembre 2010.

ce qui a une odeur de soufre, on abaisse le débat, accentue le cynisme et exacerbe le populisme[37]. Loin de se cantonner aux personnes, cette obsession de transparence concerne également les données publiques dont l'Internet s'avère un puissant moyen de diffusion, comme l'a montré de manière éclatante WikiLeaks. Si ces pratiques servent des intentions, au départ parfaitement louables, dans la mesure où elles permettent aux citoyens de contrôler l'activité de leurs élus et de leurs institutions publiques, poussées à l'extrême, elles pourraient avoir l'effet inverse de celui recherché en sapant encore davantage la confiance déjà chancelante que le peuple a dans son système politique. C'est en tous les cas l'opinion du juriste et professeur à Harvard Lawrence Lessing, pourtant farouche défenseur de la liberté sur l'Internet. Dans un article intitulé « Against Transparency » paru dans le *New Republic* le 21 octobre 2010, il met en effet en garde contre les périls d'une « transparence nue, décontextualisée », arguant que cette obsession de transparence pourrait devenir par dérive ou intentionnellement, un instrument d'opacité[38]. Dans un article du *Monde*, le politologue Thierry Vedel se fait également l'écho des effets pervers induits par cette surenchère:

> *En augmentant substantiellement la quantité de données fournies aux citoyens, on complexifie leur travail de surveillance. Démêler l'essentiel de l'anecdotique exige du temps et des compétences cognitives, et l'on risque d'instaurer de plus grandes inégalités entre citoyens. Par ailleurs, une totale transparence paralyse parfois l'action publique. Les compromis qu'elle nécessite ne peuvent être atteints en pleine lumière, celle-ci conduisant souvent les parties en présence à radicaliser ou figer leurs positions.*[39]

En outre si la liberté de parole que procure l'Internet comporte de nombreux effets bénéfiques, cette expression directe, sans filtre, est à double tranchant car tout internaute peut désormais se livrer à loisir à toutes les outrances verbales, dans une espèce de défoulement malsain.

---

[37] Virginie Picquet, *op. cit.*, p. 260.

[38] Lawrence Lessing, « Against Transparency », *The New Republic*, vol. 240, n° 19, 21 octobre 2009.

[39] Thierry Vedel, *op. cit.*

De fait, la Toile tend à faire sauter les dernières inhibitions. En conséquence, les jugements à l'emporte-pièce, les caricatures et les insultes prolifèrent, alors même que nombre d'internautes ne disposent ni de la distance ni de toutes les informations pour appréhender les subtilités d'un problème donné. Comme le notait l'historien Arthur Schlesinger Jr., l'interactivité, le manque de recul et la précipitation ne sont guère propices à un débat démocratique apaisé et constructif : « *Interactivity encourages instant responses, discourages second thoughts, and offers outlets for demagoguery, egomania, insult, and hate*»[40]. La tournure qu'a prise le débat sur la réforme de l'assurance maladie au cours de l'année 2009 en a donné une illustration saisissante. Il a, en effet, été l'occasion d'un déchaînement de propos outranciers et de contre-vérités assénés avec une violence inouïe. De nombreux blogs conservateurs ont redoublé d'agressivité pour diaboliser certains volets de la loi, accusant Barack Obama d'incitation à l'avortement et à l'euthanasie, les plus jusqu'au- boutistes – dont Sarah Palin sur *Facebook* – allant même jusqu'à affirmer que le président démocrate avait l'intention de mettre en place des tribunaux de la mort (*death panels).* De fait, l'un des aspects les plus préoccupants de la blogosphère réside, sans conteste, dans le fait que l'information circule de manière anarchique et sans aucun garde-fou. N'importe qui peut poster un commentaire injurieux, donner une information erronée, voire totalement fallacieuse sans être inquiété. La Toile bruisse de rumeurs et dénouer le vrai du faux relève souvent de la gageure. Un phénomène que Barack Obama avait jugé suffisamment préoccupant pendant la campagne pour créer *fightthesmears.com*, un site exclusivement consacré à neutraliser les rumeurs, déjouer les attaques et tuer dans l'œuf les insinuations[41]. Cela ne l'avait toutefois pas empêché d'être la victime de multiples campagnes de manipulation orchestrées par certains blogs conservateurs et relayées par quelques ténors de la droite radicale tels Bill O'Reilly ou Rush Limbaugh. Des sites proches du Parti républicain comme *Newsmax.com*, avaient, par exemple, tenté d'instiller le soupçon sur la confession religieuse du candidat démocrate en postant des titres volontairement équivoques tels que : « *Was Obama a Muslim?* ». Dans

[40] Arthur Schlesinger Jr., *War and the American Presidency*, New York: Norton, 2004, p. 111-112.
[41] *Ibid.*, p. 340.

la même veine, le blog *wnd.com* avait titré : « *Muslim Photo Raises Obama Connection Questions* », faisant allusion à la photo mise en ligne sur le *Drudge Report* où l'on voyait Barack Obama porter une tenue traditionnelle africaine. Les résultats d'un sondage réalisé par le *Pew Research Center*, peu de temps avant l'élection, montrèrent que la manœuvre avait partiellement porté ses fruits puisque seulement 47% des sympathisants républicains pensaient que Barack Obama était chrétien et, parmi les partisans de John McCain, 16% croyaient qu'il était musulman[42]. Bien d'autres allégations, notamment celle selon laquelle Barack Obama ne serait pas né aux Etats-Unis et ne pourrait donc pas être président, avaient également tenté de semer le doute et créer la confusion dans les esprits[43]. Outre le fait que ces campagnes de désinformation et de diffamation sont potentiellement dévastatrices pour toute personne publique, elles sont également délétères pour la démocratie car elles exacerbent la défiance des citoyens à l'égard de leurs institutions représentatives et constituent un terreau fertile pour la montée en puissance du populisme. Enfin, sans constituer une menace à proprement parler, il faut aussi préciser que la blogosphère a ses limites car si elle a la volonté louable d'impliquer le citoyen ordinaire, les blogueurs sont dans leur très grande majorité des hommes blancs, éduqués, issus de la classe moyenne supérieure, qui s'adressent à des lecteurs qui présentent les mêmes caractéristiques ethniques et socio-économiques[44] :

> *If blogs derive their credibility from being the "voice of the people," surely we should be concerned about which opinions get attention over others. The question of representation affects not just who is blogging – and with great success—but also the audience of these blogs. What kind of democratic consensus does the blogosphere reflect when the people participating in it are most likely to be white, well-educated men?*[45]

---

[42] Mary Lu Carnevale, *The Wall Street Journal*, 21 octobre 2008.

[43] Cass R. Sunstein, *On Rumors: How Falsehoods Spread, Why We Believe Them, What Can Be Done*, New York: Farrar, Strauss and Giroux, 2009.

[44] « Blogging in 2010: What You Need to Know», http://www.searchenginejournal.com, 17 mars 2010.

[45] Lakshmi Chaudhry, *op. cit.*

Ce manque de diversité constitue indéniablement une forme de faiblesse. Car si les principaux acteurs de la blogosphère se targuent de redonner le pouvoir à la base, cette ambition apparaît quelque peu illusoire. De fait, la difficulté pour tout citoyen issu d'un milieu intellectuellement et socialement défavorisé, ne réside pas tant dans sa capacité à se procurer un ordinateur que dans son absence de volonté de participer au débat[46]. Certains blogueurs, à l'instar de Markos Moulitsas Zùniga qui est lui-même l'un des rares à ne pas correspondre au profil du blogueur type puisqu'il est d'origine salvadorienne, balaient d'un revers de la main ce reproche et estime que les *netroots* se font, en quelque sorte, les porte-parole des sans voix.

Quoi qu'il en soit, en permettant de nouvelles formes d'exercice démocratique, en faisant pression sur les gouvernants et en donnant la parole à tout citoyen qui souhaite la prendre, les *netroots* représentent un atout incontestable pour la démocratie. Toutefois la liberté quasi-illimitée que procure la blogosphère comporte un certain nombre d'effets pervers qui ne doivent pas être sous-estimés. L'enjeu n'engage rien de moins que la qualité du débat politique et, en définitive, la démocratie.

Virginie Picquet

Université d'Angers

[46] « The Score: Profile of a Netroot », *imediaconnection*, 22 juin 2006.

L'Impact de l'Internet sur la culture politique américaine

Rerouting Politics: Networks, Netroots, and the U.S. Cultural Imaginary

We live today under a new world order.
The web which weaves together all things envelops our bodies,
Bathes our limbs,
In a halo of joy.
—Michel Houellebecq, *The Elementary Particles*

Since I end up making some bold claims, let me start out less ambitiously, by rehashing a few venerable commonplaces. First off, any polity, and any politics for that matter, rests on a reasonably shared political philosophy or at least implies one; any political project speaks, explicitly or less so, to a broader vision. In turn, any philosophy, "big picture", or whatever you might call it is culture-bound and thus informed by a certain cultural imaginary. Now, if all this is true – and because what I do is literary-cultural studies – the basic question I want to raise next goes something like this: what kind of cultural imaginary does the recent proliferation of networks foreground inside and outside politics? For, it seems to me, the wildfire spread of new media and techno-financial webs, including the digital netroots behind Howard Dean's 2002-2005 spectacular if short-lived career boost, attests, in the U.S. and elsewhere, not only to a hunger for political change but also to a change in how people view themselves and the world around them. As I have been arguing on a number of occasions lately, a new imaginary is taking center stage in post-Cold War U.S. culture. Very simply speaking, relation – seeing oneself with an other in the wider world – provides the building block of this imaginary. Therefore, I call this imaginary relational. I also suggest here, as I have done more extensively in my 2011 book *Cosmodernism*,[1] that *relationality* is the new cultural-political *rationality* of the post-1989, hypernetworked aftermath.

A crucial watershed in modern history, the Berlin Wall's fall was, not unlike the New York City Twin Towers' on 9/11, both an American and a world event. Needless to say, the U.S. Marines were not its heroes, nor did it happen in North America. And yet, for one thing, the U.S. had been deeply involved in it; for another, the Wall's collapse has been playing a remarkably transformative role across American society; like the rest of the world, the U.S. changed forever "in or about" 1989, as Virginia Woolf might have put it. Most historians agree that the 1970s and even the early 1980s had allowed only inklings of the new, post-1989 global setup. Comparatively speaking, the pre-1989 world was a world asunder. What prevailed during the Cold War was an antinomian logic of spheres, blocs, regions, and countries separated by all sorts of "curtains" and checkpoints and inherently affected by the kind of cultural-epistemological "tunnel vision" that usually comes with such geopolitical "mincing" of one's world. Instead, the period following the Cold War witnesses the acceleration of globalization, which, in essence, sets in train processes geared economically, politically, technoculturally, and otherwise, to an unprecedented expansion and thickening of the world's relational makeup inside and across national boundaries. The world of accelerated, "late," or "strong" globalization is quintessentially if not uniformly (nor fairly) more and more hypernetworked.[2]

This stage in the age-old global developments has been covered *ad nauseam* by cohorts of critics;[3] for this reason, I will refrain from rehearsing the arguments of the enormous literature on the topic. I will say, though, that, in theory, late globalization should be ideally conducive to cooperative scenarios of cultural production and

---

[1] Christian Moraru, *Cosmodernism: American Narrative, Late Globalization, and the New Cultural Imaginary*, Ann Arbor, MI: University of Michigan Press, 2011.

[2] David Held puts forth the "strong globalization thesis" in the "Afterword" to his anthology *A Globalizing World? Culture, Economics, Politics*, p. 171, London: Routledge in association with The Open University, 2000. Christopher J. Kollmeyer takes up Held's weak/strong globalization distinction in "Globalization, Class Compromise, and American Exceptionalism: Political Change in 16 Advanced Capitalist Countries," *Critical Sociology* 29, no. 3, October 2003, p. 369-391.

[3] See, among others, Martin Albrow, *The Global Age: State and Society Beyond Modernity*, Stanford, CA: Stanford University Press, 1997.

subjectivity fashioning. After all, as has been pointed out, what distinguishes our moment from earlier globalization is the former's superiorly "webbed" makeup, its high connectivity. We are living, or so we are told, in a "network society" where the fostering of identity and meaning individually and collectively, in and of "our" culture, involves, indeed, necessitates recurring references to other cultures and "others" in general.[4] The pre-1989 global setup had been less technologized and hence less networked, more country- and region-focused, in brief, "thinner." By contrast – a contrast starker, I think, that some would allow – what comes after is "denser": conspicuously more systemic, more technological and thus more integrated, transnational and cross-regional. Critics like Martin Albrow and Roland Robertson believe the transition from one to another occurs over a wider time swath (1945-1990s in Albrow, 1960s-1990s in Robertson), whereas Thomas L. Friedman revisits the "1989 argument" made in *The Lexus and the Olive Tree* and reiterated in *Longitudes and Latitudes* to conclude that a "new whole era: Globalization 3.0" commences circa 2000.[5] In my own estimation, 1989 was what Jean-Pierre Warnier would deem a true *année charnière*, a "hinge year" on which turned the doors opening, in the U.S. and abroad, onto the highly interconnected world of late globalization.[6]

A "new beginning," then? So contend Albrow, Arif Dirlik, and others who, against Francis Fukuyama's controversial "end of history" thesis, point to the globally inaugural thrust of the Cold War's end.[7] What with the downfall of the Berlin and related walls, barriers, and divisions, 1989 was the single major historical-geopolitical milestone that, at the end of the twentieth century, signaled that we meant to leave behind a divided, compartmental, cloistered world – Pierre Chaunu's *universe*

---

[4] Manuel Castells, *The Information Age: Economy, Society, and Culture*, vol. I, *The Rise of the Network Society*, 2nd ed., Oxford, UK: Blackwell, 2000, p. 500-508.

[5] Thomas L. Friedman, *Longitudes and Latitudes: Exploring the World After September 11*, New York: Farrar, Strauss and Giroux, p. 3; *The World Is Flat: A Brief History of the Twentieth-First Century*. Further Updated and Expanded, New York: Farrar, Strauss and Giroux, 2006, p. 10.

[6] Jean-Pierre Warnier, *La mondialisation de la culture*, 3rd éd., Paris : La Découverte, 2004, p. 32.

[7] Albrow, *The Global Age*, p. 77; Arif Dirlik, "Globalization as the End and the Beginning of History," http://www.scribd.com/doc/2546826/Globalization-as-the-End-and-the-Beginning-of-History (accessed July 27, 2008); Francis Fukuyama, *The End of History and the Last Man*, New York: Free Press, 1992.

cloisonné – and enter a new one, which held out the promise of experiencing itself as being-together with unrivaled pathos.[8] Thus, the post-Wall era purported to be equally post-divisional *urbi et orbi*, in Berlin and worldwide, to put an end to the East-West "bipolarity" and to the gulfs and schisms directly and indirectly derived from it.[9] On this score, Friedman's observation is not entirely off the mark: "to appreciate the far-reaching flattening [globalizing] effects of the fall of the Berlin Wall, it's always best to talk to non-Germans or non-Russians" such as Indian businesspeople *in* India, for they would explain to you how new digitizing technologies have made Bangalore into a Boston suburb.[10]

Are we talking about a happy "Fall," then? So it seemed and actually was for many in Central and Eastern Europe, in the former Soviet republics, around the world, and in the U.S. no less, for Cold War Manichaeanism had also exacted its toll on the American public imaginary, policies, and welfare. The world's "fall into relation" appeared to meet the logical, geocultural and political condition for closing the world's economic gaps and healing its historical wounds. The ensuing "postlapsarian" global certainly advertised itself as a postconflictual state of affairs of a world decreasingly apart, in which the polarizing and *disconnective* impetus of the Cold War and of modernity overall at long last took a back seat to a rationally managed worldly *connectedness* that in turn prompted people to see themselves *sub specie coniunctionis*, as embodiments of an existentially and culturally relational logic. This utopianism got resounding traction in sweeping pronouncements of the "new world order" sort made by Mikhail Gorbachev in the heyday of *perestroika*, then by George H. W. Bush as a prelude to Desert Storm. Both were belated echoes to the "new world" rhetoric of Woodrow Wilson's 1918 "Fourteen Points" speech, soon to be canceled out by the "new world *dis*order" counterrhetoric of Ken Jowitt's 1992 influential book, followed by similar interventions by Zygmunt Bauman, Tzvetan Todorov, Amin Maalouf, Immanuel

---

[8] On Pierre Chaunu's *univers cloisonné*, see his book, *Histoire, science sociale: la durée, l'espace et l'homme à l'époque moderne*, Paris : Société d'édition de l'enseignement supérieur, 1974.

[9] Roland Robertson, "Mapping the Global Condition: Globalization as the Central Concept," in *Global Culture: Nationalism, globalization and modernity. A Theory, Culture & Society Special Issue*, ed. Mike Featherstone, London: Sage, 1990, p. 27.

[10] Friedman, *The World Is Flat*, p. 53 and p. 63.

Wallerstein, and other chroniclers of "*le Nouveau Désordre mondial*."[11] Suspiciously "orderly," one smacks of wishful, arguably self-interested thinking. The other presents us with a hopelessly entropic, world-scale pandemonium. One is overly institutional and simplistically centripetal, what with its late 1980s-early 1990s roll call of accomplishments: the tearing down of the Iron Curtain; the 1993 signing of the North-American Free-Trade Agreement (NAFTA); the 1995 consolidation of the Bretton Woods institutions and agreements through the World Trade Organization (WTO); the new initiatives of the International Monetary Fund (IMF) and The World Bank; the expansion of the European Union and the North Atlantic Treaty Organization (NATO); the new non-governmental organizations cropping up all over the world while the older ones bolster their activities inside or outside the United Nations; the Internet and other advances in communications, commerce, finance, and afferent technologies. The other is exceedingly centrifugal, registering chiefly the regional crises and ethnic-religious conflicts that also multiply during this time following the breakup of former supranational and imperial entities such as the Eastern bloc, the USSR, and Yugoslavia. One hawks a ubiquitously nurturing relatedness and implicitly a top-down worldly coherence yet describes them in policy-oriented, abstract, impersonal terms. Dismissing relatedness altogether, the other makes a half-gesture toward bottom-up movements although they evoke little more than the violent incoherence of a "Balkanized" planet. Both world pictures are therefore macrostructural. In that, they describe the world as much as they shortchange it.

In reaction to this reductive picture, my take on the geocultural context arising after the Cold War is at once more modest and more ambitious. Which is to say, I do acknowledge that, a turning point in history, 1989 heralds a new world order. But this is neither of the orderly

[11] Ken Jowitt, *New World Disorder: The Leninist Extinction*, Berkeley, CA: University of California Press, 1992. Bauman refers to Jowitt's book in *Globalization: The Human Consequences*, New York: Columbia University Press, 1998, p. 59. For Todorov, see *Le Nouveau Désordre mondial. Réflexions d'un Européen*. Préface de Stanley Hoffmann, Paris : Robert Laffont, 2003. On the "chaos" of contemporary world, also see Amin Maalouf's recent book *Le dérèglement du monde*, Paris : Grasset & Fasquelle, 2009, and Immanuel Wallerstein's article "Revolts Against the System," *New Left Review*, 2nd series, n° 18, November-December 2002, p. 37.

nor of the disorderly kind. It is not an order of the world per se either, a neatly unified geopolitical or economic setup. I do find both grand narratives wanting, first and foremost because they miss the "micro" level, in particular the place of the individual and individual communities in the global scheme of things and principally the role played by the imagination in the developing of this scheme or "order." I think it is urgent that we make up for this shortcoming by refocusing the discussion on the mental picture individual and groups paint of themselves, their worlds, and the world beyond. Accordingly, what my analysis uncovers is not a "totality," a fully integrated (or disintegrating) world (dis)order, much as, again, the late-global world, and America within it, is distinct from the pre-1989 world. What I bring to light is chiefly an order of the imagination, more precisely, an imaginary in the making. Or, if this is an order of the world, it is one to the extent that the world is this order's object, gets "ordered" – taken apart, reshuffled, and put back together – in combinations that are meaningful and critical, suggestive of a structural coherence and a critical scrutiny absent from the neoliberal picture of the actual planet. Both the cohesiveness and the critique draw on a consistent and individualizing wrestling with that very distinctiveness of the post-1989 U.S. and world, namely, with a qualitatively and quantitatively unequaled relationality. Unlike grandiose statements of the geopolitical-corporate sort, the worldview I emphasize here puts this burgeoning relatedness on trial. Neither ignoring nor discounting it, I take note of its presence. In effect, I do not hesitate to pinpoint the excessive presence *in the world* of a "macro" sort of circuitry powered by economic and military flows decided "from above," and I offer up in exchange an alternative vision *of the world.* This outlook boils down to a different relational model. The model does not pull us out of the webbed world's expanding material culture of relatedness. Weary of the latter's record, it only proposes that we imagine it otherwise, ethically. What I have in mind, specifically, is an ethics of relationality that undergirds the bulk of our cultural practices and dealings and, in that, grounds – or should ground – political networking no less. Notably, the onset of this relational ethic is part and parcel of an ongoing, broader paradigm shift across discourses, disciplines, epistemologies, and areas of everyday, material-symbolic life in the U.S. and beyond. This is, once again, an epochal shift, if not completely away from postmodern society, then into a qualitatively new stage of postmodernism: the "network society" of post-1989 globalization.

To clarify what might make this sort of relationality ethical, what I must ask at this point is this: exactly what kind of relationality is Manuel Castells' network society fostering? This question too is a tough one. But we should put it because how we answer it could help us get a grip on the thorny meaning of netroots politics. A first step toward that answer might be just to own up to the complexity of what we are dealing with. Critics overall agree that, in John Tomlinson's words, the society Castells describes is a "rapidly developing and ever-dens[ify]ing network of interconnections and interdependences." But the agreement ends here because network linkages among people, cultures, and places can be construed, Tomlinson admits, "in a number of different modalities."[12] In principle, there is nothing wrong, of course, with connectivity and its planetary thickening. Yet there is everything wrong with "netocracy" that connects to exploit and disenfranchise. No question about it: networks can empower people. So did fax machines in Beijing's Tiananmen Square back in 1989 and Twitter during Iran's presidential elections twenty years later. But the networks can also enfetter. Yahoo! did nothing else a few years ago, when it turned over to the Chinese government records that led to the jailing of several dissidents. The same networks can speed up relief assistance *and* the planet's "McDonaldization." To outspoken net buffs like Friedman, Bill Gates, Alexander Bard, and Jan Soderqvist, networks are *the* solution; to net skeptics à la Alain Finkielkraut, Paul Soriano, Steven Shaviro, Fredric Jameson, and Slavoj Žižek, they are "public enemy number one," as Jean Baudrillard writes in *Cool Memories IV*.[13] In consequence, highly networked, late globalization is, Michael Hardt and Antonio Negri assure us, hardly "univocal," and, again, one must recognize that it

---

[12] John Tomlinson, *Globalization and Culture*, Chicago, IL: The University of Chicago Press, 1999, p. 2.

[13] See Alain Finkielkraut and Paul Soriano, *Internet, l'inquiétante extase*, Paris : Fayard, 2001; Alexander Bard and Jan Soderqvist, *Netocracy: The Power Elite and Life after Capitalism*, London: Reuters, 2002. For a net-skeptic rebuttal of Bard and Soderqvist, see Žižek, "The Ideology of the Empire and Its Traps," in *Empire's New Clothes: Reading Negri and Hardt*, ed. Paul A. Passavant and Jodi Dean, New York: Routledge, 2004, p. 258-261. For Baudrillard, see *Cool Memories IV: 1995-2000*, trans. Chris Turner, London: Verso, 2003, p. 24.

does run the whole gamut, from the diversification/localization of global vectors and influences to Robertson's "glocalization" to the serialization/homogenization of local cultures.[14] The majority of writers pinpoints, however, the pronounced "homo-hegemonizing" penchant of contemporary networks, as Derrida called it.[15] Many of these networks come into place to standardize and subsume the world to historically privileged locales, standards, and agendas. This aspect of planetary "flattening" cannot be glossed over. Why? Because, deceptively enough, it gestures to lateral, even bottom-up moves; because it implies challenges to extant stratifications of power, party bureaucracy, old-boys clubs, back-room deals, and other types of exclusionary, endogenous politics; and because it is otherwise suggestive of democracy, fairness, increased participation, and other things of such "horizontal" nature while its actual effects may be and often are "vertical," reworking the network into a hierarchy with its command nodes, one-way channels, preferred circuits, and unacknowledged profit schemes.

With this observation, I now circle back to the second question above to answer it as follows: to a worrisome extent, post-1989 globalization means, inside and outside the U.S., the strengthening of relationality as a rationalizing, re-centering vehicle. Insofar as it does the bidding of

---

[14] On Hardt, Negri, and the political ambiguity of global networks, see their *Empire*, Cambridge, MA: Harvard University Press, 2000, xv, and *Multitude: War and Democracy in the Age of Empire*, New York: Penguin, 2004, p. 79-91. See too Jodi Dean, "The Networked Empire: Communication and Capitalism and the Hope for Politics," in Passavant and Dean, *Empire's New Clothes*, p. 265-288. In Peter Day and Douglas Schuler's collection, *Common Practice in the Network Society*, London: Routledge: 2004, see especially the editors' introductory essay, "Community practice: an alternative vision of the network," p.1-20. For "glocalization," Roland Robertson's *Globalization: Social Theory and Global Culture*, London: Sage, 1992, is still the *locus classicus*. On "glocalization" and "heterogenization," helpful is Robertson, "Glocalization: Time-Space and Homogeneity-Heterogeneity," in *Global Modernities*, ed. Featherstone, Lash, and Robertson, London: Sage, 1995, 40. Relevant to the notion and the debate around it is, in the same collection, Timothy W. Luke's essay "New World Order or Neo-world Orders: Power, Politics and Ideology in Informationalizing Glocalities," p. 91-107.

[15] On globalization as "homo-hegemonization," see Derrida, *Negotiations: Interventions and Interviews, 1971-2001*, ed., trans., and with an introduction by Elizabeth Rottenberg, Stanford, CA: Stanford University Press, 2002, p. 373.

modernity in forms and with intensities previously unknown, our age carries on the selfsame logic according to which, in a relation, contact, exchange, affiliation, or any other kind of association, one element attempts to control and co-opt another. I call this self-serving, egocentric logic egological. So, egological for the most part, modern ontology, the logic of how things "are" in modernity, and arguably modernity as a whole have gone into egological overdrive of late. In my account, Anthony Giddens's "runaway" world is a juggernaut egology. Why? In it, the self's autoreproduction has stepped up courtesy of recent geopolitical developments such as the EU, financial-economic agreements like NAFTA, corporate mergers, and time-space compression technologies in media, communications, informatics, and elsewhere. What is becoming progressively evident on the heels of all these is how, within a "world risk society" determined as commonality of risks, the *risks of commonality* are getting higher and higher, that is, how in a world risk culture, cultural diversity and ultimately culture itself are at risk.

"Communality," philosopher after philosopher have stressed, is a primordial condition and aspiration of the human. Only, in the shrinking world of the last two decades communality of time and space has translated apace into commonality of culture. The new, world proximity of self and other has often translated into their equivalence, symmetry, and even identity. Available to "us" as never before, "they" – those "out there" – are becoming more and more like us in the global panopticon. Yes, the Walls have fallen and the Windows (with capital "W") have opened to "flatten" the world, level the playing field, and "empower" all "communities," says Friedman.[16] In this cheerful survey of the late-global landscape, the "power of globalization" and power broadly are thus seized on *in abstracto* as *access to an other*, namely, to quote Friedman again, "as the inexorable integration of markets, transportation systems, and communication systems to a degree never witnessed before, in a way that is enabling corporations, countries, and individuals to reach around the world farther, faster, deeper, and cheaper than ever before, and in a way that is enabling the world to reach into corporations, countries, and individuals farther, faster, deeper, and

[16] Friedman, *The World Is Flat*, p. 92-93.

cheaper than ever before."[17] An abundance of evidence points, however, to the frequently disempowering upshots of upgraded and generalized access. More than once, reaching across previously less permeable borders has had assimilative, "rationalizing" effects on those we wished to reach. In this respect, what bears noting is the asymmetrical structure of said symmetry: indeed, "we" here, in the U.S., in the West, or in Bangalore's upper-class, still have to become like "them."

Coping with this worldly unevenness requires, as far as I am concerned, confronting the global condition of cultural risk, dealing that is, with the ongoing *relational depletion* of the world. The statement may puzzle those who will recall that I associate late globalization with an *influx* of relationality into the world. To make myself clear, I will say first that what I am taking about is a risk and an impending crisis that pertain to cultural diversity viewed as a mark of others' presence in our common world. This presence is original and vital to the world, is its inherently relational makeup. An ethical a priori and hence, Emmanuel Levinas reminds us, an ontological *donnée*, this other-based constitution constitutes the world, makes its history possible and those in it ("us" too) what they are. As such, this type of relationality should be celebrated. But there is another type, which gets into high gear in the post-divisional world of the past two decades. Of a more corporate, managerial, and "macro" "order," this sweepingly assimilationist, self-reproductive relationality runs counter to, and threatens to eradicate, the ethical kind and with it, Baudrillard fears in his late works, the alterity on which this form of relationality is premised and which in turn affords us a world. This threat is real. It signals a crisis – a crisis of rationality, of rationality as modernity's egological rationale and distinctive cultural procedure.

How do we respond to this crisis? What the egologically poised world of networks, real-time news feed, and digitalized stock trade calls for in response is what I label an *ecology* of relations. What I mean by this is another way of thinking about being in the world and, more broadly, about being: a way of being-and thinking-*with* – with oneself, with others both like and unlike oneself, with one's country and with the

---

[17] Friedman, *Longitudes and Latitudes*, p. 3.

world beyond it. This thinking and imagining, this imaginary, traces a complex move, half in progress, half still ahead of us, a turn away *from* an egological *to* an ecological modernity; *from* a modernity that has grounded, even in its postmodern afterglow, most of its endeavors to pull the world together, map it out, and treat its "disorders," in a self-centered and self-centering relationality, in connections that assimilate and make uniform, *to* a modernity in urgent search for a new "connective reason," *raison connectique*, as Finkielkraut and Soriano call it in their 2001 manifesto *Internet, l'inquiétante extase*;[18] *from* a modernity of cultural, epistemological, and political tactics, concepts, and rationalizing modules that make scant provisions for others and their otherness *to* a genuinely "considerate" modernity.

Marking the transition from self-centering, ego-logical modernity, from *relationality as rationality*, to an other-oriented modernity and modern rationale, to a *rationality as relationality* and to being understood as a relationally "authentic" formation and thereby as obligation to an other, this consideration or concern entails post-rational "reflexivity." In turn, this reflexivity involves a sustained critique of the linking and networking setups and strategies that, under the guise of progress, access, and democratic participation, predicate their sociocultural, economic, and geopolitical arrangements on the assimilation and serialization of "subaltern," "alien," "foreign," or "exotic" singularities and thus damage cultural-political environments. The way I see it, this is a techno-cultural critique and more broadly a way of conceiving the world and of being in it that emulate Levinas's ethical departure from Martin Heidegger's *Da-sein*. That is to say, this is an effort to found comprehension, representation, and behavior not on a relation with the Heideggerian Being looming high in the background of our dealings with the world and on the ontology ingrained in that self-referencing presence, but on "conversational" commerce with an other, on the face-to-face as pre-face to understanding. This is con-versation, not conversion. Fundamentally, in Levinas and, specifically, in the network environments that I would like to see proliferating, the self turns to an other not to convert that other, or him- or herself for that matter, but *to be*. Here, the self must

[18] Finkielkraut and Soriano urge a "critique of connective reason" in *Internet, l'inquiétante extase*, p. 72.

turn to an other as such, other, *autre*, in order "just" to exist, thus acknowledging that which warrants his or her own being. In this particular webbed horizon, self and other may converge *on* certain subjects (on which they may otherwise disagree), but they do not merge into a single subjectivity. As Leslie Head argues, this is the only "non-allergic relation with alterity," for it does not flow from, nor is designed to confirm, the self, its ideas, or historical incorporations.[19] If Heideggerian ontology is an "ontology of sameness," an egology, the emerging imaginary or, more pugnaciously put, the counter-imaginary one hopes to see emerging, is an ecology, an imaginal domain of ethical relations.

What I mean by ecology is *cultural ecology*. Around since the 1950s, this umbrella term has been tacked recently to a direction in environmental studies that approaches landscape as a "bioculturally collaborative project,"[20] a site where local traditions of "language and knowledg[e] both shape and are shaped by" the natural settings "in which the culture exists," to quote Head and P. B. Bridgewater, respectively.[21] I do retain the correlative ("collaborative") aspect, but what interests me is chiefly culture, while I also ascertain that the cultural, the topological – culture's shared topology or space – and the ethical – an obligation following from "proximal" living under late globalization – dovetail, in other words, that cultural analysis of webs and other types of culturally-politically geared interface leads logically (eco-logically, I am tempted to say) to an ethics. I do not ignore

[19] Levinas, *Totality and Infinity: An Essay on Interiority*, trans. Alphonso Lingis, Pittsburgh, PA: Duquesne University Press, 1961, p. 47. On recent applications of the Levinasian egological vs. ecological distinction, see Adam Potkay's article, "Wordsworth and the Ethics of Things," *PMLA* 123, no. 2, March 2008, p. 391. Potkay refers to Silvia Benso's book *The Face of Things: A Different Side of Ethics*, Albany, NY: SUNY Press, 2000.

[20] Leslie Head, "Cultural ecology: the problematic human and the terms of engagement," *Progress in Human Geography* 31, no. 6, 2007, p. 840. Important interventions in cultural ecology along postmodern lines rather distinct from the present discussion have made of late Paul Maltby, Laura Barrett, John W. Coletta, and Jim Tarter. On "cultural ecosystems," see Armand Mattelart's *Diversité culturelle et mondialisation*, Paris : La Découverte, 2005, p. 92-100. Mattelart calls for an "info-ethics" (p.100), that is, for an ethics of bio-cultural diversity in the "new world order of networks" (p. 99).

[21] P.B. Bridgewater, "Biosphere reserves: special places for people and nature," *Environmental Science & Policy* 5, 2002, p. 9.

natural habitat either, nor do I buy into a hard-and-fast nature-culture distinction. But the environments I am scouting are by and large cultural, and, alongside critics from Ursula Heise and Hubert Zapf – whose *kulturelle Ökologie* has been making inroads in Germany since 2002 – to Joseph Tabbi, Michael Wutz, and Henry Sussman, I argue for a certain cultural environmentalism.[22]

It is from such a culturally environmental standpoint that I claim that the world is at risk. The world's relational equilibrium, I further suggest, is being jeopardized by egological trends, to which I oppose an ecologically minded picture of the world. This picture is ecological not because it takes into account nature, although, again, it does, but because it challenges the egotistic penchant of late-globalization systems of cultural-electronic integration. In response, and this time around against recent interventions by cultural ecologists, I suggest that we think of culture's well-being in terms of an ecological balance understood as co-presence, co-implication, and co-responsibility of self and his or her cultural other, in short, as ethical relatedness. This correlation runs deeper than the classically environmental, human-natural nexus. For, in my view, otherness may be distinct from the self but is neither isolated nor external to it. Not just environment or background to the self's figure, otherness authenticates selfhood in the sense specified above, participates massively and originally – from the moment of origination – in the self's production, performance, and auto-conceptualization. The ecological is thus deeply correlative; it acknowledges and thrives on the presence and stories of others. The

[22] Hubert Zapf, *Literatur als kulturelle Ökologie. Zur Kulturellen Funktion imaginativer Texte an Beispielen des amerikanischen Romans*, Tübingen, Germany: Max Niemeyer, 2002, and the anthology *Kulturökologie und Literatur. Beiträge zu einem transdisziplinären Paradigma der Literaturwissenschaft*, Heidelberg, Germany: Universitätsverlag Winter, 2008; Ursula Heise, *Sense of Place and Sense of Planet: The Environmental Imagination of the Global*, Oxford, New York: Oxford University Press, 2008; Michael Wutz, *Enduring Worlds: Literary Worlds in a Changing Media Ecology*, Tuscaloosa, AL: University of Alabama Press, 2009. Worth mentioning here is too the anthology published by Wutz and Joseph Tabbi, *Reading Matters: Narrative in the New Media Ecology*, Ithaca, NY: Cornell University Press, 1997. Also, in the preface to *Idylls of the Wanderer: Outside in Literature and Theory*, New York: Fordham University Press, 2007, Henry Sussman touches on the "ecology of writing" (p. xv).

egological is illusorily self-referencing and self-relative; it stands as its own, superficially self-sufficient relation, relative (or kin), and explanatory narrative (or myth, in Roland Barthes's sense). An egological self is therefore quite inconceivable. More exactly, its authenticity is. On this account, this co-relationality cuts both ways: it is as significant to others and their own selves "out there" as much as it is to those "from around here" who have a hard time seeing themselves "with," i.e., either as shaped by others' perceptions and stories or, conversely, as shaping those perceptions, stories, and the identities behind them. At the dawn of the third millennium, U.S. literature and culture forefront, I maintain, a deepening and quite refreshing awareness of this mutually fashioning process. Stronger than ever before in our history, this awareness is ethical – it marks out a distinctly ethical project in post-Cold War America – in that it testifies both to our indebtedness to others, to what others have done for us, and to what we have done *unto* them. Furthermore, this testimonial entails a moral stance insofar as such recognition lays out implicitly what we ought to do (or *not* to do) to honor that debt. The latter injunction is no less important given the asymmetry of identity-fashioning co-relationality, what with Western culture and U.S. media popular culture in particular aggressively reproducing themselves across and at times at the expense of selves "other" worldwide. As a critic of contemporary American culture, I cannot overstate this enough: not only does this tendency threaten to remake other presences and cultural practices into similes and echoes of our selves and worldviews; it also denies these selves to ourselves by inscribing us into expansionist-assimilationist scripts of identity where others are there to reflect our self-gratifying gaze back to us.

To summarize, and offer a tentative, sort of open-ended conclusion: netroots are techno-political vehicles and socio-digital sodalities whose advent is symptomatic of something bigger, of a *Weltanschauung*, more precisely, of a contest between competing worldviews. One is egological; the other is ecological. One is already in place; the other is on the rise. The egological, on the one hand, much like technology in Heidegger, betrays a certain instrumental view of things, the worrisome notion that the world, its resources, citizenry, and electorate are available, within reach, and potentially if not effectively something to be manipulated. Technology makes something handy, brings resources, natural and human, to the disposal of its handlers so that the technocrats or the values they embody can reembody, reproduce themselves under the guise of open-access rhetoric. Netroots can be and have been used to communicate but also to deceive, manipulate, and hide – and, to go back one last time to Howard Dean, I cannot help recalling his fall: whether you like him not, what came out during his January 2004 celebratory speech – in his infamous scream, more exactly – was something until then largely unknown and that, for better or worse, brought his presidential bid to a halt (on a second thought, David Letterman could be right: Iowans realized that night that they just did not want a commander-in-chief with a personality of a hockey dad). Further, netroots, blogospheres, and their managements do raise issues of competence, professional authority, identity, anonymity, and neo-populism (alternatively, of elitism); they include but can also keep out; they professedly serve public interest but are also ideally set up to disguise their financing.

On the other hand, there is hope, hope of the ecological kind described earlier – hope one might pin on the interface that does not de-face, in which we preserve our faces, figures, and postures, our positions and singularities. An interface or coming together – a form of togetherness – that both safeguards the individual – what I term, following Jean-Luc Nancy and others, "singularity" – and which at the same time retools traditional American individualism for the necessarily communal projects of twenty-first century progressive agendas. Having already occurred in recent U.S. "e-lections," this retooling is what I call, giving the technological Caesar what it belongs to him (or it) rerouting: rerouting of politics *around* self-catering party machines, privileged nomenclatures, and their ingrown culture, but also rerouting or reorientation of quintessentially American values, perceptions, and self-perceptions.

Christian Moraru

University of North Carolina Greensboro

On the U.S. Reception of *L'Insurrection qui vient*

Ce tract présente de nombreux inconvénients...mais surtout il ne cadre pas avec la fable médiatique sur notre compte, celle du petit noyau de fanatiques portant l'attaque au cœur de l'Etat...[1]

- Julien Coupat, *Le Monde*

There are too many people that want to have their dream world...I'm going to show you the coming insurrection...[2]

- Glenn Beck, *Fox News*

Among the varied historical lenses used to interpret the often vitriolic tenor of conservative political punditry accompanying the 2008 U.S. presidential election and subsequent rise of the Tea Party movement, Richard Hofstadter's classic 1964 diagnosis of Goldwater conservatism "The Paranoid Style in American Politics" has been perhaps the most resilient. Defined as a cognitive manner characterized by "*heated exaggeration, suspiciousness, and conspiratorial fantasy*,"[3] and typically delivered in an "*uncommonly angry*," bellicose tone, current journalistic evocations of this paradigm have run the gamut from genuine innovations on its influential hypothesis to generic descriptive[4] writ large for reactionary antagonisms real and imagined. Following this popular logic, the

[1] "*This tract is inconvenient for numerous reasons...but especially because it does not fit the media fable that surrounds us: a small core of fanatics attacking the heart of the State....*" See "J*ulien Coupat: La prolongation de ma détention est une petite vengeance.*" *LeMonde.fr*. Le Monde, 25 May 2009. Web. 15 January 2011.

[2] *Glenn Beck. Fox News Channel*. 31 January 2011. YouTube. 31 January 2011.

[3] Richard Hofstadter, *The Paranoid Style in American Politics and Other Essays*, 1965; New York: Vintage, 2008, p. 3.

[4] For a more generic application of the concept, see Noam Scheiber, "Zeke Emanuel and the Right's Paranoid Style." *The New Republic*, 12 August 2009. Web. 15 January 2011.

paranoid style's problematic reputation as default "*style of mind*"[5] for a resurgent American conservative philosophy has found no greater exemplar than *Fox News* commentator Glenn Beck, arguably the most vociferous exponent of large-scale conspiracy among contemporary commentators on the political right. An observation first made by *Salon* columnist Laura Miller,[6] who briefly noted the close correspondence of Hofstadter's key tenets to the host's obsessive approach, Beck's apparent elevation to chief architect of a deliriously concatenated paranoid political imaginary was perhaps as unsurprising as it was inevitable, his show having "uncovered" a wide range of would-be news stories – from imminent worldwide economic control at the hands of a "shadow government" funded by George Soros' financial empire, to the instigation of civil unrest in the Middle East by an "Islamic caliphate" bent on global domination.

Of course, one qualifies references to "breaking news" of any kind reported by Beck in the conditional tense given the improbably fantastic nature of his commentary, a "*vast theater for his imagination, full of rich and proliferating detail, replete with realistic clues and undeniable proofs of the validity of his views*," as Richard Hofstadter so presciently remarked over four decades ago.[7] Yet repeated applications, however reductive, of an eminent historian's academic thesis to a current conservative media phenomenon surely introduces the possibility of a more thoroughgoing account, one that might perhaps move discussions about how the *Fox News* host enacts certain characteristic traits of Hofstadter's paradigm, to questions regarding the paranoid style's function as a useful heuristic for understanding interactions between twenty-first century world events and media representations of those events. Does Hofstadter's paradigm remain a relevant construct for contemporaneity, or are there more nuanced approaches available to properly address political paranoia's evolving concept? [8] How does the

[5] Hofstadter's categorical emphasis for this brand of mediated political paranoia, p. 3.

[6] See Laura Miller, "The Paranoid Style in American Punditry." *Salon.com*, 15 September 2010. Web. 15 January 2011.

[7] Hofstadter, p. 24.

[8] This paper's emphasis on the paranoid style as a rhetorical mode rather than a clinical condition removes it from the exhaustive body of research on paranoia as political psychopathology. For an excellent survey of this subfield, see Robert S. Robins and

intersection of multiple technologies – print, televisual, and digital, contribute to one's understanding of a distinctly twenty-first century paranoid style? Taking these convergent[9] concerns for its point of departure, my paper interrogates the structural contours of one notably transnational case featured on the *Glenn Beck* show, and, more precisely, examines its forceful emplotment of the paranoid style's wider historical and theoretical utility.

In the following media reception analysis, I explore a variation on the paranoid style through the contemporary example of Glenn Beck's 2009 television review of *L'Insurrection qui vient* (*The Coming Insurrection*), an obscure French anarchist tract used to recurrent, increasingly grandiloquent effect on the pundit's controversial show. Developed via literary theorist Emily Apter's concept of "oneworldedness," in which the author outlines a Hofstadter-inflected paranoiac worldview as a decidedly exportable form of American national allegory, I illustrate the way a number of current theoretical conversations speak to that classic study – focusing particularly on how paranoia theory explains the ease with which a mistaken national security incident translates to a widely misunderstood transnational media event. Specifically, I trace the paradigm's trajectory from unconstitutional French police action taken against a radical political commune suspected of authoring the tract, to its dramatization for a U.S. audience through the *Glenn Beck* show's report. Concentrating predominantly on the latter context, I identify the key features of Beck's performative "oneworldedness" through media theorist Richard Grusin's notion of "premediation," in which low levels of fear or anxiety are perpetuated by socially networked media during periods of heightened securitization.[10] An outgrowth of Grusin's

---

Jerrold M. Post, *Political Paranoia: The Psychopolitics of Hatred*, New Haven, CT: Yale University Press, 1997.

[9] Though relying on Jay Bolter and Richard Grusin's "remediation" premise throughout this article's discussions of mediality, I use the favored synonym "*convergence*" to avoid terminological confusion with a term more central to my thesis: Grusin's more recent "*premediation*" premise. Evoked in order to more clearly articulate intersections of varied media technologies in the production of a hypermediated paranoid style, *convergence* has a wider but related utility in references to Henry Jenkins' influential *Convergence Culture*, New York: New York University Press, 2006, to be further elaborated at a later point in this article.

[10] Richard Grusin, *Premediation: Affect and Mediality after 9/11*, New York: Palgrave, 2010. p. 1-2.

pioneering work with Jay Bolter in *Remediation: Understanding New Media* (1999), *premediation* diagnoses various media affects in the aftermath of America's globally scaled "war on terror." Thus, my analysis charts an emergent form of the paranoid style, one in which the pundit's alarmist polemical agenda is advanced via an intermedial, transnational exchange of cross-cultural political rhetorics.

1. "Oneworldedness": Transnationalizing 'the Paranoid Style'

Near the conclusion of "The Paranoid Style in American Politics" Richard Hofstadter gestures toward the "international" applicability of his thesis, an underdeveloped prognostication on the part of this important essay that nevertheless serves as a crucial point of departure for Emily Apter's recent global reimagining of paranoia theory, termed "oneworldedness" by the critic. Though never directly engaging Hofstadter's model, Apter's definition repurposes his three-part criteria of "*heated exaggeration, suspiciousness, and conspiratorial fantasy*" by "*envisag[ing] the planet as an extension of paranoid subjectivity vulnerable to persecutory fantasy, catastrophism, and monomania.*"[11] With its central emphasis on subjectivity, the critic's expanded brief reinstates the foundational assumption of paranoia as a rhetorical-eschatological mode[12] rather than a politico-philosophical complex – its very term a belated echo of Hofstadter's observation that, "*The paranoid spokesman sees the fate of conspiracy in apocalyptic terms – he traffics in the birth and death of whole worlds, whole political*

[11] Emily Apter, "On Oneworldedness: Or Paranoia as a World System." *American Literary History*, n° 18, 2, 2006, p. 365-389.

[12] Through this more general referent, I will show how Apter's concept takes up Hofstadter's evasion of an expected analysis of the paranoid style in various international contexts. The hinge point of that evasion is Hofstadter's reference to Norman Cohn's *The Pursuit of the Millennium*, a foundational work of scholarship on millenarianism and paranoid formations among religious sects of the sixteenth century that foregrounds his own paradigm's origins in the sacred. Toward specifically tracing a lineage between Cohn, Apter, and ultimately, Richard Grusin's notion of premediation, I am here suggesting that Hofstadter's selection of "*the megalomaniac view of oneself as the Elect, wholly good, abominably persecuted yet assured of ultimate triumph*" (quoted in Hofstadter, p. 38) from Cohn provides the universalizing impulse that unites these often disparate thinkers.

orders, whole systems of human values. He is always manning the barricades of civilization. He constantly lives at a turning point."[13]

Driving this totalizing sensibility in Apter's comparatively muted study is the urgency of a given nation's relative place in the "*competition for cultural hegemony*,"[14] a condition that asks which culture is the most globally ubiquitous, and how this ubiquity is projected rhetorically as a fundamental part of the culture's national identity. The author concludes portentously that not only is America the nation most visibly concerned with the scale of its competitive influence, but that also the very form of its concern – again, the *effect* of ubiquity or omnipresence – now functions as a metonymy for America and "Americanness."[15] Whether in its various modes of cultural production or, even more manifestly, in its unilateral military actions throughout the world, the United States' performance of paranoia as a global system has for Apter become inextricably embedded in the forms of mediality through which it imagines itself in, of, and ultimately over, the world. In their analysis of emergent forms of new media, Bolter and Grusin have outlined the technological conditions which make this effect of ubiquity possible, the conduit through which America's commitment to the "war on terror" is delivered: news and information shows that "*promote…[their] own version[s] of immediacy*."[16] The authors locate the motive force behind these networked communications systems in the experience of instantaneity, in which the ubiquity of technology imagines a fully "realized" networked society. Hence, Bolter and Grusin's assertion that "*news and information shows (…) claim to immediacy is based on the shared belief that they are presenting what 'really happened'*."[17] Furthermore, the authors assert that,

> *The insistence on the liveness of the action is what gives television news its special claim among journalistic media. (By contrast, analysis, especially political analysis, is regarded as inappropriate for television almost a violation. It remains the province of print journalism, ostensibly – because television networks are not allowed to play political favorites, but in fact*

---

[13] Hofstadter, p. 29-30.
[14] Apter, p. 366.
[15] *Ibid.*, p. 366; p. 379.
[16] Bolter and Grusin, p. 224.
[17] *Ibid.*, p. 189.

> *because a consistent and prolonged point of view required for analysis or reflection is incompatible with televisual immediacy.) Television news and information shows are [also] increasingly willing to use digital technology in the service of hypermediacy without giving up their claim to be live. In commercials, news shows, and sports broadcasts, television is borrowing the windowed and multimediated look of the computer screen. Paradoxically, the windowed style is most evident in shows that purport to offer us a transparent view of real-time events.*[18]

The seeming up-to-the-minute immediacy of his delivery notwithstanding, Glenn Beck's broadcasts, it should be noted, tend to violate the parenthetical caveat listed above by embedding an unapologetically ideological tone in the premediated interactions between events and their representation. This strategy motivates a rhetoric that creates, and in turn is created by, a spectacle that more or less reflects itself through the constitutive pressure of time, and particularly the timeliness that mitigates such interactions.

On a practical rhetorical level, the key elemental pressure motivating both Hofstadter and Apter's respective theories is their tacit acknowledgment of an inverted contextual exigency within paranoia's controlling logic: a distortion of the classic Aristotelian notion of *kairos*.[19] Proceeding from a top-down impetus, this inversion modifies the conventional *kairotic* sense in which the timely event's arrival occasions the appropriate response, however overheated or trivialized. By contrast the paranoid style, in its often hysterically oracular register, manufactures that urgency and then attaches it to the conveniently susceptible set of stimuli under examination.

Accordingly, one might argue that "oneworldedness" revises Hofstadter's paranoia theory to accommodate the medial reflexivity of contemporary current events in relation with the forms of reportage that attempt to capture them, a premediated model that more precisely anticipates the "intersubjective feedback loop" of reaction and reception to those events. Apter encourages the recognition of this reflexive turn by framing the "*paranoid planetarity*" of "oneworldedness" in "*a*

---

[18] *Ibid.*, p. 189.

[19] For an overview of the various interpretations of *kairos*, see John T. Kirby, "Occasion." *The Oxford Encyclopedia of Rhetoric*, Ed., Thomas E. Sloane, et al. New York: Oxford University Press, 2001, p. 529-532.

delusional model of subjective recognition that apprehends itself in global schemata."[20] Thus, the reflexivity inherent in the act of a manufactured *kairos* "stage manages" the apocalyptic conditions whereby the world is continually on the brink – a set of conditions strongly reminiscent of one of Hofstadter's central tenets: the important role temporality plays for the paranoid's conspiratorial revelations, in which danger is imminent and *"[t]ime is forever just running out.*"[21] Toward understanding this tendency through a national political "crisis"-as-media spectacle, I now turn to the events surrounding *The Coming Insurrection's* volatile French reception.

Writing for *The Guardian* in January 2009, acclaimed translator and social theorist Alberto Toscano reflects the emergent nature of "oneworldedness" with the warning:

> *We are losing the political literacy, and the legal capacity, to distinguish between sabotage and terrorism, vandalism and mass murder, as every oppositional alternative to the status quo is swallowed up under the umbrella of terrorism. In times of crisis and possible turmoil, this one-dimensional thinking is profoundly dangerous, and an insidious threat to everyone's "security.*"[22]

A response to the November 2008 arrest of the alleged "anarcho-autonomous" terrorist cell branded the "Tarnac 9" by the French media, Toscano's remarks deem the incident emblematic of the Sarkozy administration's preemptive mode against a variety of countervailing ideologies while reflecting its narrower status as *cri de cœur* among continental academic philosophers and public intellectuals alike. Openly accused by French Minister of Justice Michèle Alliot-Marie of having authored the tract, the indicted collective's media-designated leader Julien Coupat has repeatedly maintained his innocence for the series of rail network vandalisms that inspired the arrests, as well as denying responsibility for the book's revolutionary message (said to carry coded references to the above *nuisances*).

---

[20] Apter, p. 371.

[21] Hofstadter, p. 30.

[22] Alberto Toscano, "Criminalising Dissent," *The Guardian.co.uk*, 28 January 2009. Web. 15 January 2011.

With no evidence forthcoming in either context despite Coupat's controversial sixth month prison detainment, the French public has borne witness to a scenario that Toscano has since defined as "*deeply symptomatic [of] the very notion of 'preterrorism,' ...mak[ing] patent the link between the obsessive identification of 'dangerous individuals' and the imagination of future revolts that call for repressive pre-emption.*"[23] Following the close relationality between Hofstadter and Apter's concepts, Richard Grusin's reception theory of premediation likewise finds a practical corollary in Toscano's apt descriptor. Generated in the aftermath of a national trauma, premediation first operates through a mode of governmentality[24] grown increasingly vulnerable to the aforementioned *kairotic* inversion (the November 2005 riots in the banlieues outside of Paris perhaps serving this traumatic function). Insofar as a police action can be construed as a form of discourse reception, the government's overwrought response to the manifesto seems to have been fomented through successive waves of mediated paranoid rhetoric leveled by the French press. However, what makes this particular instance premediated is the fact that widespread interest in the text did not occur until *after* the arrests happened (the original 2007 reception of *L'Insurrection qui vient* having been limited only to brief recognition by activist newsletters and journals). Under these conditions, it becomes quite clear that the continuous media revaluation of the police action and the sense that it was motivated by divergent social and political values (expressed in the text) rather than with concrete evidence, premediated the book's *kairotic* reception as a purported blueprint for the alleged terrorist actions against the French rail lines. "Preterrorism," Toscano's word for the forms of preventative action taken by government agencies to circumvent terrorist activity, thus figures as a powerful analog for the reactionary global trend among government administrations in the wake of the Bush administration's War on Terror.

---

[23] Toscano, "The War Against Pre-terrorism: The Tarnac 9 and *The Coming Insurrection*," *Radical Philosophy*, n° 154, 2009. Web. 15 January 2011.

[24] Grusin follows the Foucauldian conception of governmentality, a securitization-obsessed "*biopolitical discourse formation that followed upon both sovereignty as the dominant juridical form of ruling a state or managing its territory and upon discipline as the dominant juridical form of surveillance and punishment of individuals*" (quoted in Grusin, p. 73).

These conditions suggest a greater degree of power and control by the media, far beyond the mere chance effect of rhetorical immediacy by network news shows' remediation of the Internet's formal characteristics. Hence Grusin's revision of earlier remarks with the observation that "*Rather than a desire for the immediacy of the catastrophe, premediation seeks instead to protect the American media public from having to experience again the shock or cultural trauma experienced on 9/11 by concerning itself with the remediation not of the present, but of the future.*"[25] Such logic aligns with Apter's notion of paranoid planetarity as an American export of distinctly transnational utility, premediation accounting for both the preemptive behavior of the French government, and Glenn Beck's similarly inflammatory coverage of the event. Additionally, it serves as an instructive lens through which audiences can better understand Beck's fortunes as a radio, television, and Internet news force. Notably, Beck's media empire, Mercury Radio Artists, Inc., relies on exactly the three technologies Bolter and Grusin foreground as the most convergent: telephone (via interaction with callers on his radio show *The Glenn Beck Program*); television (through Fox's *Glenn Beck*); and most currently, on the Internet with first his online for-profit educational apparatus, Beck University, and *The Blaze* – Beck's pseudo-aggregate news organ (a la *Drudge Report* or *The Huffington Post*). With the coverage surrounding the Tarnac 9 arrests providing an apt intermedial case study – and evoking a roughly concurrent chronology of his company's convergence of a variety of media formats – Beck's manufactured *kairos* continues to function as the constitutive pressure for a distinctly premediated paranoid style. Ironically, the expression "the coming insurrection" might be read less for its anticipation of revolutionary upheaval than for its reflexive prescience regarding the conservative pundit's manifold media innovations.

Featured during the show's digest segment "The One Thing," Beck's July 2009 review[26] of *The Coming Insurrection* notably begins with a reference to time and timeliness when the host briskly states, "*I was*

[25] Grusin, p. 34.

[26] For the purposes of clarification, it should be noted that *Fox News* published an article (authored by Beck) entitled "Extreme Left Calling People to Arms" concurrently with the broadcast. The piece is nearly identical to the content in Beck's broadcast but has been edited for readability. See Glenn Beck, "Extreme Left Calling People to Arms." *FoxNews.com*. Fox. 1 July 2009. Web. 15 January 2011.

handed this this morning when I got in to work (...) I've been trying to get a copy of this for a while. It is a brand new book – it is a dangerous book. It is called The Coming Insurrection."[27] Briefly summarizing the tract's status as a violent, anti-capitalist call-to-arms and making passing references to its origins in the French riots of 2005 (among other subsequent uprisings in Greece and Iceland), Beck's opening commentary seems poised to begin one of the show's key features: "academic" history lesson replete with chalk drawn maps, or ideological tirade on twentieth century social and political movements?

Such features align with one of the core tropes of Hofstadter's paranoid style, exemplifying what the author characterizes as an exorbitant concern with "pedantry," a "*heroic striving (...) for 'evidence' to prove that the unbelievable is the only thing that can be believed.*"[28] This overweening compulsion to accumulate facts, often in an ostentatiously voluminous manner, reflects the "*higher paranoid scholarship's*" preoccupation with the appearance of totality: the "*imputed total competence (...) that [leaves] nothing unexplained and comprehend[s] all of reality in one overreaching, consistent theory.*"[29] Though a staple of Beck's show – with its hall of mirrors blackboard set design[30] relentlessly triangulating the latest imagined network of cabals in an infinite regress behind its animated host – pedantry is all but nonexistent in the original *Coming Insurrection* review. Instead, Beck supplants the expected flood of analysis with the subsidiary rhetorical strategy of "privileged access," repeatedly filling air time with references to the difficulty of obtaining the book, its apparently heralded publication in the U.S., and even referring to the copy in hand as "*one of the first copies finished in English.*"[31] In this way, Beck's *kairotic* inversion reverses the normative trend that privileges the forward march of technological advance and anachronistically places a high value on print technology – a seeming scarcity in the midst of ubiquitous information. This evasive strategy sets the stage for the host's premediation of *The Coming Insurrection*,

---

[27] *Glenn Beck. Fox News*. 1 July 2009. YouTube. 15 January 2011.
[28] Hofstadter, p. 35-36.
[29] *Ibid.*, p. 36-37.
[30] For a notably unrestrained example of Beck's use of stagecraft, see *The Glenn Beck Show*. Fox. 31 Jan. 2011. YouTube. 15 February 2011.
[31] *Glenn Beck. Fox News*. 1 July 2009. YouTube. 15 January 2011.

introducing its status as a potentially combustible commodity to which only he has access.

2. Premediating *The Coming Insurrection*

Beck's analysis of *The Coming Insurrection* takes a dual-layer approach. The first involves his show's use of textual excerpts from the tract that are displayed digitally on the viewer's screen as the host reads them; the second centers on Beck's delivery. The latter, supporting Bolter and Grusin's remarks about the hypermediated nature of twenty-four hour cable news channels, is positioned with an "*aim to provide viewers with as much information as possible in the shortest possible (...) fill[ing] up the screen with visible evidence of the power of television to gather events. This leads to what we might call the 'CNN look,' in which the televised image of the newscaster is coordinated with a series of graphics and explanatory captions, until the broadcast begins to resemble a web site or multimedia application.*"[32] Likewise, the pundit's content supports this saturated digitally-influenced approach with commentary that tends to be broadly historical and gestural rather than careful and complete – a sound bite format that jumps to the tendentious association or incendiary conclusion as a hallmark of his individualized variant of the paranoid style. The passages excerpted are all culled from the most "directive" portion of the text close to its end, selections that have obviously been chosen for their high incitement premium. For example, the host cites the following excerpts, in effect indicting the group by skipping over a large portion of the text: "*Take up arms. Do everything possible to make their use unnecessary. There is no such thing as a peaceful insurrection*"; and "*[i]t's a question of knowing how to fight, pick locks, to set broken bones and treat sicknesses, how to build a pirate radio transmitter.*"[33] Thus, roughly a quarter of *The Coming Insurrection*'s length stands in for almost a hundred pages of carefully conceived rationale filled with copious historical referents and allusions to the work of critical thinkers such as Michael Hardt and Antonio Negri, Ulrich Beck, Manuel Castells, and Pierre Bourdieu. Based on the material presented, the tract could be mere mischief (a

[32] Bolter and Grusin, p. 189.

[33] *Glenn Beck. Fox News.* 1 July 2009. YouTube. 15 January 2011.

Francophone *Anarchist's Cookbook*), or it could be considerably more: one of those little red or green books[34] its French editor, Eric Hazan, resolutely denies is its intent.

Following this ambiguous logic, Beck's rhetorical strategy feigns in one direction, seemingly exercising the paranoid trope of pedantry in which specific events are exhaustively contextualized in their respective historical moments, only to undercut the contemporaneous force of those details through conflation. In other words, the host maximizes the potential for multiple, unrelated events to serve as "opportunities" for reactionary sloganeering, though such opportunities – which Beck usually seeks under a crass pretense of analysis – are shunted off in preference for calling attention to and aggrandizing his own reputation as a radical. Relating the story of Coupat's alleged visit to New York City via an illegal Canadian border crossing (apparently to avoid leaving a finger print record with U.S. authorities), Beck protests, "*Remember the media will tell you that people like me are the ones to be feared. That I am racist because I say 'protect the borders,' or I am somehow dangerous because I tell you 'start using common sense'.*"[35] Delivered in a tonally eccentric voice that careens wildly from heartfelt concern to reflexive self-parody, this set piece nevertheless retreats from charges of seriousness in its projection of the "amiable entertainer" persona – a defensive pose in the name of "showmanship." Again, a manufactured *kairos* provides the ground note for Beck's premediation.

Delivery is a particularly fascinating measure of Beck's ethos because it telegraphs his performance of sincerity in a way that registers the host's interpretation of the values ostensibly shared with his audience. Walking a line between earnest concern and cynical opportunism, Beck vacillates between a pandering expression of the *vox populi*, first imagining his audience as the lowest common denominator "too busy working hard to pay close attention"[36] before shifting into the ebullient rhetoric of the "average Joe" autodidact, just trying to encourage a little intellectual curiosity in the midst of everyone's busy lives. In both contexts, the subject of feelings replaces rational inquiry, even serving as

---

[34] See note 37.

[35] *Glenn Beck. Fox News*. 1 July 2009. YouTube. 15 January 2011.

[36] See especially Beck's introduction to *Common Sense: The Case of an Out-of-Control Government, Inspired by Thomas Paine*. New York: Threshold Editions, 2009.

a kind ideologically overdetermined placeholder for the conventions of reasoned discourse, as when Beck asserts:

> *Most Americans remain convinced that the country is on the wrong track. They know that SOMETHING JUST DOESN'T FEEL RIGHT but they don't know how to describe it or, more importantly, how to stop it. But just because you may not know exactly what your gut is saying, doesn't mean what your feeling is wrong...[and] now, after supposedly massive change, not only are we still on the wrong track, but it feels as though our new conductor has just increased the speed at which our misdirected train is traveling.* (emphasis author's)[37]

Later in the same textual passage, his quasi-Tea Party manifesto *Common Sense: The Case against an Out-of-Control Government, Inspired by Thomas Paine*, Beck contradicts this preternatural ability to divine the truth through "feelings," when he mocks so-called "Progressive" educational policy as one driven by "feeling": "*Because so much of what the Progressives stand for feels good, it wasn't a hard sell to educators and sociologist experts...as a result, kids have been taught for years that they are all equals in the classroom and that feelings matter more than test scores.*"[38] A parental force lies behind this pathos-driven persona: that of the world-weary, socially conscious family man, lone light of sanity in a world gone mad. With a kind of mock-maudlin exasperation, Beck closes by saying, "*I'm going on vacation today and I'm taking this on the plane. I promised my family I was going to read happy books but I have to read this one first, so I can come back after vacation and tell you what's in it. Because I'm telling you – there is trouble on the way.*"[39]

Sylvère Lotringer, professor of French and philosophy at Columbia University and general editor at Semiotext(e),[40] made perhaps the single most acute observation about the *The Coming Insurrection's* eventful trajectory post-Beck broadcast: "*I would be willing to come on the show if he had read the book, but he has never read it. Nothing that he has said shows that he read it. He is incapable of reading it*" ("A Book

[37] Beck, p. 8.
[38] *Ibid.*, p. 92.
[39] *Glenn Beck. Fox News.* 1 July 2009. YouTube. 15 January 2011.
[40] Semiotext(e) is the tract's English-language publisher.

Attacking"). This remark, though clearly aimed at the larger strand of populist anti-intellectualism Beck represents, inadvertently calls attention to the proverbial elephant-in-the-room enacted by the broadcast: Beck never actually *reviews* the book. By contrast, the host decontextualizes its specific meaning by immediately putting the work into conversation with Beck's own overwrought statement of purpose, *Common Sense*. Though clearly an instance of Beck's predilection for cravenly capitalizing on his endless supply of product – a review of *The Coming Insurrection* becoming a mere plug for *Common Sense* – the use of this method serves two purposes: to reestablish generally his own credibility as the authority against which all objects of knowledge confronted on the show are defined; and to interpret a text the host has not read (or perhaps, has not read carefully enough to understand) through the filter of one he has authored.

Beck's negative strategy of reviewing an unknown work through one he has written or that he, at least, strongly endorses should not be understood as a strategy intended to deliberately engender an array of antithetical positions about the texts under comparative review. Compare, for example, the rhetorical strategy deployed by French journalist Olivier Bailly in his essay and interview with *The Coming Insurrection*'s original editor, Eric Hazan:

> *Précisons que si* L'Insurrection qui vient *n'est pas l'indicateur de police des chemins de fer, il n'est pas non plus une boussole destinée à ceux qui ont perdu le sens de l'histoire, encore moins un manuel, ni un livre de recettes, ni un bréviaire, une bible, un livre rouge (vert) ou le phare de la pensée. Tout cela suffirait à le rendre déjà, en ce siècle de la vitesse, caduc.*[41]

By contrast with the *Fox News* host's ethically problematic approach, Bailly here charts the various genres into which the book has been popularly slotted as a way of constellating the respective ideological positions of its varied audiences. The effect, intended to be dialectical, is

[41] "*Let us say that if* The Coming Insurrection *is not a guidepost, it is also not a compass destined to those who have lost a sense of history, even less a manual, neither a cookbook, nor a brief, a bible, a red (or green) book or the beacon of thought. All this would suffice to render it, in this century of speed, already obsolete.*" See Bailly, Olivier, "L'Insurrection qui vient est en avance sur l'horaire," *AgoraVox.fr*. AgoraVox, 12 December. 2008. Web. 15 January 2011.

followed quickly with a positive abstraction of the book's categorical difficulty, forcing readers to generate independent thought about the artifact under discussion, as when Bailly completes the move, writing, "L'Insurrection qui vient *c'est donc moins ce qu'on lui prête et sans doute plus que ça. C'est peut-être la photographie instantanée d'une génération perdue.*"[42] Conversely, being instructed to consult Beck's own book before reading the tract in its proper social, historical, and national context functions as a deterrent for his audience, preventing it from engaging circumspectly with *The Coming Insurrection*'s ideas. Apropos of Lotringer's sharp dismissal, this strategy[43] also conveniently distracts the viewer from Beck's ignorance of the demanding continental theory that makes *The Coming Insurrection* legible to an educated readership. In this way, the review enacts Grusin's contention that, "*(...) participatory networked media threaten to produce an epistemological free-for-all that does away with the possibility of authoritative belief or credibility*"[44], a state of affairs Beck's diversionary style capitalizes on.

3. The Paranoid Style of *Common Sense*

Early in his broadcast on *The Coming Insurrection*, Glenn Beck asserts:

> *This book is the anti-Common Sense; in fact, I talk about books like this in Common Sense, the section called 'The Enemies Within.' In this book, when I wrote this, I knew people like this...I didn't know this book was coming out...but I knew people like this were going to show up. Enemies Within. And they were going to tell you to pick up a gun and they were going to use every kind of emergency and stress to get you to do it. This is a book of revolution (holds up* The Coming Insurrection*); this is a book of peaceful*

[42] "*The Coming Insurrection* is thus less than what one credits it and without a doubt, more than that. It is, perhaps, the last instant snapshot of a generation." Olivier Bailly, "L'Insurrection qui vient est en avance sur l'horaire," *AgoraVox.fr*. AgoraVox, 12 December 2008. Web. 15 January 2011.

[43] Beck's strategy has only grown more pronounced with the arrival of *The Blaze*, a clearly ideological, opinion-inflected "news" site with the appearance of a news aggregation website (inaugurated on both the right and left by the *Drudge Report* and *The Huffington Post*, respectively).

[44] Grusin, p. 35.

> *revolution (holds up* Common Sense*). This one's from the right (presents* Common Sense*) – you know, the radicals that everybody's so worried about in government? This one is from the left (presents* The Coming Insurrection*).*[45]

At its author's invitation, I will treat briefly the subsection in *Common Sense* that Beck claims relates to *The Coming Insurrection*. Part of a larger chapter entitled "The Cancer of Progressivism," "Enemies Within: Tread Carefully" takes the familiar tone of a close friend and neighbor offering sound advice, a custodial rhetoric[46] whose repetitive plea to protect the family from government intervention shrilly imagines left-liberal national education policy as serial child abduction. In the text's most relentless and strident example, Beck attacks the issue of voucher programs versus public schools and discusses at length the subject of "homeschooling" – a popular mode for many of his supporters. Rather than reasonably surveying the wide range of opinion on homeschooling, in typical paranoid style Beck introduces the subject in its most stigmatized form, manufacturing its urgency with the comment: "*Progressives label those who homeschool their children as 'backwards,' 'socially undeveloped,' or religious zealots – but those attacks are just diversions from their real concern about lack of State control.*"[47] Following this opening assault, Beck moves quickly into one of his most oft-abused pathetic appeals, a counterfactual fallacy with which the author posits a settled issue (a conservative victory, in fact) as a vulnerability awaiting "progressive" reversal at any moment.

---

[45] *Glenn Beck*. Fox. 1 July 2009. YouTube. 15 January 2011.

[46] Custodial rhetoric is a persistent rhetorical tendency for the contemporary right. This patronizing strategy aligns with Beck's general philosophy by replacing the onus of a large, invasive government system serving the well-being of its constituents with that of the family. Tonally, motifs of guardianship and the defense of values are visualized through a father-protector figure embodied in the persona of the pundit (see, for example, Bill O'Reilly's *Who's Looking Out For You?* and *Culture Warrior*). It is notable that only Glenn Beck has pursued this strategy in arguably its most logical, albeit extravagantly sentimentalized, venue: the children's book (see *The Christmas Sweater*, New York: Threshold Editions, 2008).

[47] Glenn Beck, *Glenn Beck's Common Sense: The Case of an Out-of-Control Government, Inspired by Thomas Paine*. New York: Threshold Editions, 2009, p. 94.

Introducing the overturning of a California appellate court's judgment on the unconstitutionality of home-schooling,[48] Beck cautions:

> *Many will counter that this decision was reversed and that homeschooling is alive and well in California today. While that may be true, I would remind you that Progressive policy makers are patient. They know how to bide their time, waiting for the right combination of public opinion and judicial appointees to take hold before making their case again (...) Progressives do not care about minor setbacks. They will continue their assault because they do not fear us. And, truthfully, they have no reason to. We have failed to stand up to them time and time again even as they've worked tirelessly and openly to restructure and reshape America.*[49]

The strategy of recasting a victory as an all-but-imminent defeat strongly aligns with Hofstadter's contention that "*the paranoid style is aroused by a confrontation of opposed interests which are (or are felt to be) totally irreconcilable, and thus not susceptible to the normal political processes of bargain and compromise.*"[50] With the homeschooling example as a case in point, Beck reads as pathology a characteristic of political debate that is bi-directional, a neutral strategy as readily available to conservative interlocutors as it is to progressives (or *anyone* on *any* side of an issue). In other words, the alleged edge-of-the-seat Progressive obsession with overturning the possibility of homeschooling in California can stand in for any subject, and, as could be argued about all of the writer's pet issues, goes both ways. Emily Apter has explored this unusual approach to logic in her conception of "oneworldedness", writing: "*[P]aranoia reinforces unipolar thought, specifically, a model of oneness as allness (...) [T]he paranoid theorist devises a system of omniscience capable of binding everything into coherence, thereby rendering discrepant orders of signs mutually intelligible or pantranslatable.*"[51] This cosmic expansion develops Hofstadter's remarks on the paranoid's hypothetical "enemy," in which the oppositional figure achieves an almost monolithic status in the practitioner's mind, and so "*seems to be on many counts a projection of*

[48] See *Jonathan L. v. Superior Court*, 165 Cal. App. 4th 1074 (Cal. App. 2 Dist. 2008).
[49] Beck, p. 95.
[50] Hofstadter, p. 39.
[51] Apter, p. 371.

the self: both the ideal and the unacceptable aspects of the self are attributed to him."[52] Toward better understanding this interaction in Beck's review of *The Coming Insurrection*, I will now highlight explicit passages that reinforce the host's odd injunction that readers interpret the tract through his own triumphalist lens.

Especially ironic when read in tandem with *The Coming Insurrection*, *Common Sense* inadvertently mirrors the revolutionary "manual," if only because both seem to be brokered across the same perilous "*battlefield of ideas*"[53]: the family versus an all-powerful state apparatus. But where the former text deploys the rhetoric of bourgeois domesticity, for example peppering its assault with melodramatic claims such as, "*We have so little trust in the character of the people we elected that most of us wouldn't invite them into our homes for dinner, let alone leave our children alone in their care*"[54] – the latter imagines a subjectivity governed by a total freedom outside of government and the family structure.[55] Announcing the "moribundity" of social relations in general, and branding "the couple" a sign of "*the final stage of the great social debacle*,"[56] the anonymous authors nevertheless reserve the majority of their criticism for the subject of institutional education; for example, when they echo Beck's aggressive sentiments with a warning about France's national school system, and particularly its production of "*a type of state subjectivity that stands out among all others*."[57] In the spirit of Beck's own somewhat antinomian sensibilities, the collective celebrates their belief that "*this construction of subjectivities by the state that is breaking down every day a little more, with the decline of the scholarly institutions*."[58] Yet, at the level of basic values, stark differences emerge of the sort that generate Beck's favored polemical

---

[52] Hofstadter, p. 32.

[53] This phrase, or a variation on it ("a revolution that won't be fought on battlefields, but in the hearts and minds of the three hundred million people lucky enough to call America home") Beck often misattributes to George Washington. (See Beck, *Glenn Beck's Common Sense: The Case of an Out-of-Control Government, Inspired by Thomas Paine*, New York: Threshold Editions, 2009. viii; p. 17.

[54] Beck, p. 10.

[55] See The Invisible Committee, *The Coming Insurrection*. Trans. *L'Insurrection qui vient*. Los Angeles, Semiotext(e), 2009, p. 32.

[56] *Ibid.*, p. 40-41.

[57] *Ibid.*, p. 37.

[58] *Ibid.*, p. 37.

turns; for instance, the pundit's use of rhetorical appeals that reflect a yearning for some purist, nostalgia-inscribed idea of revolutionary America before the encroachment of a "parent-like state" – a phrase that refreshes his audience's anger about the U.S.'s "Progressive" deterioration into "*a place that bears less and less resemblance to the America we remember from our childhoods*."[59] Conversely, the Invisible Committee's wish to tear down France's existing educational apparatus acknowledges its inculcation of certain "*excessively scholastic*"[60] and even activist principles; in fact, the authors suggest that the schools have nurtured revolt in French society, an expression of free-thinking the inspiration of which Beck would undoubtedly argue should be fostered in the home. Despite such departures, Beck's prescribed comparative assessment of the two texts seems the classic case of an embattled misreading failing to recognize its own combative stance reflected back through the object it so heatedly derides. Uncannily, Hofstadter's essay is again instructive, pointing up that "*the fundamental paradox of the paranoid style is the imitation of the enemy*."[61]

Opening with a plea "*to return to the place we were on September 12, 2001... [when] we were not obsessed with Red states, Blue states or political parties*"[62] *Common Sense* coalesces around the idea of common sense as an ideologically neutral impulse "felt" by all Americans, assembled and at the ready to defend the common values and principles of the country they love.[63] When applied to Glenn Beck's emotionalist rhetorical style, the assumption that conservative punditry can be understood through the sense that "everything comes back to 9/11," might be considered reductive and even offensive if it was not already such an explicit part of the pundit's agenda. The "9-12 Project," Beck's most programmatic aim to flatten out ideological differences, takes as its central purpose the sort of unipolar, either-or understanding of the world earlier described as a key feature of "oneworldedness". Moreover, this variation on the paranoid style exemplifies Apter's provocative conclusion that the intended exportation of "American-style

[59] Beck, p. 7.
[60] The Invisible Committee, p. 37.
[61] Hofstadter, p. 32.
[62] See Beck's introduction to *Common Sense: The Case of an Out-of-Control Government, Inspired by Thomas Paine*, New York: Threshold Editions, 2009.
[63] *Ibid.*, vii.

democracy" to various strategically selected countries in the Middle East strongly suggests "*a group psychosis of defense has taken hold (...) [one] that builds on a mandate for open-ended war justified by an unfathomably deep sense of injury, a conviction that the entire life of the world would not be enough to compensate for 9/11.*"[64]

Reconsidered through Beck's evaluation of *The Coming Insurrection*, in which the host's misinterpretation premediates his audience's understanding of a text, one of Beck's most indomitable theoretical bogeymen – the transnational – comes back to haunt him. In classic unipolar fashion, the pundit writes: *HISTORY DEMANDS A CLEAR ANSWER. One response leads us to transnationalism and the end of American sovereignty, while the other leads us to a restoration of our liberty. But time is running out. We must answer the question and face the consequences, or our reckless apathy will answer it for us* (emphasis author's).[65] A fascinating counterpoint to *The Coming Insurrection*'s apocalyptic celebration of the "*end of the 'national' period of History (...) and all of its consequences,*"[66] Beck's inflammatory comments reinforce the sense that an interanimation of governmental and media logics through the premediated lens of rhetorical exigency will continue to provoke the explicit politicization of "oneworldedness" as not only a necessary emphasis, but also quite dire given the extraordinarily rapid growth of a paranoid political imaginary in the U.S. and abroad. Mirroring *The Coming Insurrection*'s own smug tone of inevitability, in which the anonymous authors' write, "*It is hard for a country [France] which created, out of nothing, the ideological framework of nationalism and exported it to the whole world to recognize that all that remains of it now is a document to be filed in the historical archives*"[67] – Beck's transnational synthesis of French and American political rhetorics retrofits the staid tradition of opinion/editorial commentary, creating a fluid, interconnected, and ultimately all-encompassing vehicle for mediated paranoia.

On a larger scale, this vehicle occupies an even more elemental intersection between participatory and commercial culture, a space Henry Jenkins has termed "convergence culture," writing:

---

64 Apter, p. 379.
65 Beck, p. 11-12.
66 The Invisible Committee, p. 88.
67 *Ibid.*, p, 89.

> *Convergence does not depend on any specific delivery mechanism. Rather, convergence represents a paradigm shift – a move from medium-specific content toward content that flows across multiple media channels, toward the increased interdependence of communication systems, toward multiple ways of accessing media content, and toward ever more complex relations between top-down corporate media and bottom-up participatory culture.*[68]

With its zealous sloganeering and claims to a prelapsarian purity of political vision, the nostalgic register voiced by Beck and best exemplified by the Tea Party's reactionary reversal on the rhetoric of the American Revolution illustrates Jenkins' notion of the "*grassroots convergence*"[69] of participatory and commercial culture as generative force *par excellence*. Despite harnessing the illusion of grassroots activism as a catalyst for his message – most provocatively displayed in Beck's organization of the August 28, 2010 Restoring Honor rally[70] held at the Lincoln Memorial – the host's powerful ability to gesture toward participatory culture is, as Jenkins argues about convergence culture generally, seemingly "*driven by economic calculations and not by some broad mission to empower the public*."[71] Of course, the rally's influential impact on certain political groups on the right as precisely (and even beyond) the sort of spontaneous grassroots creativity Beck's publicity machine designed it to be transcends mere profit motive to support Jenkins' most powerful point. Though commercial culture may have a decisive advantage in terms of funding structure and professional polish, the boundless freedom afforded grassroots creativity via its ability to harness exposure through new technologies – whether inspired by the entertainment industry or through the political process – suggests that "*grassroots convergence presents the folk process accelerated and expanded for the digital age*."[72] In its ironic alignment with and unusual exploitation of The Invisible Committee's tract, the fortunes of Beck's multimedia empire since the rally continue to tell a very interesting story

---

[68] Jenkins, p. 254.
[69] Jenkins, p.18 and p. 57.
[70] Significantly, *The Blaze*, Beck's news and opinion site, was launched three days after the Restoring Honor rally.
[71] Jenkins, p. 254.
[72] Jenkins, p. 140.

about the powerful media realignments possible with convergence culture.

Following in the long line of *agents provocateurs* from both sides of the Atlantic published by Semiotext(e), theorists such as Félix Guattari, David Wojnarowicz, Jean Baudrillard, and most importantly Guy Debord, the Invisible Committee's tract demands to be put in its appropriate generic context – regardless of its tone of revolutionary foreboding. Indeed, *L'Insurrection*'s style compares well with the pranksterish, proto-punk sensibility of Debord's Situationist International group (the publisher has notably collected the latter group's correspondence from 1957-1960, so the comparison is perhaps irresistible). Such clarification in the interest of understatement seems unlikely however, given Beck's entrepreneurial talents, which have had the unintended effect of boosting sales of the text he so avidly demonizes in the 2009 broadcast. In a follow-up story to their initial report about the book's New York debut, *The New York Times* related the tract's post-Beck show sales spike, in which *The Coming Insurrection* rose to Amazon's number one spot in July – truly an astonishing feat for a work published by a press known for relatively obscure critical and social theory. The infamy drawn to the book through Beck's attacks shows most prominently via Semiotext(e)'s unlikely public relations move in response to the pundit's overwrought assessment of *The Coming Insurrection.* Humorously reversing the default setting of positive feedback for an advertising strategy, Beck's damning pronouncements against the pamphlet have been adopted by Semiotext(e)'s web site as "blurb copy." This welcome, if unintended "endorsement" likely accounts for the work's swelling sales, Beck trumpeting its infamy as, "*Quite possibly the most evil thing I've ever read.*"

Though one might imagine a happy accident emerging from this elevated interest, having the opposite effect of Beck's intended use of the text by influencing thousands of readers to engage with critical and social theory – the more likely eventuality has already come to pass. Beck's penchant for apocalyptic opportunism has gone still further, as the pundit has continued to distance the tract from its original context by making it a catch phrase for his recent series of reports on civil unrest in the Middle East. At the time of this writing, Beck's latest programs carry the banner "The Coming Insurrection" with the name of the country under siege following the phrase. Occasionally flashing a copy of the tract's dark blue cover – a prop for his apocalyptic harangues – Beck rarely mentions its actual contents, instead intoning dire warnings such as, "*This is not just happenstance. This is not just poor people mad at rich people. This is coordinated.*"[73] As Sean Wilentz has remarked in a lengthy article on the Cold War influences of the pundit's paranoid posturing, "*[p]art of Beck's allure is the promise that he will reveal secret information.*"[74] But the excitement generated by such suspenseful tactics – a constructed urgency to which Beck provides the proverbial calm at the center of various political storm systems – may have outpaced the zeitgeist it once relied on to such polarizing effect. According to one report, a perceived decline can be traced to roughly the point at which the host began escalating his increasingly eschatological commentaries. At the time of this writing, the once unflappable multimedia force "*has lost over a third of his audience on Fox – a greater percentage drop than other hosts at Fox.*"[75] Regardless of the host's ideologue status, the Glenn Beck phenomenon clearly exemplifies a political crossroads between old and new media, a turning point which Henry Jenkins defines elsewhere as "*a critical moment of transition during which the old rules are open to change and companies may be forced to renegotiate their relationship to consumers. The question is whether the public is ready to push for greater participation or willing to settle for the same old relations to mass media.*"[76] While the short

[73] *Glenn Beck. Fox News.* 31 January 2011. YouTube. 31 Feb. 2011.

[74] Sean Wilentz, "Confounding Fathers: The Tea Party's Cold War Roots." *The New Yorker.* NewYorker.com. 18 October 2010. Web. 10 Mar 2011. Also see Wilentz's "The Delusional Style in American Punditry" (*The New Republic.* TNR.com, 19 Dec. 2007. Web. 15 January 2011) for an ideologically bi-directional revision of the paranoid paradigm, rooted, the author argues, in Bush-era "instinct"- and "intuition"-based policy decisions but now having bipartisan utility on similarly specious grounds as the "celebrity personality-worship" that surrounded the candidacy of Barack Obama. An expert on Hofstadter's milieu, the Princeton historian has also previously reviewed a critical biography of Hofstadter's career (See Wilentz, "What Was Liberal History?" Rev. of *Richard Hofstadter: An Intellectual Biography. The New Republic* 235 (2006): 21-28), and, most notably, has written the introduction for a recent reissue of *The Paranoid Style in American Politics and Other Essays*, 1965; New York: Vintage, 2008, p. xi-xxx.

[75] David Carr, "The Fading Power of Glenn Beck's Alarms." *The New York Times*, 6 March 2011. Web. 10 March 2011.

[76] Jenkins, p. 254.

term analysis suggests that in the aftermath of the tract's repurposing as "The Coming Insurrection: Egypt" or "Libya," the host's wild-eyed conjecture might have run its course, one can nevertheless be certain that regardless of Glenn Beck's particular career trajectory, the paranoid style will continue to create the conditions by which such conspiratorial imaginings come to define a distinctly premediated political landscape for many generations to come.

Daniel Burns

University of North Carolina Greensboro

Bibliographie sélective

ACKLAND Robert, « Mapping the U.S. Political Blogosphere: Are Conservative Bloggers More Prominent? », March 4, 2005, http://voson.anu.edu.au/papers/polblogs.pdf.

ADAMIC Lada, GLANCE Natalie, « The Political Blogosphere and the 2004 U.S. Election: Divided They Blog », May 7, 2005, http://www.blogpulse.com/papers/2005/adamic.pdf.

APTER Emily S., « On Oneworldedness: Or Paranoia as a World System», *American Literary History*, vol. 18, n° 2, Summer 2006, 365-389.

ARMSTRONG Jerome, MOULITSAS ZUNIGA Markos, *Crashing the Gate: Netroots, Grassroots, and the Rise of People-Powered Politics*, White River Junction, VT: Chelsea Green, 2006.

BALKIN Jack M., « Digital Speech and Democratic Culture: A Theory of Freedom of Expression and Information Society », *New York Law Review*, n° 79, 1, 2004, 1-55.

BAODONG Liu, *The Election of Barack Obama: How He Won*, New York: Palgrave Macmillan, 2010.

BARD Alexander, SODERQVIST Jan, *Netocracy: The Power Elite and Life after Capitalism*, London: Reuters, 2002.

BENKLER Yochai, « From Consumers to Users: Shifting the Deeper Structures of Regulation towards Sustainable Commons and Users Access », *Federal Communications Law Journal*, vol. 52, n° 3, 1999, 562-579.

BENKLER Yochai, *La richesse des réseaux. Marchés et libertés à l'heure du partage social*, Lyon : Presses Universitaires de Lyon, 2009, Traduction en français de *The Wealth of Networks : How Social Production Transforms Markets and Freedom*, New Haven, CT: Yale University Press, 2006.

BENNETT Lance W., *Civic Life Online*, Cambridge, MA: The MIT Press, 2008.

BERNERS-LEE Tim, *Weaving the Web/ The Original Design and Ultimate Destiny of the World Wide Web by Its Inventor*, San Francisco, CA: HarperSanFrancisco, 1999.

BLOOD Rebecca, *We've Got Blog: How Weblogs Are Changing Our Culture*, Cambridge, MA: Perseus Publishing, 2002.
BOEHLERT Eric, *Bloggers on the Bus: How the Internet Changed Politics and the Press*, New York: Free Press, 2009.
BOWERS Chris, STOLLER Matthew, « Emergence of the Progressive Blogosphere: A New Force in American Politics », *New Politics Institute*, August 10, 2005. http://www.newpolitics.net/node/87.
BUFFA Dudley, WINOGRAD Morley, *Taking Control: Politics in the Information Age*, New York: Henry Holt and Co., 1996.
CARDON Dominique, *La démocratie internet. Promesses et limites*, Paris : Seuil, 2010.
CASTELLS Manuel, *The Information Age: Economy, Society, and Culture*, vol. I, *The Rise of the Network Society*, 2nd ed., Oxford, UK: Blackwell, 2000.
COLEMAN Stephen, BLUMER Jay G., *The Internet and Citizenship. Theory, Practice, Policy*, Cambridge, UK: Cambridge University Press, 2009.
DAVIS Richard, *The Web of Politics: the Internet's Impact on the American Political System*, New York: Oxford University Press, 1999.
DAVIS Richard, *Politics Online. Blogs, Chatrooms, and Discussion Groups in American Democracy*, New York: Routledge, 2005.
DAVIS Richard, *Typing Politics. The Role of Blogs in American Politics*, New York: Oxford University Press, 2009.
DEYSINE Anne (dir.), *Etats-Unis : une nouvelle donne,* Paris : La Documentation Française, 2010.
FARRELL Henry, « Do the Netroots Matter? », *The American Prospect*, August 13, 2009, http://www.prospect.org/cs/articles?article=do_the_net roots_matter.
FELD Lowell, WILCOX, Nate, *Netroots Rising: How a Citizen Army of Bloggers and Online Activists Is Changing American Politics*, Westport, CT: Praeger, 2008.
GILLMOR Dan, *We the Media: Grassroots Journalism by the People, for the People*, Sebastopol, CA: O'Reilly, 2004.
GOLDSMITH Jack, WU Tim, *Who Controls the Internet? Illusions of a Borderless World*, New York: Oxford University Press, 2006.
GRAFF Garrett M., *The First Campaign: Globalization, the Web, and the Race for the White House*, New York: Farrar, Straus and Giroux, 2007.

GRUSIN Richard, *Premediation: Affect and Mediality after 9/11*. New York: Palgrave, 2010.
GRUSIN Richard, BOLTER Jay D., *Remediation. Understanding the New Media*, Cambridge, MA: MIT Press, 2000.
GRUSIN Richard, CROWLEY David, HEYER Paul, *Communication in History, Technology, Culture, Society*, Boston, MA: Allyn and Bacon, Pearson, 2011.
HINDMAN Matthew, *The Myth of Digital Democracy*, Princeton, NJ: Princeton University Press, 2009.
HARFOUSH Rahaf, *Yes We Did! An Inside Look at How Social Media Built the Obama Brand,* Berkeley, CA: New Riders Press, 2009.
JENKINS Henry, *Convergence Culture*, New York: New York University Press, 2006.
KARPF David, « Unexpected Transformations: The Internet's Effect on Political Associations in American Politics », Ph.D. dissertation, University of Pennsylvania, June 2009, http://davekarpf.files.wordpress.com/2009/03/dissertation.pdf
KAYE Kate, *Campaign '08. A Turning Point for Digital Media*, CreateSpace, 2009.
KERBEL Matthew R., *Netroots: Online Progressives and the Transformation of American Politics*, Boulder, CO: Paradigm Publishers, 2009.
KENSKY Kate *et al*, *The Obama Victory: How Media, Money, and Message Shaped the 2008 Election*, New York: Oxford University Press, 2010.
LASICA J. D., « Election News from the Wired Right », *Online Journalism Review*, November 11, 2000, http://www.ojr.org/orj/work place/1017962484.php.
LESSIG Lawrence, *L'Avenir des idées. Le sort des biens communs à l'heure des réseaux numériques*, Lyon : Presses Universitaires de Lyon, 2005.
LESSIG Lawrence, *Code Version 2.0*, New York: Basic Books, 2006.
LESSIG Lawrence, « Against Transparency », *The New Republic*, vol. 240, n° 19, 21 October 2009.
MARGOLIS Michael, *The Prospect of Internet Democracy*, Burlington, VT: Ashgate Publishing Co., 2009.

McGRATH Ben, « The Movement. The Rise of Tea Party Activism », *The New Yorker*, February 1, 2010, http://www.newyorker.com/report ting/2010/02/01/100201fa_fact_mcgrath.

McKENNA Laura, POLE Antoinette, « What Do Bloggers Do: An Average Day on an Average Political Blog », *Public Opinion*, n° 134, 2008, http://ideas.repec.org/a/kap/pubxcho/v134y2008i1p97-108.html.

MITCHELL Greg, *Why Obama Won? The Making of a President,* New York: BookSurgePublishing, 2009.

MORARU Christian, *Cosmodernism: American Narrative, Late Globalization, and the New Cultural Imaginary*, Ann Arbor, MI: University of Michigan Press, 2011.

PARKER Richard A. (Ed), *Free Speech on Trial: Communication Perspectives on Landmark Supreme Court Decisions*, Tuscaloosa, AL: University of Alabama Press, 2003.

PERLMUTTER David D., *Blogwars*, New York: University Press, 2008.

PICQUET Virginie, *L'Image du président de John Kennedy à Barack Obama*, Paris: Ophrys, 2010.

ROGERS Everett, *Diffusion of Innovations*, Glencoe IL: Free Press, 1962.

RUSSOMANNO Joseph, *Defending the First. Commentaries on the First Amendment Issues and Cases,* Mahwah, NJ: Lawrence Erlbaum Associates Publishers, 2005.

ROSENBERG Scott, *Say Everything: How Blogging Began, What it's Becoming, and Why it Matters*, New York: Crown, 2009.

RUIZ Jean-Marie, *Une tradition transatlantique. L'Impact du réalisme politique sur la fondation des Etats-Unis et la pensée politique américaine au 19e siècle,* Chambéry : Editions de l'Université de Savoie, 2010.

SABATO Larry J., *The Year of Obama: How Barack Obama Won the White House?,* New York: Longman, 2010.

SHIRKY Clay, *Here Comes Everybody: the Power of Organizing without Organizations*, New York: Penguin Press, 2008.

SMITH Aaron, RAINIE Lee, « The Internet and the 2008 Election », Research report, *Pew Internet and American Life Project,* 2008, http://www.pewinternet.org/Reports/2008/The-Internet-and-the-2008-Election.aspx.

SUNSTEIN Cass R., *Republic.com*, Princeton, NJ: Princeton University Press, 2002

SUNSTEIN Cass R., *On Rumors: How Falsehoods Spread, Why We Believe Them, What Can Be Done*, New York: Farrar, Strauss and Giroux, 2009.

SUNSTEIN Cass R., *Going to Extremes: How Like Minds Unite and Divide*, Oxford, UK: Oxford University Press, 2009.

SUNSTEIN Cass R., *Republic.com 02*, Princeton, NJ: Princeton University Press, 2007.

TEACHOUT Zephyr, STREETER Thomas, *Mousepads, Shoe Leather, and Hope: Lessons from the Howard Dean Campaign for the Future of Internet Politics*, New York: Paradigm Publishers, 2008.

THE POYNTER INSTITUTE, *President Obama, Election 2008*, New York: Andrews McMeel, 2009.

THOMAS Evan and *Newsweek*, *A Long Time Coming: The Inspiring, Combative 2008 Campaign and the Historic Election of Barack Obama*, New York: Public Affairs, U.S., 2009.

THOMPSON Gary, « Weblogs, Warblogs, the Public Sphere, and Bubbles », *Transformations* 7, September 2003, http://www.transformationsjournal.org/journal/issue_07/article_02.shtml.

TRIPPI Joe, *The Revolution Will Not Be Televised*, New York: HarperCollins, 2004.

TUNNEY Sean, MONAGAN Garrett, (Eds), *Webjournalism:// A New Form of Citizenship*, Portland, OR : Sussex Academic Press, 2010.

WARNIER Jean-Pierre, *La Mondialisation de la culture*, 3rd éd., Paris, La Découverte, 2004.

WU Tim, « Network Neutrality, Broadband Discrimination », *Journal of Telecommunications and High Technology Law*, n° 2, 2003, 141-175.

WU Tim, *Master Switch. The Fall and Rise of Information Empires*, New York: Albert Knopf, 2010.

ZITTRAIN Jonathan, *The Future of the Internet and How to Stop It*. New Haven, CT: Yale University Press, 2008, et en lecture sur le site : http://futureoftheinternet.org/static/ZittrainTheFutureoftheInternet.pdf.

Note sur les auteurs

Aurélie Blot

Doctorante à l'Université de la Sorbonne Paris 4 et ATER à l'Université de Paris-Ouest Nanterre la Défense (spécialité civilisation américaine, séries télévisées et média), Aurélie Blot prépare une thèse sur l'image de la famille dans les *sitcoms* familiales américaines et son évolution depuis les années 1950, sous la direction de Monsieur le Professeur Pierre Lagayette. Dernières publications: « Lucille Ball, the Queen of Show Business versus Lucy Ricardo, the Failed Actress. When the Actress Plays the Role of the Businesswoman », *Transatlantica, The Businessman as Artist in American Civilization*, avril 2011. « *Married...With Children* versus *Father Knows Best*: The parody of a Loving Family », *The 2010 History and Film Conference*, publication sur CD Rom, Milwaukee, Wisconsin, juin 2011.

Aurélie Blot is a PhD student at the Sorbonne (Paris 4) and an ATER at l'Université de Paris-Ouest Nanterre la Défense. She specializes in American Civilisation, Television sitcoms and the media. Her PhD is entitled « l'image de la famille dans les sitcoms familiales américaines et son évolution depuis les années 1950 ». Her supervisor is Professor Pierre Lagayette. Latest publications: « Lucille Ball, the Queen of Show Business versus Lucy Ricardo, the Failed Actress. When the Actress Plays the Role of the Businesswoman », *Transatlantica, The Businessman as Artist in American Civilization*, April 2011, « *Married...With Children* versus *Father Knows Best*: The parody of a Loving Family », *The 2010 History and Film Conference*, a CD Rom Publication, Milwaukee, Wisconsin, June 2011

Elisabeth Boulot

Est Maître de Conférences HDR honoraire en Civilisation américaine de l'Université Paris Est Marne-la-Vallée. Sa recherche porte essentiellement sur la jurisprudence de la Cour suprême des Etats-Unis Elle est membre d'IMAGER et participe aux travaux de recherche du CIMMA. Récentes publications: « Gérer l'héritage des réformes passées et réformer le système de santé américain. Politiques étatiques, proposition des candidats à la présidence », Marie-Françoise Alamichel, éd., *Héritage(s) dans le monde anglophone. Concepts et réalités*. Paris : L'Harmattan, 2009, p. 289-307. « La Cour suprême et la politique environnementale du gouvernement américain sous la présidence de G. W. Bush : Les raisons d'un désaveu ». *La géographie dans le monde anglophone*. Textes réunis par Marie-Françoise Alamichel et Olivier Brossard, Paris : Michel Houdiard, 2010, p. 262-273. « Liberté d'expression, liberté de la presse et droit de vote : le rôle de la Cour suprême dans les années soixante ». Frédéric Robert, éd., *Révoltes et utopies. La contre-culture américaine des années soixante*. Paris : Editions Ellipses, 2011, p. 87-102.

Elisabeth Boulot is a former senior lecturer at the University of Paris Est Marne-la-Vallée (She retired in December 2010), accredited to supervise doctoral studies. She was also a visiting professor at the Law faculty at Paris Est Créteil (UPEC). She specializes in American Civilisation and in the study of the U.S. Supreme Court jurisprudence. Latest publications: « Gérer l'héritage des réformes passées et réformer le système de santé américain. Politiques étatiques, proposition des candidats à la présidence », Marie-Françoise Alamichel, éd., *Héritage(s) dans le monde anglophone. Concepts et réalités*. Paris : L'Harmattan, 2009, p. 289-307. « La Cour suprême et la politique environnementale du gouvernement américain sous la présidence de G. W. Bush : Les raisons d'un désaveu ». *La géographie dans le monde anglophone,* Textes réunis par Marie-Françoise Alamichel et Olivier Brossard, Paris : Michel Houdiard, 2010, p. 262-273. « Liberté d'expression, liberté de la presse et droit de vote : le rôle de la Cour suprême dans les années soixante ». Frédéric Robert, éd., *Révoltes et utopies. La contre-culture américaine des années soixante*. Paris : Editions Ellipses, 2011, p. 87-102.

Daniel Burns

Daniel Burns est étudiant en Master à l'Université de Caroline du Nord à Greensboro. Il étudie la littérature et la culture américaine du vingtième siècle. Sa recherche porte sur le discours encyclopédique de la période l'après-guerre, l'histoire intellectuelle et la théorie des réseaux. Il a reçu pour son travail de recherche en Master le prix de l'AWRN (Atlantic World Research Network) 2010-2011.

Daniel Burns is a graduate student in twentieth century American literature and culture at the University of North Carolina-Greensboro. His research focuses on the postwar encyclopedic narrative, American intellectual history, and network theory. He was awarded the Atlantic World Research Network Graduate Student Research Prize 2010-2011

Aurélie Godet

Ancienne élève de l'École normale supérieure de Lyon (ENS-LSH), agrégée d'anglais depuis 2003 et lauréate d'une bourse Fulbright en 2008, Aurélie Godet est aujourd'hui maître de conférences à l'Université Michel de Montaigne – Bordeaux 3. Ses recherches portent essentiellement sur les mouvements conservateurs aux Etats-Unis. Sa thèse de doctorat, soutenue à l'Université Paris Diderot – Paris 7 en 2009, portait sur la pensée d'Irving Kristol (1920-2009), généralement décrit comme le "parrain" du néoconservatisme. Elle prépare à présent un ouvrage sur le *Tea Party*, à paraître en 2012.

A former graduate student in Anglo-American studies at the Ecole Normale Supérieure and former Fulbright grantee, Aurélie Godet passed the Agrégation (France's highest competitive teaching examination) in 2003 and completed her PhD at Paris Diderot University in 2009. She is now an Assistant Professor of U. S. History at Bordeaux University.
Her research focuses on conservative thought and political culture in the United States, more specifically on the writings of the late Irving Kristol and the history of the creation-evolution debate. She is now working on a new book on the Tea Party movement, to be published in 2012.

Erica Johnson

ATER à l'Université Paris Est Créteil, Erica Johnson prépare une thèse de Doctorat sous la direction du Professeur Vincent Michelot à l'Université Louis Lumière (Lyon 2). De nationalité américaine, elle a fait des études de français et d'informatique. Depuis qu'elle est en

France, elle enseigne l'anglais à l'université. Elle a obtenu un Master en Etudes Anglophones. Son mémoire portait sur le rôle des blogs dans la campagne présidentielle de 2004. Sa thèse de doctorat analyse la formation et la structure des communautés sur les blogs politiques et comment ces communautés politiques changent les concepts en matière d'activisme politique. Ses domaines de recherche sont : les liens entre les nouvelles technologies, la communication et la politique.

Erica Johnson is an ATER at Université Paris-Est Créteil in Créteil, France, and is doing her doctorate at Université Lumière Lyon 2 with Professor Vincent Michelot. American by birth, she graduated from college with a dual degree in French and computer science. After moving to France to teach English at the university level, Erica started a Master's degree and studied the role played by American political blogs in the 2004 presidential election. Her doctoral research analyzes the formation and structure of communities on political blogs and how these political communities are changing concepts of political activism. Field of research: the intersection of technology, communication and politics

Christian Moraru

Professor of English at the University of North Carolina, Greensboro, Christian Moraru specializes in critical theory, American literature, as well as comparative literature with emphasis on history of ideas, narrative, postmodernism, new material studies, and the relations between globalism, community, and culture. His latest books include *Rewriting: Postmodern Narrative and Cultural Critique in the Age of Cloning* (SUNY Press, 2001), *Memorious Discourse: Reprise and Representation in Postmodernism* (Fairleigh Dickinson University Press, 2005), *Cosmodernism: American Narrative, Late Globalization, and the New Cultural Imaginary* (University of Michigan Press, 2011), and the edited collection *Postcommunism, Postmodernism, and the Global Imagination* (Columbia University Press, 2009).

Professeur d'Anglais à l'Université de Caroline du Nord à Greensboro, Christian Moraru est un spécialiste de théorie critique, de littérature américaine et comparée, d'histoire des idées (narration, postmodernisme, nouvelles études matérialistes, relations entre mondialisation, communautés et cultures). Dernières publications : *Rewriting: Postmodern Narrative and Cultural Critique in the Age of Cloning* (SUNY Press, 2001), *Memorious Discourse: Reprise and Representation in Postmodernism* (Fairleigh Dickinson University Press, 2005), *Cosmodernism: American Narrative, Late Globalization, and the New Cultural Imaginary* (University of Michigan Press, 2011), et *Postcommunism, Postmodernism, and the Global Imagination* (Columbia University Press, 2009).

Virginie Picquet

ATER à l'Université du Maine, Virginie Picquet est titulaire d'une thèse de Doctorat intitulée « La dégradation de l'image du président dans la presse américaine de John F. Kennedy à George W. Bush ». Sa recherche porte principalement sur les présidents américains modernes, la presse et le rôle de l'image en politique. Elle est l'auteur de *L'Image du président de John Kennedy à Barack Obama* paru aux Editions Ophrys en 2010.

Virginie Picquet is an ATER at l'Université du Maine. Her Doctoral dissertation was about the deterioration of the image of presidents in the press from John F. H. Kennedy to George Bush. She is the author of *L'Image du président de John Kennedy à Barack Obama* published by Les Editions Ophrys in 2010.

Jean-Marie Ruiz

Jean-Marie Ruiz est Docteur en sciences politiques et Maître de conférences en Civilisation américaine à l'Université de Savoie. Ses recherches portent sur la politique étrangère des Etats-Unis et sur l'histoire des idées politiques américaines, particulièrement dans ses interactions avec les idées européennes. Il a récemment publié : *Une tradition transatlantique. L'Impact du réalisme politique sur la fondation des Etats-Unis et la pensée politique américaine au 19e siècle*, Chambéry : Editions de l'Université de Savoie, 2010).

Jean-Marie Ruiz is Associate Professor of American Studies at the Université de Savoie, France. His research deals with American political theory and foreign policy and he is the author of the recently published *Une tradition transatlantique. L'Impact du réalisme politique sur la fondation des Etats-Unis et la pensée politique américaine au 19ᵉ siècle*, Chambéry : Editions de l'Université de Savoie, 2010.

Table des matières

L'HARMATTAN, ITALIA
Via Degli Artisti 15; 10124 Torino

L'HARMATTAN HONGRIE
Könyvesbolt ; Kossuth L. u. 14-16
1053 Budapest

L'HARMATTAN BURKINA FASO
Rue 15.167 Route du Pô Patte d'oie
12 BP 226 Ouagadougou 12
(00226) 76 59 79 86

ESPACE L'HARMATTAN KINSHASA
Faculté des Sciences sociales,
politiques et administratives
BP243, KIN XI ; Université de Kinshasa

L'HARMATTAN CONGO
67, av. E. P. Lumumba
Bât. – Congo Pharmacie (Bib. Nat.)
BP2874 Brazzaville
harmattan.congo@yahoo.fr

L'HARMATTAN GUINÉE
Almamya Rue KA 028, en face du restaurant Le Cèdre
OKB agency BP 3470 Conakry
(00224) 60 20 85 08
harmattanguinee@yahoo.fr

L'HARMATTAN CÔTE D'IVOIRE
M. Etien N'dah Ahmon
Résidence Karl / cité des arts
Abidjan-Cocody 03 BP 1588 Abidjan 03
(00225) 05 77 87 31

L'HARMATTAN MAURITANIE
Espace El Kettab du livre francophone
N° 472 avenue du Palais des Congrès
BP 316 Nouakchott
(00222) 63 25 980

L'HARMATTAN CAMEROUN
BP 11486
Face à la SNI, immeuble Don Bosco
Yaoundé
(00237) 99 76 61 66
harmattancam@yahoo.fr

L'HARMATTAN SENEGAL
« Villa Rose », rue de Diourbel X G, Point E
BP 45034 Dakar FANN
(00221) 33 825 98 58 / 77 242 25 08
senharmattan@gmail.com

592796 - Décembre 2014
Achevé d'imprimer par